Sociological Analysis

Sociological Analysis
Methods of Discovery

John A. Hughes

Nelson

Thomas Nelson and Sons Ltd
36 Park Street London W1Y 4DE

Nelson (Africa) Ltd
PO Box 18123 Nairobi Kenya

Thomas Nelson (Australia) Ltd
19-39 Jeffcott Street
West Melbourne Victoria 3003

Thomas Nelson and Sons (Canada) Ltd
81 Curlew Drive Don Mills Ontario

Thomas Nelson (Nigeria) Ltd
PO Box 336 Apapa Lagos

First published in Great Britain by Thomas Nelson and Sons Ltd,
1976
Copyright © John A. Hughes 1976

ISBN 017 7111178 (Boards)
     017 7121173 (Paper)

Printed in Great Britain by
Clarke, Doble & Brendon Ltd
Plymouth

to
Jacky

Contents

Preface

My reasons for writing this text originate from a disquiet about the branch of the sociological curriculum familiarly known as 'research methods'. Students tend to see such courses as a chore grudgingly recognized as necessary, but one not really germane to the 'central issues' of the discipline—whatever these may be. This attitude is often reinforced by the methods teacher's colleagues, who occasionally relegate him, one hopes unjustly, to the dispiriting role of a 'numbers man' who may be able to count, but who is illiterate as far as anything of importance is concerned. Although he may retaliate with references to the 'How-many-Durkheim's-can-you-get-on-the-head-of-a-needle-school' or 'armchair theorizing', none of this is particularly conducive to collaborative communication between those who 'do' theory and those who 'do' methods.

Such a gap between sociological theory and research methods is bad for the discipline. More and more frequently does the theoretical work of sociologists tend to be ignorant of the problems to do with the empirical verification of their theories, thus taking on the character of what Martindale terms 'terminological pyrotechnics', or commentaries upon commentaries on Marx, Weber, Durkheim, or whoever currently occupies the place of honour in the pantheon of master sociologists. Not that such activity is useless or irrelevant, but sociological theory ought to be a great deal more than this. Similarly, courses in methodology too often tend to offer an uninteresting recipe of techniques which fail to relate to the theoretical problems arising from the attempt to understand and explain social relationships. Too often does it lead to a narrowness and naïvety of methodological usage. Too often does the sociologist leap for his or her questionnaire, participant observer role, tape recorder, or whatever, without thinking of the kind of commitments in which he thereby becomes involved and how they might connect with the theoretical ideas of the discipline. This is the beginning of what Kaplan calls 'the law of the instrument': 'Give a small boy a hammer, and he will find that everything he encounters needs pounding.' In other words, methods teaching often results in a trained incapacity to visualize the limitations of a technique as much as to extend its use imaginatively.

In this book, I have tried to portray as honestly and as clearly as possible some of the major research methods and approaches used in sociology. While criticisms will be made, these will, hopefully, be offered in a constructive spirit rather than constitute a holistic attack on the legitimacy or otherwise of various strategies of research. No claims will be made as to what should be the only true source of sociological knowledge. I do not wish to claim that any particular method or any particular approach is *a priori* superior to any other. All methodological positions should be assessed by how far they enable the researcher to understand, explain and describe the relationships between human beings in social contexts. This is not meant to imply that on practical grounds every approach is as good as any other. Judgements as to the merits or otherwise of an approach or strategy have to be made, but the grounds upon which they are made are crucially important. This is the beginning of a new school of sociological thought: Systematic Theoretical Cowardice!

It cannot be said that what follows in this volume will always be neat and tidy. In my view, 'methods', indeed sociology in general, is not a static, dead language, but something that has to develop as time and experience accumulate. One of the reasons why courses in research methods appear so dull is, I am sure, because they are made to appear uncreative and not situations in which the student can and should use his or her imaginative faculties. After all, in a neat and tidy world, nothing needs clearing up.

What this text will try to do is present an introduction to research methods through what might be broadly and loosely termed theories of data, or, in Cicourel's terms, theories of instrumentation. It will attempt to give an account of the various methods and approaches used in empirical sociological research and will raise some of the theoretical issues which arise from these procedures.

A word about the exercises which appear at the end of each chapter. Most of the textbooks which offer exercises for the student tend to present very constrained, highly organized projects. While there is a great deal to be said in its favour, I have tried to avoid this pattern, primarily because the approach of this book attempts to encourage imagination in the use of methods. They are intended to raise questions of importance, not only for methodology, but also for sociological theory. Obviously, the ability to carry out any of these exercises will depend upon available resources. In institutions which have access to the most up-to-date research facilities, quite ambitious projects can be mounted. In other cases, more modest but no less useful efforts will have to suffice. But whichever is the case, the important thing is to try to do *some* empirical research, and to try to be aware of what it is to make sense of data. To my mind, research methods cannot be successfully taught without the student being involved in practical work of some kind. Whatever else it is, sociology is an empirical discipline, and creating data, analysing it and making it relevant to certain theoretical ideas is central to the sociological 'trade'.

Finally, I would like to extend my thanks to the following people for the various kinds of assistance they offered during the preparation of the text. Professor Eldridge read through the entire manuscript and gave much needed advice and encouragement. Bob Hinings, Doug Benson, Keith Soothill, Paul Drew, Suzette Heald and Ray Pawson, the latter the best graduate student one could ever wish for, all gave valuable advice, and made not always complimentary comments. Charlie Wilsher and Ian Turner often provided suitable liquid refreshment when ideas and inclination ran dry. I should also like to thank Bob Dowse, a long-time colleague and friend, who thinks he taught me everything I know, but only taught me a lot. Also, thanks to Brenda Wright, who, apart from being departmental secretary, also enlivened many a drab morning with her delightfully risqué innuendoes. Annie Barré typed some of the manuscript and also cheered the place up. Thanks are also due to my colleagues—especially John Wakeford, whose experience and support were invaluable—and to my many students who suffered my teaching of research methods. Finally, thanks and tribute are due to Ken Fox, an incomparable editor, who was always full of encouragement, help and support. If it were possible to blame all these for the weaknesses in the book, I would not hesitate to do so. But, as always, one can honestly say that this is impossible. Whatever virtues there are in it, the credit belongs to others.

Introduction:
Background Ideas and a Man from Mars

Date: 5th March, 1973
Place: Somewhere on the planet Earth

Ardd Vonrosh, a graduate student of the Mars Academy of Non-Martian Studies, lands on the planet Earth to collect information for his thesis, provisionally entitled, 'Self-Inquiry Among Humans: The Case of the Sociologist'. Concealing the spaceship and assuming the physical appearance of a middle-aged but trendy human male, Ardd, the ninth scholar of the Prchxxl nest, proceeds towards one of the major centres of learning somewhere on Earth, his goal to talk to and analyse as many sociologists as possible. He carefully notes what the members of the clan who call themselves sociologists do as part of their everyday lives. Some he finds talking to other humans and making marks on sheets of paper. Others are peering at a huge roll of paper which has just been produced by a large, chattering machine with blinking lights. Others are punching oblong holes on pieces of card. Becoming more and more puzzled, Ardd proceeds to other places in his constant search for further examples. These he finds sitting in libraries reading large tomes by people long dead and carrying out strenuous argument about what someone or other really meant. Others set about joining juvenile gangs, becoming workers in factories for a period, and so on. All in all he finds that sociologists are embroiled in an almost incredible variety of activities and rituals. 'XCV-*DFRESS*MULLTIPLI*XXCC*A* SS**' (translated, 'What (expletive deleted) are they doing?'), he asks himself. On being told, at some considerable length, that they are studying people, he quickly jets back to Mars and reregisters for a post-graduate course in Insect Midwifery.

This trivial little tale suggests two things. First, that sociologists do many different kinds of things and are many different kinds of people who work in varied ways. Secondly, it suggests that if it is claimed that sociologists study people, they do so in 'odd' and unexpected ways: by manipulating figures on paper, by asking people questions, studying conversations, playing games of various sorts, operating with mathematical routines, and so on. All of which may appear (not only to the Martian but to fellow humans) too remote from the living, breathing, loving, hating people with whom we are familiar in our everyday lives. Both the layman and the student have often voiced puzzlement about what sociologists do.[1]

What does, however, emerge from this is that the sociologist normally works with data. This may consist of answers to a questionnaire, observations made in a factory, figures of suicide rates, attitude scales, the results of a laboratory experiment and so on; but whatever it is, it is important to understand how this data has been created and why it is considered to do the job asked of it. Data does not suddenly appear out of nowhere; it has to be created, and, in my view, it is necessary to understand what is involved in creating, processing and theorizing with data if we are to enjoy the richness of the sociological enterprise. Answers to a questionnaire item, descriptions of what people did in natural settings, long strings of figures, scores on an attitude scale, and so on, are not data until they are considered within a meaning context. Even fundamental kinds of data, such as sense impressions of sights, sounds and smells, are not data until they are made so by being placed within a particular meaning context. A tool, whether a ruler, chisel, questionnaire, or whatever, is only such because it is part of a system or context of meaning that defines it as a tool of a particular sort. A wooden stick of a particular length is useless, except perhaps for making a fire, throwing for a pet dog or stirring a pot of paint. However, if we develop a system of meaning so that this stick is adopted as a standard, we can then compare the length, breadth and height of things around us. In other words, objects in the universe can be given spatial magnitudes. We can do this not because the stick is of a certain length (its physical character), but because we choose to put it into a meaning context which defines ways in which we can talk about reality. This meaning context could become quite sophisticated. With our notion of a 'ruler' we can talk about the world in terms of its scale, the relative location of objects, their volume, and so on. In combination with another meaning system, weight, we can go on to stipulate an even more complex description of the universe, reality or whatever we choose to call it at this stage.

The point is that these meaning systems or meaning contexts are, in a strict sense, a human product: they are not given in what we perceive, though what we perceive may well suggest some kind of a clue. Indeed, our perceptions themselves are structured by the meaning system. Once, say, we are familiar with the meaning system incorporating the idea of length, we tend to 'notice' lengths of objects, distances between them and so on. In short, we provide a structure to the world, the universe, by the meaning systems we happen to employ.

These meaning systems or contexts, as I have called them, may come to be agreed on by a number of people. For example, physicists, at any one time, may be broadly in agreement upon the meaning of such terms or concepts as 'mass', 'length' or 'time'. Other concepts may have a more negotiable meaning. In fact, even such an apparently unproblematic notion as weight, within certain areas of the physicist's meaning system, assumes a much more controversial, problematic nature. Some terms in the system may be clearer than others, but the general point is clear: there are meaning contexts familiar to groups or aggregates of people.

Up to now I have been discussing what I have called 'meaning systems' or 'meaning contexts' only very generally and it is perhaps time to consider their nature more fully. A meaning system is a set of understandings related to each other in ways that make sense.[2] A set of signs, as '+', '−', '*', 'A', 'B', 'C', '%', ' ', ' ', are all meaningful when we place them in a meaning context. By itself, the sign 'A' means nothing. If, however, it occurred at the beginning of a sentence in English, we would immediately recognize it as a word with a function to perform within an English sentence. Similarly, to carry out the symbol manipulation '$2 + 2 = 4$' correctly is to move from marks on paper to place them in a meaning context known as arithmetic.

Perhaps language is the most basic meaning system familiar to all of us, and the one which probably underlies most other meaning systems. But what is it that makes the sounds, the signs which are part of language, meaningful? This is a very difficult question to answer satisfactorily and briefly. It used to be thought that the signs were meaningful because they referred, rather like labels, to things in the word. The neat simplicity of this view collapsed through difficulties over such ubiquitous terms as 'this' and 'that', which referred or labelled nothing uniquely. An alternative view was that meaning comes from the use of the terms within some kind of 'language game'. 'This' and 'that' are meaningful, even though there reference shifts from occasion to occasion of use, and their meaning has something to do with the function they perform within an act of speech or communication. Meaning, then, has a lot to do with the 'contexts of use' and our understanding of the situations in which the signs occur. Learning a language is not only learning to operate with sounds and other signs according to certain rules, but also of learning the meaning and the contexts of meaning in which the sounds and signs appear. As Chafe points out, '. . . meaning is in every way as important as sound in . . . understanding language as a whole'.[3]

Without language, it would be difficult to construct anything like a complex meaning system. The symbols in the language and the meanings we attribute to them not only give men a sense of their commonality with other men, but also provide a link with past experiences and a mode of talking about the world. Language helps us to communicate the meaning systems we use to shape, discuss, perceive and generally structure the universe about us, and is a major element in the formation of social thought.[4]

Meaning systems are, then, our link with and within the world. They are the medium through which we define, interpret and understand the world. In a word, we construct reality by means of our meaning systems. An infant, or the Man from Mars mentioned earlier, might organize his knowledge in a manner very differently from ours. 'Instead of placing things in categories such as living and non-living, animal and plant, gallons, liquid, and solid, he might categorize in different dimensions, such as autonomous or dependent, growing or decaying, self-regulating or "wild".'[5] This has a number of serious implications. If one poses the argument that, since we cannot know reality except through the organization of our sense impressions by means of some meaning system, then, as meaning systems change, so must reality. Or, to put it another way: if two people see reality in different ways does this mean that there are two realities, or is there some way of choosing between them? Hallowell is making much the same kind of point when he states:

> It has not always been emphasized sufficiently that the very existence of varying culture patterns carries with it the psychological implication that the individuals of these societies actually live in different orders of reality. . . . Reality in this sense of the term does not primarily refer to discrete objects or persons as existent. . . . It defines the relations of human beings to the objects of their . . . environment . . . in terms of the meanings and practical significance which they have had for them.
>
> Human beings, that is to say, never live in a world of bare physical objects and events. They live in a meaningful universe.[6]

A way of appreciating the force of this kind of argument is to imagine a primitive hunter and a suave urbanite walking through a forest. The perceptions of the hunter would be infinitely more complex than those of the city-dweller. Among other signs, the hunter would note the tracks of different animals as meaningful in terms of food, wealth and survival, and not just as a mess of muddy marks. Of course, in a reverse situation, the primitive hunter would be as lost among the neon lights of the city. There are many practical examples of this, such as that of the Eskimo. Their perceptual work is quite different from that of men living in industrial societies. An important feature of this difference is the Eskimo's use of his senses to orient himself in territories where there is no horizon separating earth from sky, where there is nothing for the eye to fix on except snow, snow and more snow. How does the Eskimo find his way? Apparently by natural reference points such as the relationship between contours, types of snow, wind, salt air, ice crack and so on. Quite different reference points to, say, those a driver uses when finding his way through a large city.[7] In a way, these people would be living in different realities. But, is it only 'in a way'? Is 'living in different realities' merely a way of speaking, of emphasizing forcefully the implications of the fact that people notice different things about the world? Could we not more correctly say that they notice different things, but that the reality in which they live is exactly the same? The urbanite, never faced with the necessity of hunting his food and clothing, is not likely to pay any special perceptual attention to those features necessary to the hunter's task. Similarly, the hunter, never knowing the need or pleasures of attending nightclubs, would have no incentive to sort out the neon signals impinging on his senses. In short, the hunter and the urbanite do not live in different worlds or realities; it is merely that their perceptual structure, based on past experiences and learning, is different. We find it difficult to accept in anything but a metaphorical sense that there are several, ultimately billions, of realities; more comforting is the position that there is one reality, but many different ways to perceive it. We admit, then, a relativity in perceptions, but believe in a unity underlying this variation. There is the implicit belief that experience is what men share; that when two human beings are subject to the same 'experience', virtually the same data are fed into the two central nervous systems and the two central nervous systems and the two brains record similarly.[8] Our language assumes it and our commonsense screams for it. How else could we communicate, unless there were some reality agreed upon by most people? The short answer to this is that people may come to agree on a *description* of reality, agree on a meaning system about the nature of reality, but that ultimately there is no way of knowing whether that description is 'true' for all time and all places.

What can be done, however, is to work within the often loose and vaguely defined parameters implied by particular ways of talking about reality. Even though ultimate and unquestionable criteria of truth are elusive, working within less ambitious confines can be both profitable and fascinating. While agreed-on ways of describing reality are more than plentiful—ranging from astrology, Buddhism, physics, witchcraft and so on—this text is primarily concerned with those covered by the term 'sociology', especially in so far as they have to do with ways of formulating descriptions of social life and how data is both defined and structured to answer questions felt to be relevant. Moreover, the question raised in the preceding paragraphs concerning single or multiple realities is not purely metaphysical, since these have a bearing, as we shall see, on fundamental conceptions about the nature of sociology and sociological research. To this end, Chapter 1 begins with a discussion of the meaning system of science leading on to a consideration of the meaning systems of sociology. The remaining chapters have as their topics various methods and methodological problems.

'Methods' and 'methodology' are used here to refer to ways in which a researcher tries to gather data relevant to his purpose and to ways in which the data are justified as relevant. As such, the matters subsumable under these terms are exceedingly wide, including, unless one is careful, pretty near everything it is possible to discuss. The term 'methods' is normally reserved for the technology of research, the actual tools by which data are gathered and analysed. while 'methodology' refers to the logic or philosophy underlying particular methods. Taking rather more care to be specific, the text will be concerned, at various times, with matters to do with 'research design', or how the researcher marshals and organizes his endeavours to create data able to answer the questions posed; the 'logic of analysis', or how the data is manipulated and formed into a meaningful structure; and ways of formulating different kinds of theories or accounts of the phenomena of social life.

The subject of sociological methodology I do, to be frank, find increasingly difficult to regard as neatly organizable into watertight compartments. Unfortunately, the exigencies of presentation necessitate some plausible chapterization taking the reader through basic principles on to more particular applications. Perhaps the favourite rational is to divide chapters into 'Research Design', 'Forms of Data', 'Data Analysis', or their equivalents, or to cite the various methods in order of some felt pre-eminence. Neither of these has been particularly followed here. The first substantive chapter on the experiment comes early, even though it is less used than other methods, because in my view it neatly raises issues relevant to the study of other methods. The next two chapters on observation and verbal methods could be regarded as discussions of primary data sources, the remaining chapters dealing, in the main, with matters of design and analysis. In any event, none of these chapters should be studied in isolation from the others. The later chapter on the survey, for example, is incomplete without some understanding of the verbal methods discussed earlier. Like most subjects, there are many ways of 'cutting the cake', as it were, all having their advantages and disadvantages, and I am not entirely satisfied that the way this has been done is the best. However, it is the way I found it easiest to write, and so hopefully it will serve the purpose.

Notes and References

1. Natural scientists rarely have to face this issue. To most laymen, what the natural scientist does is often beyond their ken, but it is expected to be so: it is a matter for experts. However, sociologists frequently have to face the charge that what they do is nothing special since every human being is qualified by virtue of the fact of being human!

2. I hope the notion of meaning system is reasonably clear, since I feel reluctant at this stage to offer a more formal definition. If you like, treat it as a 'sensitizing concept' given meaning, according to Blumer, by 'means of exposition which yields a meaningful picture, abetted by apt illustrations which enable one to grasp the reference in terms of one's own experience'—'What is Wrong with Social Theory', *American Sociological Review*, 19, 1954, p. 9. For those wishing to read an empirical account of the ways in which meaning can be organized in social interaction, see P. McHugh, *Defining the Situation*, Bobbs-Merrill, New York, 1968.

3. W. L. Chafe, 'Meaning in Language', *American Anthropologist*, 67, 1965, p. 23. See also a difficult but rewarding piece by J. Coulter, 'Language and the Conceptualization of Meaning', *Sociology*, 7, 1973, pp. 173–89.

4. See D. G. Mandelbaum (ed.), *Selected Writings of Edward Sapir*, University of California Press, Berkeley, 1951; and J. B. Carroll (ed.), *Language, Thought and Reality: Selected Writings of Benjamin Lee*

Whorf, Technology Press, Cambridge, Mass., and John Wiley & Sons, New York, 1956.

5. F. K. Berrien, *General and Social Systems*, Rutgers University Press, New Brunswick, 1968, p. 6.

6. A. Irving Hallowell, 'Psychological Leads for Ethnological Field Workers', in D. G. Harding (ed.), *Personal Character and Cultural Milieu*, Syracuse, 1949, pp. 309–10. Other relevant perspectives on this are illustrated by G. E. Swanson, 'Marx and Freud: Their Relevance for Social Psychology', *Sociometry*, 24, 1961; and A. Schutz, 'Commonsense and Scientific Interpretation of Human Action', in M. Natason (ed.), *Philosophy of the Social Sciences*, Random House, New York, 1963, pp. 302–46.

7. E. V. F. Carpenter and R. Flaherty, *Eskimo*, University of Toronto Press, Toronto, 1959.

8. E. T. Hall, *The Hidden Dimension*, Doubleday, New York, 1966, p. 2.

1
Meaning Systems and Their Relevance for Sociological Methods

Any discipline or way of looking at the world contains certain presuppositions which serve as justifications for the descriptions and explanations offered. Any item of data, evidence or argument is so because of its place within a system of meaning defining it as *such*. Moreover, the quality of the data, evidence or argument is subject to rules of judgement which serve, as it were, as licences or warrants justifying what is done with the data. There is no such thing as a fragment of data independent of some system of meaning which gives it sense. To explore these ideas further, let us look first at a meaning system often offered as providing the most sophisticated method of describing, explaining or understanding the world: the *scientific method*.

Some Elements of the Meaning System of Science

'Science', whatever we mean precisely by the term, has an honoured and exalted place among all the instruments of the human mind. The spectacular achievements of technology—in a way, a direct offspring of developments in the natural sciences—have further established the status of 'science', which has now become almost the final arbiter of what is, in truth, reality. By use of 'the scientific method', it is claimed, we can attain closer and closer approximations to accurate descriptions and explanations of the universe, reality or whatever we call it. It has already been suggested that a meaning system is simply a set of signs or symbols invested with some integrated meaning by an individual or group, though the group can be very broad ('all people who speak the English language') or very narrow ('all those who can understand the theory of quarks'). A meaning system can be a sub-class of a larger one, and thus the

meaning system involved in quantitative mechanics is part of the
larger meaning system known as 'physics', which, in turn, is part
of the meaning system of natural science. Also, any particular
meaning system can form part of more than one higher-order
meaning system. Physics can be treated as part of the meaning
system of the English or the German languages, though for this to
be the case, certain commonalities between the higher-order meaning systems have to be assumed.[1] Thus to talk about the meaning
system of science can be to talk about many things, including
physics, chemistry, biology or neuro-physiology, or, at the other
extreme, about those meanings and beliefs common to all activities
that call themselves scientific. It is the latter kind that I wish to
discuss here,[2] while examining the kind of assumptions and 'nest
of commitments' involved in attachment to the meaning system of
science: to explicate close to what Kuhn at times refers to as a
'scientific paradigm': 'a locus of scientific commitment including
metaphysical presuppositions, substantive concepts, methodological
rules and problem directives'.[3] At this stage, we need not deal in
any detail with specific scientific disciplines, but will stick mainly
to those 'metaphysical presuppositions' referred to above. In a
sense, this is rather like trying to extract the basic elements out of
a culture and looking at the main themes which as it were, form a
'deep structure' to that culture. In this case, the culture is 'science'.

Ontological Assumptions

The first element in the meaning system of science concerns specific
ontological assumptions about the character of the universe.
Generally, such assumptions consist of certain fundamental beliefs
about the nature of reality, the universe and what it contains. Often
these are fairly commonsense notions, such as that there are certain
things which are soft and others which are hard, some which are
hot and others which are cold. However, within the scientific community they tend to have a more exalted and precise metaphysical
status, as they do within theology and philosophy: that the world
outside is real, that the universe is ruled by God, or that the universe
follows certain inexorable laws of nature. Such beliefs underlie all
human activity: religion, politics, economics or sex. As Diesing puts
it, they serve 'to organize and explain the otherwise disorderly flow
of experience by suggesting the basic realities that underlie the
flux of appearance'.[4] Many, it is true, sound so trivial that it is
almost embarrassing to assert them. Nonetheless, philosophical
inquiry has a nasty habit of making them appear rather less trivial

and much more problematic than may be first realized. But, however they appear, trivial or otherwise, scientific activity begins and ends with such ontological postulations. To use an image offered by Gouldner, the ontological assumptions (Gouldner calls them 'background assumptions') are the top of an inverted cone, the area of greatest circumference, and 'have no limited domain to which alone they apply. These are beliefs about the world that are so general that they may, in principle, be applied to any subject matter without restriction. . . . They serve to provide the most general of orientations, which enable unfamiliar experiences to be made meaningful.'[5] Of course, the highest level of ontological beliefs within one meaning system may, in another system, constitute lower-order beliefs. At a more specific level, ontological assumptions, when applied to a particular area, become what Gouldner terms 'domain assumptions'. In sociology, for instance, beliefs about the nature of man and society would be domain assumptions, such as a belief that men are rational (or irrational), that social life is conflict-ridden, that behaviour is unpredictable. Such beliefs are of less generality than the kind of universal hypotheses spoken of earlier which may have virtually unlimited applicability. The kind of beliefs to be considered below are domain assumptions of science, but, of course, to the extent that one takes them as general descriptions of the universe even outside a scientific context, they can become general ontological postulates.

One such belief, and one on which the whole scientific activity as presently conceived is predicated, is that there is a universe apart from our senses which scientific activity seeks to understand. Commonsense would seem to indicate that this is a necessary belief, otherwise effort and expenditure on scientific inquiry would seem pointless and irrational. Though we cannot strictly *prove* there to be a reality outside our senses, this is not to say that the belief is trivial or of no concern. The fact that it would seem to underpin and legitimate the whole of the scientific (and the human) enterprise would be evidence enough of its importance. However, the implications of the beliefs are something else again, especially when it comes to describing the nature of that reality. Even at a day-to-day level of activity, we can be deceived and find our senses open to 'error'. This happens every day of our lives, and it is unnecessary to quote such uncommon and dramatic phenomena as mirages or distorting mirrors. Accordingly, it is necessary to provide other sets of assumptions and rules to define what is to count as 'error', and what is to count as a 'true' perception. In other words, we have to have a theory that the universe operates on our senses and instruments in particular ways which can be taken as yardsticks by which to define what is true and what is false. We need, in other words, an epistemology. The belief that there is a universe to perceive is the bedrock of all scientific activity.

In another way, similar sets of ontological postulates are crucial to the way in which we decide to look at and talk about this universe which we assume to be present. It is the scientist (as a generic category rather than a particular person) and not nature which furnishes the substantive content of the ontological assumptions and postulates. In a significant sense, it is the observer—the scientist, in this case—who defines what is and is not in the universe. He asserts the kind of things that exist, and this has important implications for what he does in the way of scientific activity. Kuhn gives an excellent example of the kind of thing meant:

> After about 1630 . . . particularly after Descartes's immensely influential scientific writings, most physical scientists assumed that the universe was composed of microscopic corpuscles and that all natural phenomena could be explained in terms of corpuscular shape, size and motion, and interaction. That nest of commitments proved to be both metaphysical and methodological. As metaphysical, it told scientists what sort of entities the universe did and did not contain: there was only shaped matter in motion. As methodological, it told them what ultimate laws and fundamental explanations must be like: laws must specify corpuscular motion and interaction and explanation must reduce any given natural phenomenon to corpuscular action under these laws. More important still, the corpuscular conception of the universe told scientists what many of their research problems should be.[6]

Many similar examples could be cited—Newtonian mechanics and Darwin's theory of evolution among them—and it applies equally to any system of thought which makes some reference to the universe, or, if preferred, to reality. The ontological assumptions, then, define what it is that we understand to exist within the universe. But not only this, for we also begin to become involved in a meaning system which puts a framework on sensory experience.[7] If we think God rules the universe and intervenes in the affairs of men, then certain kinds of event will be interpreted as supporting evidence. If, on the other hand, we do not admit the existence of such an entity as God, these same events will require some other kind of explanation based on a meaning system which includes other kinds of ontological assertion but rejects others. In the history of scientific activity, these ontological postulates are crucial in determining the sphere of active research. They set 'puzzles' to solve: to make data fit theory and vice versa, to incorporate new 'facts' into the framework, to deal with inconsistencies in theory and data, and so forth. In short, they create the normal pastimes of the researcher and investigator.[8]

Rules of Evidence

We have identified two elements within the meaning system of science: the ontological postulates which define the nature of the universe; and we have discussed briefly the 'rules of evidence' by which the various elements within the meaning system are related. A great deal of scientific activity is, consciously and unconsciously, geared to understanding rules of evidence. Talk about 'good experimental work', 'precise observation' and so on, is concerned to indicate that certain kinds of link within the meaning system are legitimate, while others are not. Thus a scientist who asserted that there was a causal link between X and Y solely on the basis of a correlation between them, would be accused of breaking a rule to the effect that 'correlation does not establish cause'. (In practice, of course, this particular rule is far more complicated.) So, to adopt the meaning system of science is also to adopt, as part of that meaning system, a whole set or cluster of rules for evaluating evidence, for establishing links within the system of meanings, for establishing what is to count as good evidence, what is to count as a tentative conclusion, and so on. Again, these 'rules of evidence' are arbitrary in the sense of being non-natural, not given in nature. Their ultimate validity depends upon our strength of attachment to them, psychological, moral or whatever. Within the meaning system concerned, of course, they are internally valid. If we accept the premises of the meaning system, and the rules specifying what links may be made between elements within the meaning system, then we become involved in an activity—in this case, science.

Part of our use of the terms 'truth' and 'falsity' are about what I have termed 'rules of evidence' or 'rules of procedure'. One kind of rule with which we are familiar, and grasp as part of our everyday life, is that a statement is true if it corresponds to some empirical fact, but false if it does not. For example, we regard the statement, 'Jim is 38' to be true if, in fact, Jim is thirty-eight years old. But, while this might seem commonsensically obvious, there are a number of hidden assumptions and understandings implicit in the judgement. For one thing, the fact of being 38 assumes a number whereby each unit of a year is related to some appropriate number system. In a society where age was calculated from the approximate time of conception, 'Jim is 38' would not be true unless we assumed the relevant age-grading principle appropriate to that society. Again, we also make assumptions in such cases about how the world is and what is in it. Many years ago in Britain most people believed in witches. The meaning system incorporating these entities also included procedures for detecting them, including the technique of 'pricking'. If a witch, it was reasoned, was pricked through his or her 'witch's mark' (today we would probably call such a mark, a mole), the witch would feel no pain and no blood would flow on the pin being withdrawn. Naturally enough, there were cases where this happened, where no pain was felt and no blood flowed from the wound, and these people were accordingly dubbed witches and brought to a brutal end.

To our sentiments, such practices seem not only barbaric but to be based on quite extraordinary beliefs about reality. Of course, we know better. Those eager 'witch finders' of the Middle Ages or the seventeenth century lacked our sophisticated science. They knew little about physiology or psychology. The women and men brought to public trial for witchcraft were no doubt in a terrible state of fear. Possibly many fainted, so becoming anaesthetized to the pin's prick, and then, depending on the location of the 'witch's mark' on the body, blood may well have flowed away from the area, so refusing to flow when the pin was withdrawn. This example shows the ways in which ontological assumptions can be reinforced by rules of truth, in spite of the fact that today, in terms of different meaning systems, we would regard such beliefs as false. The general point is as McHugh puts it: 'nothing—no object, event, or circumstance—determines its own status as truth. . . . An event is transformed into truth only by the application of a canon of procedure, a canon that truth-seekers use and analysts must formulate as providing the possibility of agreement.'[9]

But, whatever the detailed difficulties of the notions of truth and falsity, there are one or two agreed principles within the scientific meaning system according to which we decide on the truth value of various assertions. One of these is that a statement must be testable against sensory experience, even if this is mediated through instrumentation: the statement must be objective in the sense that other observers could come to the same conclusion if they followed the same procedures. Herein lies the importance of the norm of publicity within the scientific community. Findings must be public so that checks can be made on them by other interested researchers.[10] But note that rules or canons of truth derive their validity from the meaning system to which they belong, even though the criteria involved in scientific work may have currency in other fields.

It has already been claimed that to be a scientist is to be involved in a system of meaning which not only defines the reality studied but also provides the ways of studying it and the criteria for evaluating that study. A good illustration is the ontological belief that the universe is subject to unalterable laws and is, in this sense, determined. This belief may be expressed in many ways, among them, 'every event has a cause'. This not only immediately suggests something about the universe, but also gives a framework or provides a strategy for its study. Thus, if we have an event, we look for a cause or causes that we assume to be there because we accept the premise that 'every event has a cause'. We do not admit, in other words, that there is such a thing as a 'cause-less event'. So not only is 'every event has a cause' a statement about what the universe is believed to be like, but also a recommendation for how we might analyse that universe. In addition ancillary premises constitute rules of evidence. If we find that an object falls at a particular rate of acceleration, we are told to look for a cause and go on to see if this has similar effect on other objects. After suitable examination of a definite, if large, number of falling objects, we will feel confident enough to generalize about all falling objects. We cease to feel the necessity to check the law or generalization every time an object falls. We believe that everything is caused, and once we have found the cause we feel fairly confident that this cause will operate throughout time and place.

This does not imply that we will not change the law in the face of other evidence. But, as Kuhn amply demonstrates, laws in science are changed only grudgingly. Our confidence is derived from belief in the ontological postulates defining what the universe is and what it is fundamentally like.

So to 'do' science is to accept certain elements of a particular meaning system: a meaning system that is man-made, whatever else we believe it to be. If we think that science gives a better description of reality than religion, it does so only because we accept the premises and assumptions in the meaning system of science. This does not mean that there are no criteria by which to evaluate the ultimate postulates, only that there are no *absolute* criteria. There are plenty of criteria, rules of evidence, of procedure, and so on within the system of meaning itself, but our confidence in them comes from the attachments and human commitments we make to them.

There is an inevitable circularity in this argument. Science, or any other human activity, may become like a game, morally neutral and with no point beyond the playing of it. This argument also suggests that science and the scientist are not, after all, possessed of some marvellous secret of the universe beyond human judgement. They are men like other men, influenced by all the factors that influence men. This is not to say that scientists are not biased and prejudiced. They are, but so is everyone in this sense. 'Bias' and 'prejudice' in scientific or any other activity is a matter for the particular system of meaning involved. It also suggests that commitment to the meaning system of science is a human and a social matter : a fact of considerable importance.

This discussion has considered the meaning system of scientific activity in very general terms. It still needs to be pointed out that each discipline within the scientific enterprise will have its own sub-system of meaning. In these cases, the ontological postulates and assumptions will contain particular references about the nature of the universe, specific rules of procedure and evaluation, but all linked to the larger meaning system indicated above. Again, at this more specific level, there are other elements within the scientific meaning system not yet discussed, namely, the rules of procedure involved in the creation of concepts, theories and the like. Consideration of these will be left until later.

Finally, a large part of the meaning system of science is latent within the scientific enterprise. Some of this is not derived from science *qua* science, but is part of the social context in which scientific activity goes on. For example, a scientist, when writing a paper, will simply state his hypothesis, his method and his conclusion in the rather aseptic manner expected of such papers. Thus he will state the hypothesis baldly, without specifying or referring to any of the influences which led him to entertain the hypothesis in the first place.[11] This is in due conformity with the rule that lays stress on objectivity and the irrelevance of other factors not 'germane' to the study. There is an unconscious obedience to such rules, many of which are part and parcel of everyday life, that may exert an influence.

The Meaning System of Sociology

The time has come to link some of the above points with sociology. Properly speaking, of course, the title of this section should be the meaning *systems* of sociology, for, as we shall see, there is no one paradigm agreed to by all sociologists equally. While many of these differences are attacks and defences of straw men, they nonetheless often reflect deep and important differences in approach and thinking.

The purpose of the sociologist's meaning system is to make sense of the social world. But we immediately strike a difficulty attaching to the notions of 'make sense of' and 'social', about which there is a veritable mountain of comment and invective within sociology. This is not surprising, perhaps, since both are key notions. It is less problematic to presume that the sociologist does study something, and that this something is sufficiently different from what physicists, economists, chemists or biologists study to warrant the establishment of a separate discipline.[12] Briefly and simply, sociologists study that which is a product of men entering into relationships with other men. Beyond this simple formulation, a great deal more can be said and argued about. But once we have demarcated a particular area of inquiry, certain other questions begin to follow as a matter of course. The very demarcation of the world into 'social' and 'non-social' is part of some set of ontological beliefs. But what are we to include within 'the social'? Do we include all possible social relations as the province of sociology, or only certain kinds? What about 'buying and selling goods'? Should this be a part of sociology or a part of economics? Again, do sociologists need to study 'man's inner life', or can we leave this to the psychologists or psychiatrists?

None of these and similar questions admit of a definite answer. Nor perhaps should they. Nor are many of them questions to be answered empirically by reference to 'facts of the world', for, in a way, they are questions and issues about what kind of facts are in the world. There is nonetheless an empirical component to them. Many of the disciplinary demarcation disputes within the social sciences are the product of particular sets of historical circumstances. The social sciences began their development in Western Europe in the early nineteenth century. At first, practitioners were exceedingly catholic in their interests and inquiries, and many of them would be rather puzzled by the present-day division of the social sciences into such subjects as sociology, politics and economics. They were men for whom the whole of social life and not just a set of narrow, professionalized problems was the focus of inquiry. With the expansion of higher education in all industrial societies throughout the later nineteenth century and especially during the twentieth processes of professionalization and differentiation began to operate until progressively narrower professionalisms began to emerge.[13] But this has not been only a matter of profesional expediency. The distinctions essential to defining the subject-matter of the various disciplines derive from meaning systems within the culture. Historically, sociology depended upon a cultural realization that differences between peoples existed, and a further realization that ways of life could change or be changed by circumstance.

The Industrial Revolution is a classic case in point, and one very relevant to the development of European sociology. The changes brought about by the introduction of inanimate sources of power to production, meant great changes in modes of work, life style methods of making war, and so on. Soon, the cultural idea took shape in some men's minds that 'the social' was an area of inquiry worthwhile in its own right, and not something natural or God-given. In other words, there began the development of a meaning system granting some autonomy to the 'social' and the recognition that human beings and the ways in which they behave has a lot to do with the ways in which they form social bonds with others.[14]

Imagine, for a moment, a small-scale, technologically primitive society entirely cut off from contacts with other societies. Assume also that the society is in some sort of balance with its environment in that neither birth nor death rates pose challenges to the social organization of the society in its present form. For most members of the society, life would be relatively unproblematic. From birth to death people could conform to custom, plying their trades, growing or hunting their food, marrying, setting up families and worshipping their deities in a routine and unreflecting manner. Such a society would feel little need for a sociology in the sense of encouraging a discipline to inquire into the nature of social life. (It would also feel little need for any sort of science or technology beyond the rudimentary one assumed.) There would be little that was puzzling for them to explain. No doubt explanatory meaning systems would evolve, but once established, they would go unchallenged. The current pattern of behaviour would seem inevitable, and the only sociological proposition would refer to the dependence of behaviour upon convention. It is no accident, then, that the rapid development of sociology took place when and where it did. The Industrial Revolution posed new problems, for which certain people found that existing systems of meaning had no answer.

Of course, having made the distinction between the 'social' and the 'non-social', it is not enough to rest content. The content and other ramifications of the distinction must be elaborated. Other assumptions and statements need to be made about the 'social' and its relationship to the 'non-social', or to use a better, more familiar term, the 'natural'. Indeed, much of the activity on the sociological agenda is precisely this: the attempted clarification of concepts related to the definition of the 'proper province' of the discipline. However, fundamental to the discussion here and to follow are two contrasting themes of thinking which have relevance not only for substantive theorizing in sociology but also for methodological questions.

The 'Natural' and the 'Social'

One sort of justification for making the distinction between the 'social' and the 'natural' is that this division represents the dualistic nature of the world. On the one hand, there is the natural world of inanimate matter and motion, subject to vast, impersonal laws; while, on the other, is the world of life, of animate and (very important) conscious entities. The methodological consequences of this view are that the former are to be studied by the methods well established in the natural sciences, and the latter by other non-naturalistic methods. The contrasting position is that the distinction between the social and the natural merely reflects a matter of convenience; there is no dualism in the world, but simply different aspects of the same underlying natural phenomena. The implication for methodology of this position is that both the social and the natural, as they are termed here, can be studied by the same methods, or, at least, by methods based on the same logic or principles.[15] As sets of ontological postulates, they represent meaning systems crucial to the understanding of both theoretical and methodological issues within the history of sociology. In a way, they represent competing sets of 'domain' assumptions which overarch particular theories about the relationship between man and society. For example, if a naturalistic image of man were adopted that emphasized his organic origins, and the argument posed that man's inherent neuro-physiological structures and primitive motives are moulded and refined by interaction with his environment, then we are likely to proceed to our study with a different armoury of concepts, theories and methods than if we adopted a view that man was a spiritual being, possessed of free will and the ability to choose his fate. Although this example might perhaps pose the differences between the positions far too sharply, it should serve to make the point. In the former case, we would tend to interpret man's behaviour as a conflict or adaptation process between his needs (perhaps physiologically defined) and the demands or problems set by the pressures of his environment, both natural and human. In the latter case, we would begin to interpret man's doings primarily as a spiritual and moral process, serving perhaps some great religious or other human purpose, but certainly in language far from that typical of the naturalistic approach.

The history of sociology is full of presuppositions and ideas which fall, more or less, to one side or the other of the hypothetical line dividing the naturalistic from what Catton calls the 'animistic' positions. Darwinism had just such a classic impact on the development of sociology. The idea that man was a creature like any other animal had massive consequences for nineteenth-century thinking. Man, with all the paraphernalia of civilization, was fundamentally like the ape, his nearest relative in the animal kingdom, and subject to the same processes of life, birth, death and development. Any differences were quantitative rather than qualitative. Indeed, man's 'great chain of being' stretched back to the first slimy virus that managed to reproduce itself in the primeval mud. This had a tremendous impact on a society only slowly emerging from religious interpretations of the universe, and a profound impact on the development of social thought.[16]

All the implications of these 'domain assumptions' for theory and method are not, as Gouldner himself points out, strictly logical. Indeed, '. . . it is the essential nature of background assumptions that they are not originally adopted for instrumental reasons, the way, for example, one might pick a screwdriver out of a tool kit . . .'; but because they are familiar to us, they strike resonance with what we believe to be obvious as a product of our experience and learning within a particular cultural tradition from childhood onwards.[17] They have links, in other words, with the contexts of meaning provided by the culture, both societal and professional, within which the sociologist works. In this way, Gouldner goes on to argue, we have a predilection for certain kinds of ontology because of our socialization into the meanings characteristic of a particular culture and their deep-rootedness within the personality. Earlier we spoke of language in connection with meaning system, and how, as we learn linguistic forms, we learn the meanings and ontologies behind them. Those brought up within the Judeo-Christian tradition with its notions of 'soul' might find it difficult to rid themselves entirely of 'animistic' notions since these are so deeply embedded in our language and meanings.[18] Also at a more specific level, the sociologist is, in a way, the creature of his culture because of this link between the 'domain' assumptions and the culture in which he is born, bred and earns his living. Because of this, it is not quite nonsensical to talk of *American* sociology, *British* sociology, *French*, *Polish* or *Russian* sociology. Sociological developments in different national societies are based not only on peculiar social contexts, but also partly on the ideas and concerns stemming from the cultures of these societies. British sociology, to take one example, is noted for the attention it has paid to social class, reflecting, in large part, the cultural belief that Britain is, above all else, a class society.[19]

Moreover, the social scientist, be he sociologist, economist or whatever, does not only take or receive his 'domain' assumptions from the parent ideas which constitute the culture of the society in which he lives. He also interacts within specific social contexts. He is a member of a group of fellow professionals, a member, more likely than not, of a family, maybe even of a church. These contexts also play a part in the kind of things he chooses to study, how he studies them and how he interprets them. Denzin states it baldly when he asserts that the social scientist 'follows a theory because it is in vogue, because it is espoused by powerful persons in the discipline, and many times simply because it complements his personal, or political values'.[20] So, in a real way, the theory and methods employed by the sociologist in going about his business has a lot to do with the meaning contexts in which he operates; not just the meaning contexts of a substantive theory, but those that form part of his wider culture.

It remains now to look just a little more closely at the two themes mentioned earlier, since these do, reasonably well, pose the major issues to be met within sociological theory and methodology.

Positivistic Meaning Systems and Sociological Inquiry

The 'naturalistic' meaning system is associated with many labels, 'physicalism', 'determinism', 'behaviourism', empiricism' and 'positivism' among others, which do not all mean quite the same things, and which should not be confused. Nonetheless, they do share some intellectual affinity, Philosophically, in modern history this theme was developed by the British empiricists Locke and Hume, who stressed sense experience as the source of all knowledge as against the rationalist view which allowed that some sources of knowledge had innate, non-sensory origins. In sociology, of course, the tradition goes back to Comte, the putative founder of sociology who argued for a science of man. Today, it appears as the dominant meaning system within contemporary sociology, though, let it be said, not without its vigorous challengers.

As indicated earlier, the fundamental ontological postulate which really refines this point of view is that the universe is all matter which we apprehend, sometimes incompletely, with our senses. This material world conforms to certain fixed and unalterable laws in an endless chain of causation. Though it may take a long time, the aim of scientific human inquiry is to elucidate these laws of the universe. Important for our immediate concern is that this view does not draw a consequential distinction between the material universe and the human: both are part and parcel of the same universe, subjected to the same principles of cause and effect. Man is simply one element in the orderly material universe.

If this ontological position is seriously entertained, it is important to notice the implications it has for the meaning contexts in which we talk about human behaviour. 'Free will', 'choice', 'voluntary action' and like terms, simply refer to '*epiphenomena*', only to be understood as products of the material laws determining human behaviour, which, in turn, are a sub-set of those laws which determine the pattern of the universe. A man does not *choose*; his 'choice' is simply a vector determined by the interplay of various forces acting upon him. It is an image associated with the models employed in classical mechanics.[21] Though we may not yet be able to determine the nature or the values of these forces determining human behaviour with the precision we associate with the physical sciences, time will surely enable the social scientist to do so.

Naturally enough, this view leads on to an easy association with the methods regarded as typical of the natural or physical sciences; not necessarily as a matter of logic, but certainly as a matter of what we might call 'natural affinity'. Thus, those that tend to accept something like the ontological position set out above, stress quantification, the formalization of concepts and theories, the use of so-called objective methods and techniques, and the crucial necessity of empirical observation as a theory-validating procedure.

Their approach, their justifications and typical accounts follow, more or less, the paradigm attributed to the natural sciences.

However, not all who accept this general position go all the way, which is why it is important to look at these connections as part of a flexible meaning system or context. In other words, some would accept some elements while rejecting others. For example, some accept those ideas stressing 'rules of procedure', such as systematic observation, the development of formal theory, the general principle of causation or quantification where possible, but do not accept that one can simply take over images and models directly from the physical sciences and employ them in the study of human behaviour. In other words, to accept some elements of the paradigm of the natural sciences is not at the same time to accept a slavish copying of its techniques and concepts and incorporate them entirely into sociological thinking. To accept that man is part of the material universe is not necessarily to accept also that he can be studied with the same techniques used by the physical sciences. However, it does mean adopting a methodological tenet, a rule that, in work called 'scientific', verifiable data is required, and in cases where concepts appear to refer to 'non-material' or subjective entities—values, goals, norms, purposes and so forth—any assertions should be supported by observables. By 'observables' is meant behavioural or observable indices of these non-material and subjective states. Nonetheless, it also involves accepting the postulate that such data is in principle obtainable; that behavioural indices, or whatever, have this systematic link to the non-material. That is, even so-called subjective states are part of the pattern of causation that rules the working of the universe.

Another important element of this naturalistic position is that the only source of knowledge derives from the logic and the methods and senses of the scientist, not in the subjects he studies. Common-sense meanings and the explanations of the common man have no 'scientific' status, for he cannot be an independent observer, unlike the scientist. Put another way, it is a stress on the necessity for objective standpoints in order to gain 'true knowledge'. The scientist is invoked to rid himself of personal prejudices and biases which might stand in the way of the dispassionate and objective verification or falsification of his theories. He must 'stand outside' the phenomena he studies. While this particular injunction might seem unnecessary in connection with the physical scientist, for the sociologist, or the social scientist in general, it is clearly bound to be an important and central methodological issue.

Non-Positivistic Meaning Systems and Sociological Inquiry

The alternative theme is, like the first, associated with many labels —'vitalism', 'idealism', 'voluntarism', 'rationalism', 'animism'—and, again, not all these terms mean quite the same thing. Nonetheless, while philosophies under this label might differ in detail, they generally hold to the view that 'as bodies, human beings may look like material stuff (in the same way as rocks and planetary bodies do), but that, as thinking bodies, humans are very unlike rocks and planetary bodies. The "forces" that move human beings *as* human beings rather than simply as physical bodies, are not gravitational forces or the forces of elementary particles. They are "meaningful stuff". They are internal ideas, feelings, motives.'[22] In other words, human beings are purposeful, goal-seeking, feeling, meaning-attributing and meaning-responding creatures. Moreover, and this is the important idea, this kind of 'stuff' cannot be studied with the same logic or techniques used to study the material universe. MacIver many years ago stated the position very forcibly:

> Those who would make sociology a 'natural' science, unconcerned with values, would leave out of account the special characteristics of the world of which it treats, in a vain attempt to ape those sciences where such characteristics are unknown. We are overmuch inclined to see in physical science the type and model of all science, and to imagine that measurement alone is knowledge. Purposes are incommensurate; the movements of thought among people cannot be estimated by counting heads; the power of personality is not to be measured like the power of an engine; institutions are ideal constructions without quantitative length or breadth.[23]

The distinction being argued here stresses the crucial difference between the natural and the social world: the natural possesses no intrinsic meaning system, but is meaningless, and, as a consequence, the natural scientist can more or less please himself how he constructs nature so that it is suitable for his cognitive purpose. As Schutz states it:

> It is up to the natural scientist to determine which sector of the universe of nature, which facts and which events therein, and which aspects of such facts and events are typically relevant to their specific purpose. These facts and events . . . do not reveal intrinsic relevance structures. Relevance is not inherent in nature as such, it is the result of the selective and interpretative activity

of man within nature. . . . The facts, data and events with which the natural scientist has to deal are just facts, data and events within the observational field does not 'mean' anything to the molecules, atoms, and electrons therein.[24]

What this view asserts is that there is an irreducible 'something' which is not captured by positivistic, naturalistic modes of inquiry, but which is nonetheless essential to any study claiming to inquire into the behaviour and nature of human beings. Human beings are not 'things' to be studied in the way one studies ants, plants or rocks, but are valuing, meaning-attributing beings to be understood as subjects and known as subjects.[25] Sociology (indeed any human science) deals with meaningful action, and the understanding, explanation, analysis or whatever, must be made with consideration of these meanings that make the ordering of human action possible. But these meanings cannot be studied by making man an object, as the positivist allegedly does; rather, the 'inner' subjective life of man must be made central as a methodological and theoretical canon. Durkheim's rule, 'Consider Facts as Things', is within this perspective, simply misguided and wrongheaded.[26] To impose positivistic meanings upon the *realm* of social phenomena is to distort the fundamental nature of human existence. The methodological task is to seek ways of using these subjective meanings, of entering the subject's inner domains and incorporating it within sociological theory.

Once again, sociologists falling roughly on this side of the onto-logical-epistomological fence do not necessarily have a disagreement with all that positivism stands for, or is supposed to stand for. Midway positions have been and are held. Weber, for one, while arguing the necessity for sociological analysis 'adequate at the level of meaning', also stressed the need for verification of this kind of analysis by the canons of science as normally understood.[27] Others, however, are prepared to go much further. They argue that social phenomena cannot be studied in terms of distinct and formalized categories defined in advance by the social scientist independently of the commonsense notions of men acting in their everyday concerns. To do so would be to study not human action but 'scientified' action.[28] The phenomena of everyday life must be studied in its own terms by methods that retain the integrity of that phenomena, not phenomena created by experimental situations or other positivistic methods. The prime task of sociology is to study and understand everyday life, and sociological theory begins and ends at this point. 'Any scientific understanding of human action, at whatever level of ordering or generality, must begin with and be built upon an understanding of the everyday life of the members performing those actions.'[29]

So far so good, except that part of everyday life is the sociologists' carefully constructed accounts, explanations and understandings of the people he studies. These, also, are legitimate areas of inquiry, and the sociologist, his positivist claim to being an objective observer notwithstanding, is simply another observer, like the common man, working with common understandings shared by his fellow sociologists but having no absolute view on truth. This position, then, goes quite far in rejecting any notion of an absolute objectivity, or an absolute standard of truth, or an ontology standing above all others as the criterion of reality. They reject the idea that the observer, by 'externalizing' his concepts, by using procedures of experiment, quantitative methods of measurement, and so on, can eliminate all human affects on the knowledge gained. 'By the use of these procedures . . . the human mind was presumed capable of grasping the "thing in itself" and of locating those "noumena" within a pure realm of universal co-ordinates that would enable any knowing mind to grasp or know them independently of the concrete situations in which they were originally known or in which the knower grasped them at a particular time.'[30] The alternative epistemology presented is that all human knowledge, whether we call it scientific or not, is gained and 'grounded in our human purposes in the situations in which we find ourselves, it can never be fully independent of the properties of our minds or of our practical situations'.[31] There is no absolute objectivity, only the shared agreements on truth and validity common to men who hold, in the language used earlier in this chapter, to the same meaning system.

In short, this position stresses the qualitative difference between the material world and the world of human life. Methodologically, the implications are fairly clear. If there is this difference, they must be studied by markedly different methods: methods which retain the 'essential' nature of human life and do not analyse and externalize it away. As Znaniecki said, the essential character of 'cultural data' is a 'humanistic coefficient'. If this were lost from a study of a cultural or human system, 'the system would disappear and in its stead he [the scientist] would find a disjointed man of natural things and processes, without any similarity to the reality he started to investigate'.[32]

Conclusions

These, then, are the two themes paramount in the intellectual history of sociology. As sets of ontological postulates, they have ramifications for the whole process of thinking about, thinking in, and the doing of sociology. In the terms used at the start of this discussion, they are two meaning systems used to define, assess and evaluate, and explain the subject-matter of sociology. I have refrained from posing one viewpoint against the other since many of the detailed considerations necessary for such a task will come in later chapters. Suffice it at this point to say that these are the kinds of question which will underpin the discussions to follow. Time and time again we will return to these issues to provide a larger context necessary to judge and evaluate procedures and techniques.

There is no need to choose between the two perspectives outlined. In any case, it would be unwise to do so on the basis of the discussion here, since the issues are far more complex than may as yet appear. Doing sociology is not a matter of slavishly following rules out of some book, but of trying things out, seeing how they work and, in other words, appreciating the full richness (I cannot resist the cliché) of sociology. Criticism will always be found since criticism seldom requires much intellectual courage: to have ideas requires rather more.

Exercise: The 'It' from Mars

This exercise is designed to provoke you into seeing social life as problematical, and also to provide empirical instancing of some of the issues raised in this chapter.

Sociology, like any inquiring discipline, arises and develops because far-sighted individuals perceive something that needs to be explained, something that cannot be adequately accounted for within existing explanatory schemes. The 'It' from Mars (Martians are hermaphroditic, so there are no labels in their language to indicate sex differences), observing some pieces of everyday mundane human behaviour, would find them puzzling and would probably need to develop a specialized language to describe and account for discovered patterns. What this exercise asks you to do is imagine yourself as the 'It' from Mars, and to go out to observe such everyday human activities as, for example, standing in a bus queue, shopping in a store, listening to a lecture, drinking in a pub, a policeman directing traffic; or, even more challenging, a group of people who 'happen' to be together. Observe for a period of time and try to develop a description of what is happening. It is often useful to do this exercise in pairs, you and your partner making notes and observations about the same interaction at the same time and comparing notes afterwards. The next step is to indicate what there is to explain and what form such an explanation might take.

This means formulating the description as a problem requiring explanation. How is the phenomena to be accounted for? What is distinctively 'social' about it? For example, if you are observing a bus queue, note down all the things which seem important to it as a social phenomena. Other questions to be asked in this example might be: Do people stand in bus queues and talk to each other? Is there anything distinctive about the way the interpersonal spaces are managed? Is there any pattern to the movement of the people? How is this pattern to be described? The trick is to try to make even the most routine of activities puzzling. In class discussion, try perhaps to formulate your description in such a way that the class have to guess what kind of social interaction it was that you observed.

When you come to formulate your explanatory sketches, think about the data and the observations you have made, and how they might 'fit in' with your theoretical ideas. Depending upon how much sociology you have read prior to this exercise, you might like to try your hand at using one or two sociological theories on your data. However, the aim of the exercise is to give you an opportunity to limber up your brains so that you can think about the problems of relating theory and data.

Finally, in discussion, you might like to consider formulating theoretical ideas in terms of the 'positivistic' and 'non-positivistic' modes mentioned. That is, try to cast an explanation in terms of causality, suggesting underlying agencies that determine the sort of behaviour you observed. For example, you might formulate hypotheses about how people of different social classes behave in the situations you observed. Alternatively, try to propose a 'non-positivistic' type of explanation which is more rooted in the events you have observed, and what they consist of as topics of inquiry in their own right. What do the activities look like to the people involved, and how do they organize them? Think about any differences you may note between the two modes of explanation.

Notes and References

1. There is a danger here of making the notion of 'meaning system' do too much work. I use the term to stress the human origin of idea systems in science, or, for that matter, in anything else. Also, although the term 'system' is used, the linking of meanings may or may not be so integrated as the term might imply. The degree of constraint operating within any one meaning system is a matter for inspection. For example, mathematics or logic would seem, intuitively, to be meaning systems of high constraint, whereas those of children's games or flower arrangement would seem to be much less so and more open-ended in character. A discussion of the notion of constraint with reference to idea-systems is to be found in P. Converse, 'The Nature of Belief Systems in Mass Publics', in D. Apter (ed.), *Ideology and Discontent*, The Free Press, New York, pp. 206–61.

2. There is an obvious catch here in that it would be difficult to explicate precisely what I class as scientific. Do I include scientology, astrology or palmistry? I simply note the difficulty.

3. T. S. Kuhn, *The Structure of Scientific Revolutions*, University of Chicago Press, Chicago, 1962. See also the collection of papers in I. Lakatos and A. Musgrave (eds.), *Criticism and the Growth of Knowledge*, Cambridge University Press, Cambridge, 1970. Another image, and one which will occur frequently throughout the discussion, is that what we are about to do is try to explicate the structure of a language, the language(s) investigators use to theorize and research. This is important, since, to carry the analogy with language further, linguistic structure and use affect the way in which the world is structured and interpreted. 'Thus, science and the scientific method as means of viewing and obtaining knowledge about the world around us provide those who accept its tenets with a grammar that is not merely a reproducing instrument for describing what the world is all about, but also shapes our ideas of what the world is like, often to the exclusion of other ways of looking at the world'—A. V. Cicourel, *Method and Measurement in Sociology*, The Free Press, New York, 1964, p. 35. Kaplan uses the term 'logic-in-use' to refer to the methods of argument and inquiry in a particular science, in contrast to 'reconstructed logic', which is the abstraction, idealization and generalization of principles used in reasoning. See A. Kaplan. *The Conduct of Enquiry*, Chandler Publishing Co., San Francisco, 1964, p. 8.

4. P. Diesing, *Patterns of Discovery in the Social Sciences*, Routledge & Kegan Paul, London, 1972, p. 124.

5. A. W. Gouldner, *The Coming Crisis in American Sociology*, Basic

Books, New York, 1970, p. 30. See also E. A. Barth, *The Metaphysical Foundations of Modern Science*, Doubleday, New York, 1954, for an analysis of some metaphysical elements in the development of scientific thought.

6. Kuhn, *The Structure of Scientific Revolutions*, p. 41.

7. In case it might be thought that 'reality' as we perceive it is a self-evident construction, read Carlos Castaneda, *The Teachings of Don Juan*, Penguin Books, Harmondsworth, 1970. This is about an anthropologist's experience with a Yaqui medicine man, who as part of his tradition, used hallucinogens. It is a brilliant and sometimes frightening account.

8. T. S. Kuhn, 'Logic of Discovery or Psychology of Research', in Lakatos and Musgrave (eds.), *Criticism and the Growth of Knowledge*, pp. 1–23.

9. P. McHugh, 'On the Failure of Positivism', in J. D. Douglas (ed.), *Understanding Everyday Life*, Aldine Press, Chicago, 1970, p. 332.

10. In sociology, and, one suspects, in the social sciences in general, little in the way of replication is apparent. There seems little professional mileage in it.

11. This kind of process is illustrated by the shock exhibited by the scientific community on the publication of J. D. Watson's *The Double Helix*, Weidenfeld & Nicolson, London, 1968, which 'blew the gaff', as it were, on the norms of objectivity and the dispassionate search for truth, etc., supposed to characterize scientific practice. See also, for an analysis of the role of 'common understandings' in everyday interaction, H. Garfinkel, *Studies in Ethnomethodology*, Prentice-Hall, Englewood Cliffs, 1967, esp. Chapter 2.

12. We might do well, however, to acknowledge the force of Ackoff's remark that, 'We must stop acting as though nature were organized into disciplines in the same way that universities are'—R. L. Ackoff, 'Systems, Organizations and Inter-disciplinary Research', *General Systems Year Book*, 1960, p. 6. A great deal of sociological theorizing is about the 'domain' of the subject, which, of course, has implications for more particular and substantive explanations.

13. In recent decades there have been attempts to develop a general social science embracing all existing ones. Few have been successful, partly because of the entrenched professional structure within higher education which acts as a constraint against the adoption of such radical ideas. It may, of course, be that such attempts have little merit.

14. A similar sort of argument has been advanced by Lipset in reference to the development of political science. The claim is that such a subject could not have existed until the fourteenth century when

the link between the state and the church began to erode. See S. M. Lipset, *Political Man*, Heinemann, London, 1960, Chapter 1.

15. Obviously I have posed too stark a polarity between these two positions. A good discussion dealing with the issues in greater depth is in W. R. Catton, *From Animistic to Naturalistic Sociology*, McGraw-Hill, New York, 1966, esp. Chapter 2.

16. See D. Martindale, *Nature and Types of Sociological Theory*, Routledge & Kegan Paul, London, 1960; and R. Fletcher, *The Making of Sociology*, Nelson, London, 1971.

17. Gouldner, *The Coming Crisis in American Sociology*, p. 32.

18. A brilliant science-fiction story on this theme is Walter Miller's 'I Made You', about a machine which has been made to 'think'. The irony of the man's last appeal as he is being killed by the machine is that it should pay deference, like a child, to its creator. The tale is to be found in B. Aldiss (ed.), *Yet More Penguin Science Fiction*, Penguin Books, Harmondsworth, 1964.

19. See T. H. Marshall, 'British Sociology Today', in *Contemporary Sociology in Western Europe and America*, Proceedings of the 1st International Congress of Social Science, Luigi Sturzo Institute, Rome, 1967; M. D. Carter, 'Report on a Survey of Sociological Research in Britain', *The Sociological Review*, 16, 1968.

20. N. K. Denzin, 'Politics and Promises: The Values of Social Science', in N. K. Denzin (ed.), *The Values of Social Science*, Aldine Press, Chicago 1970, p. 9. The work of Gouldner cited earlier is an extended analysis of this kind of influence within American sociology.

21. A rather forthright exponent of this view within sociology (there are, of course, others) was George Lunberg, who not only made strenuous efforts to avoid the use of such terms as 'organic', 'spiritual' and 'mental', but also conceived the entire history of science as the expansion of the realm of the natural and physical at the expense of the spiritual and mental. Thus, 'One by one "spiritual" phenomena have become "physical" . . . The evolution of the concept of the soul is especially relevant, because its final state of transition or translation by way of "mind" into purely "physical" concepts is still underway'—G. A. Lunberg, *Foundations of Sociology*, Macmillan, New York, 1939, p. 8.

22. J. D. Douglas, in *Understanding Everyday Life*, p. 6.

23. R. M. MacIver, *Community: A Sociological Study*, St. Martin's Press, New York, 1917, pp. 56–7.

24. A. Schutz, 'Concept and Theory Formation in the Social Sciences', *Journal of Philosopy*, LI, 1964, pp. 266–7. For further discussion, see D. Walsh, 'Sociology and the Social World', in P. Filmer *et al.*,

New Directions in Sociological Theory, Collier-Macmillan, London, 1972, pp. 15–35.

25. See S. T. Bruyn, *The Human Perspective in Sociology*, Prentice-Hall, Englewood Cliffs, 1966; and, for an earlier example, F. Znaniecki, *The Method of Sociology*, Holt, Rinehart & Winston, New York, 1934. Kaplan, in *The Conduct of Enquiry*, p. 31, quotes a cautionary tale on this point. An object arrives from outer space and resists all efforts by physicists, astronomers or chemists to determine its composition, structure and function until someone has the bright idea of asking, 'What is your name?' and the object replies, 'Ralph.'

26. E. Durkheim, *The Rules of Sociological Method*, The Free Press, Glencoe, 1950.

27. M. Weber, *The Methodology of the Social Sciences*, The Free Press, Glencoe, 1949.

28. The phrase is Douglas's in *Understanding Everyday Life*, p. 14. Schutz, in a statement following on from the one quoted above (page 25, states the point as follows: 'The observational field of the social scientist . . . has a specific meaning and relevance structure for the human beings living, acting, and thinking therein. By a series of commonsense constructs they have pre-selected and pre-interpreted this world which they experience as the reality of their daily lives. It is these thought objects of theirs which determine their behaviour by motivating it. The thought objects constructed by the social scientist, in order to grasp their social reality, have to be founded upon the thought object constructed by the commonsense thinking of men, living their daily life within their social works.'

29. Douglas, in *Understanding Everyday Life*, p. 11.

30. ibid., p. 25.

31. ibid., p. 27. The same argument, posed a little differently, also appears in K. Mannheim (see his *Ideology and Utopia*, Routledge & Kegan Paul, London, 1960), and is implicit in Marx's work.

32. Znaniecki, *The Method of Sociology*, p. 37.

2
Concepts and Theories

It is perhaps as well to begin the discussion with topics at the very heart of the language of methodology: (a) the formulation of concepts and (b) theory building.

Concepts and the Language of Inquiry

Scientists, any scientists, need to agree on a language with which to communicate with each other and talk about the way the world is and how it is. In Chapter 1, we discussed the importance of language and meaning in defining what was in the universe and what it was about. Concepts, if you like, are the units out of which we construct for the world a meaning, and theories are ways of relating these meanings to each other in such a way that something is claimed as true of the world. In this sense, concepts are crucial to any form of inquiry. As Blumer says, 'To speak of a science without concepts suggests all sorts of analogies—a carver without tools, a railroad without tracks, a mammal without bones, a love story without love.'[1] In other words, concepts are crucial to inquiry and the meanings they stand for are the 'stuff' of science. Through concepts, reality is given sense, order and coherence. To use the concepts of the 'natural' and the 'social' is to put, as it were, a structure or grid on to our sensory experience by defining and saying something about what the universe is like. In this sense, a concept is a rule of judging, a 'prescription for organizing the material of experience so as to be able to go about our business'.[2] A man, for example, is not just a rational animal, a biped, a fallen angel, a sex object: a man is all of these and more, depending on how he is conceived and for what purposes. The same term can stand for many concepts depending upon the particular meaning system involved. This is why it is difficult to say quite what concepts are. Clearly they are not words, although words are used to convey concepts. In the example used, the word 'man' can stand for many different concepts depending upon circumstances. Concepts are ideas 'standing behind' words, though we must be careful not to reify them by seeing them as 'things': as objects in some curious world only remotely connected with our experience. In general, it might be preferable to see concepts as the media through which we make sense (moral, empirical or religious) out of experience.

Within all the sciences there is constant discussion about particular concepts and their meaning. In sociology, for example, there is wide-ranging discussion over such commonly accepted ideas as 'social role', 'culture', 'social structure' or 'social system'. Where there is less disagreement is on the necessity or otherwise for such concepts. If concepts are the medium by which we structure a reality, then clearly it is of some importance within each discipline for certain concepts to be given a more fundamental status than others—even if there may be disagreements over meanings. These are the concepts which define the locus of the subject, and define its ultimate subject-matter and the rationale of the whole disciplinary enterprise. In sociology, they are not hard to spot: 'social' is an obvious one, 'action', 'behaviour', 'society', 'groups', 'interpersonal relations' are others. They indicate the attribute space for the attention of inquiry, and about which theories are formulated. Not that there is no disagreement about the meaning of these concepts: indeed, much important work is concerned to propose and elaborate new meanings and interpretations.

Concepts, then, are crucial in two main ways: as representatives of reality under study, and as the basis by which images of reality can be incorporated into some shared meaning system by which we can give various sorts of accounts of that reality. Concepts achieve this by classifying experience, however remote that experience might be. The concept of 'social class', for example, offers a rule, a grid, even though vague at times, to use in talking about certain sorts of experience that have to do with economic position, life-style, life-chances, and so on. It serves to identify aspects of experience, and by relating the concept to other concepts we are able to construct theories about experiences in a particular order or sphere.

Concepts and Meaning

To look more closely at the issues involved it is necessary to examine how concepts are given meaning. A concept is a 'relationship' between a symbol, usually a word, and some idea or conception. A typical manner in which this relationship is maintained is by defining the concept word in terms of other concept words: a process known as nominal or lexical definition.[3] A dictionary operates in this way. Thus, the concept of 'democracy' is defined by a set of other words, such as 'the regime of civilian rule through representative institutions and public liberties'.[4] Providing we understand the meanings of the other terms—that is, understand the language—we understand the idea behind the concept 'democracy'. Of course, it is open to us to disagree with the definition offered—as in the case of an example such as 'democracy' is more than likely—but we nonetheless understand the alternative formula. The concept with the word to which it is attached is linked to other associated ideas through other associated words.

Important to this definitional procedure is its reliance on similarities and equalities within a meaning system. This is the course of its circular and tautological character. A meaning is elucidated by making it more or less commensurate with other meanings within the system. However, this circularity does not render the procedure valueless, quite the contrary. For one thing, elucidating the meaning of concept can often best be served by relating it to other more familiar concepts. Alternatively, precision can be given to a concept by specifying clearly what the concept means in terms of other similarly precisely defined meanings. This is the kind of precision claimed to be essential for scientific concepts. 'Speed' might colloquially be defined as 'how fast an object is travelling', which, providing the English language is understood, should be clear enough for most purposes. For other purposes, however, it might not be sufficient. Instead we might offer, 'Speed means the distance travelled between any two points divided by the time taken to travel between the same two points'. Since this is related to the meaning system of mathematics, a precise numerical value can be given to the concept: for some a major step forward. In addition, to emphasize the relative precision of the scientific concept over the colloquial one, a different term may be proposed to stand for the concept of speed—say, 'velocity'.

In a sociological context, this kind of precision-creating process is claimed to be necessary by those who adopt some of the positivistic/naturalistic tenets discussed in Chapter 1. Since it is the assumed goal of the scientific enterprise to provide ever more accurate descriptions of the world, and one of the prime means to this end is by more and more refined measurement procedures, an essential step towards this goal is precise definition of what it is intended to measure. A prerequisite to measurement is the precise conceptual definition of the phenomena being measured. However, sociology, it is often claimed, faces special problems not met with in quite the same degree in the natural sciences, namely, that many of its concepts are taken from everyday life with their consequent vagaries and inelegancies of expression. So the sociologist, if he is to maintain his role as a detached, external observer, must remove the clutter and noise from terms also current in colloquial usage and give them precision.[5] Examples of such concepts in colloquial as well as scientific usage are legion, including 'politics', 'opinion', 'democracy', 'person', 'society', 'mass', and so on throughout almost the entire lexicon of the social sciences. Deriving from this is the rule that the social scientist must stipulate and refine the concepts he uses so that precise theories and explanations can be forthcoming.

An example of the danger of inadequate conceptual clarity occurs in Powers's study of the role of counselling in the prevention of delinquency. This study is important in another way in that it is one of the first (and few) attempts to use a strict experimental design in the field—that is, outside a laboratory. The point about an experiment is that it is a research design to test fairly specific hypotheses, and to do this, definitional precision is essential. In other respects, Powers's study took considerable care in design. Subjects were carefully matched and then randomly allocated to control and subject groups so that the effect of the experimental factor, 'warm and friendly counsel', could be studied as a causal factor in the prevention of delinquency. Unfortunately, the study was a failure in the sense of providing evidence for or against the hypothesis that 'warm and friendly counsel' did or did not have a material affect on the delinquency rate. Part of the failure was due to imprecise definition of the experimental factor, 'warm and friendly counsel'. Counsellors' behaviour and their interpretation of what this meant was highly variable. So whatever had been the outcome of the experiment in terms of enhancing or reducing delinquency rates, the investigators would have been unable to identify the cause since 'warm and friendly counsel', as it turned out, meant so many things. In short, the concept was too imprecisely defined.[6]

Sensitizing Concepts

Of course, to many sociologists efforts to impute precision into concepts for such purposes is fundamentally misconceived. They argue that while we must be reasonably clear what we mean, the search for precision must not make us lose sight of, or define out, the reality which we, as sociologists, purport to study. To describe, say, behaviour in terms of some precise and prior definition of role categories is to ignore one very serious and important component of human behaviour: its ambiguity, fluidity and very lack of precision. In other words, the social scientist must apprehend the original meanings with all their subtleties, since they are an essential part of what determines the course of social action. In a word, it is not always desirable in social scientific procedure to have exact definitions prior to inquiry. For one thing, they may well put a premature closure on research by too tightly formulating the nature of the problem. Any definitional precision should be the outcome of an exploration of the situation or event being studied. It is a claim, in other words, for the use of sensitizing concepts, the meaning of which is given 'by means of exposition which yields a meaningful picture, abetted by apt illustrations which enable one to grasp the reference in terms of one's own experience'.[7] But not only is it an argument against too strict prior definition and specification of concepts, since this might result in the foreclosure of important research questions, it is also a recommendation that commonsense meanings be allowed to speak. This goes back to the view put forward earlier that sociological analyses include, as a matter of explanatory necessity, the viewpoint of the actor, which, in turn, requires that concepts be derived, with all their confusion and noise, from the meanings the actors themselves employ.

Official Statistics: a Case of Spurious Clarity?

This is undoubtedly an important warning to bring against a great deal of naturalistic/positivistic work done in sociology, and one amply illustrated by a salient and much discussed example of the use of official statistics in research work. One of the available sources of data much used by positivistically inclined sociologists are official statistics gathered for governmental and other administrative purposes: crime figures, birth and death statistics, trade indices, and so on. Indeed, one of the factors enhancing the status and position of positivistic sociology was the ready availability of such data. Whatever else may be said about the pro's and con's of using officially collected statistics for sociological research, the criticism germane at this point is that the categories employed for official purposes may be seriously at variance with the sociological ideas they are intended to illuminate. The classic study using official

material of this kind was Durkheim's of suicide.[8] Durkheim, like
the majority of later sociologists interested in suicide, used data
derived from official sources—in other words, from figures based
on prior definitions of suicide. A death, in being processed for official
records, goes through a fairly complex social process in which judgement is made as to whether, for instance, the death in question
was from natural causes, was self-administered or administered by
someone else, or was accidental. In short, the persons involved in
the process of producing the official figures (in the case of suicide,
coroners, policemen or doctors) are operating on meanings and
concepts which lead them to label one kind of death 'suicide' and
another, say, 'murder' or 'accidental'. Moreover, the meanings
associated with suicidal behaviour vary within a single society and
between different societies. Is the soldier who charges an enemy
position with no chance of escaping death a hero—or a suicidal
maniac? The question itself is silly: what is important is not that
the researcher has to choose how to label the act, but that actors
in the situation label it in particular ways as 'suicide', 'heroic',
'bloody silly', or whatever. Accordingly, if one starts from the
premise that suicide is a socially rather than a naturally defined
form of behaviour, its definition becomes problematic and moreover
varies with time and location.[9]

Though this point is particularly apt with respect to official
statistics, it is also a general point against the many positivistic
strategies and techniques of inquiry that depend upon the prior
definition of concepts. While it is necessary to have some broad
idea of what it is intended to study, ideas and concepts should not
be so strictly defined that the very process of interest is also lost.[10]
A researcher must be more than a little sensitive to the way the
actors themselves perceive and give meaning of their activities. As
Douglas says most forcibly, 'Rather than putting society upon the
rock, bending and distorting the fundamental nature of man and
society to fit the narrow quantitative prejudices of officials and
their supporters in the social sciences, we must begin by studying
the fundamental nature of the phenomena, experiencing them as
directly as possible. . . .'[11]

Operational Definitions and Meaning Validation

But, whatever position we take on this matter, sociology lays claim
to being an empirical science, meaning that it tries to assert something about the social world about us. Accordingly, the nominal
mode of defining discussed earlier is hardly a complete procedure,

since concepts require some kind of link with the 'external world'. Accepting this, at least some of the concepts we use in talking sociology must be given empirical import. The typical procedure is to give meaning to concepts in terms of *observables*: things that have some sense-data content and some empirical reference. Thus the concept of aggression is given meaning in terms of certain kinds of observable behaviour, such as heavy breathing, clenching fists, vituperative language or fighting. This kind of definitional procedure is close to what is known as 'operational definition': defining a concept in terms of the operations required to measure it. Another typical example is the concept of 'intelligence', which is operationally defined as whatever is measured by an intelligence test. An extreme form of this position is to regard no concept as plausible or valid unless it can be objectively specified as applying to, or measuring, something in the external world. The difficulty with this extreme view, even in the context of the positivistic tradition with which it is usually harnessed, is that no general concepts can be admitted as legitimately meaningful. There are as many meanings of intelligence as there are tests to measure it, since, on this criterion, we cannot abstract and talk about intelligence in general. (There may, of course, well be a case for not talking about 'intelligence in general' as a kind of single intelligence factor, but rather of various sorts of intelligence.)

In fact, concepts and abstractions are used even by the most rigorous operationalists: they cannot avoid them. Statements about measuring operations are themselves abstractions since they require a commitment to at least the abstract axioms of mathematics. Moreover, as no two phenomena or occasions are exactly alike, a test situation is never exactly repeatable. As Bergmann has pointed out, an extreme operationalist would have to refuse 'to generalize from one instance of an experiment to the next if the apparatus had in the meantime been moved to another corner of the room'.[12] Clearly this kind of position if taken too seriously becomes far too extreme to be useful. Nonetheless, operational definitions, whether precisely specified or not, are essential in any sort of empirical inquiry if only to the extent that some concepts should have some empirical import.

The precise nature of this import is, however, something a little more difficult to determine. Suppose that we wish to give some empirical meaning to the concept of 'alienation'. A reasonable strategy would be carefully to go through all that we understand by the concept. We would likely as not come up with such similar terms as 'estrangement', 'separation', 'isolation' or 'apart'. Digging further, we might begin to feel the full flavour of the concept by asking such hopefully pertinent questions as, 'Alienated from what?' 'What kind of behaviours characterize an alienated person?' 'How would the term be used, in what contexts and by whom?' The procedure is rather like drawing out a sample of meanings from a universe (in the sense of population) of meanings. If it is our intention to measure this concept, to give 'alienation' some operational definition (for such reasons as constructing an attitude scale, or using it to characterize observed behaviours), then we have to select out of this universe a sample of meanings representative of the concept. Immediately this poses problems of validity: does the measure (sample of meanings) really measure (stand for) what it is we want to measure (the universe of meaning)? Does it over-represent certain nuances of the concept and under-represent others? Unfortunately, there is a lack of adequate criteria to decide on these questions, especially since we have no means of specifying any limits to the possible universe of meaning, or, even in principle, of giving a complete enumeration of these meanings. One alternative and tempting tactic to remove the frustration discussed is *stipulation* by simply stating that what is being used to measure the concept is that meaning of it which is relevant. These points will be taken up in subsequent chapters.

There are other procedures. If it is agreed that meaning has a lot to do with the consensual agreement among interested parties, then deciding on the adequacy of any empirical rendering of a concept is a matter of somehow creating agreement or using agreement as a criterion for the validity of the measures selected. This is the method known familiarly as 'face validation'. The researcher simply presents his empirical version of the concept to 'judges' who can be reasonably expected to give a considered opinion on whether or not the empirical version represents the hypothetical universe of content. In other words, one sets up a criterion of validity—in this case, the agreement of other persons—and this becomes the rule by which some objectivity is assured in the selection of representative measures. Using the procedure, the researcher sets up an arbitrary set of criteria, that is, the agreement among a certain class of people that meaning A is representative of, equal to, or can stand for meaning B. But one important catch lies in the selection of the 'certain class of people'. Who should they be? Fellow sociologists with some experience of the concept under scrutiny? Or, alternatively, people whom the concept is intended to describe? A moment's consideration of these and like questions would suggest that the judgement of validity could vary as between any two or more groups of people. How then could we decide between them? There is no easy answer, except that the issue goes back to the ultimate perspectives on sociology. If we adopt the view that judging the validity of an empirical version of a concept is a technical matter to be decided by experts, then all we need are experts. In other words, we would adopt a criterion consistent with the sociologist being somehow the privileged observer. If, on the other hand, we argue that it is the meanings of the subjects that are important, then the validation procedure will be dependent upon the subjects' judgements.

Of course, to the non-positivist all this is a waste of time. For one thing, there would seem little need to be so precise when the understandings that need to be studied are not in themselves precise (by the standards of academic logic), but rather full of ambiguity and confusion. Further, the establishment of such criteria as some objective validation procedure does not, as a matter of fact, provide any absolute standard at all. Rather it is simply the view of a set of people who are themselves operating on particular viewpoints.

Nonetheless there still remains the problem (whether we solve it or not) of giving some concepts some empirical import. It is essential to have some agreement on the ontological structure of the world. But as we might expect, this is not quite so easy as it sounds. Many concepts in all sciences, including many of the important ones, are not easily translatable into empirical terms in the sense of observables. 'Gravity', to take an obvious one, is not observable, though its inferred effects may be. Sociology is replete with such examples. 'Role' is not observable as such, nor is 'norm', 'social relationship', 'society', 'social structure', 'consensus' or 'status', even though we may talk as if we recognize them and make conversation using the concepts meaningfully. All relational concepts, so important to sociology, fall into this category. What are we to make of such concepts?

Let us first take gravity, since it is probably easier to make the point here than in the case of less familiar sociological examples. Gravity is not directly observable (unless we adopt the extreme operationalist position, and then gravity is simply the observations one must make to measure it), but its effects are. We regularly see falling bodies, such as raindrops, and may even fall ourselves. By any standards, these observations are as close to sense-data as most things. How are they to be explained? They are explained by means of a theory in which is contained a concept known as 'gravity', defined as a force belonging to objects of considerable mass which causes objects to be 'attracted' to that mass. Now, gravity is not observable, but the theory in which the concept appears offers an explanation of why objects heavier than air fall towards the earth (and why objects lighter than air do not). So, by examination of the rates of fall of these objects, we can even give a quantitative expression to the concept. In other words, we can make the link between the empirical world (falling objects) and the abstract concept (gravity) because we assume, or have evidence, that some theory (theory of gravitation) is true.

In social science, much the same kind of principle is involved, if with less precision and certainty and implicitly rather than explicitly. For example, suppose we had observed that, in a population, there is a four-year cycle in which the proportion of communication content that consists of vituperative discussion rises to a peak around the end of October in each leap year. Early in November, the rate falls and is replaced by a corresponding rise in congratulatory messages from one group to another. Suppose, further, that we had recorded a number of successive cycles of this type and can predict them with some accuracy. How are we to explain such a pattern?[13] Part of our explanation might be that the American electorate in general desires to uphold the constitution and conform to the express will of the majority more than it desires the election of particular candidates. In other words, a theory is formed about the efficacy of certain values in American society, how they are held, by which people, and how they affect political behaviour within that society. An integral part of the explanation is the concept of values which, like gravity, is not directly observable, though, it is assumed, its effects are. And, as with the concept of gravity, the link between the empirical world (observed behaviour) and the abstract concept (values) is taken as valid because some theory (a theory of the relationship between values and behaviour) is assumed to be true. (Of course, if the theory were found to be false, then the inference would be invalid.)[14] Take the earlier example of 'alienation'. Whatever decision is taken as to how it is to be given empirical import, whether by an attitudes scale or observed behaviour, the validity of the method will depend upon the adequacy of some theory, or, less strongly, supposition, linking the behaviour as instances of the concept 'alienation'.

Theory

The term 'theory' has already been used fairly freely. As already pointed out, theory is, at its most general, one way in which concepts are related to each other so that the claim can be made to have explained certain aspects of reality. The notions of theory and explanation are inseparable.

Modes of Sociological Theorizing

This brings us to some rather involved issues about the nature of theory and explanation. Unfortunately there is within sociology little agreement about what is meant by 'theory' and 'explanation', and it may be as well to look at some of the ways in which sociologists theorize and conceive of the activity of theorizing.

Few of the categories to be discussed are mutually exclusive in the sense that they represent logically distinct types of theory. Rather they are categories which describe modes of theorizing, or activities which sociologists call theorizing. 'Theory' is a term loaded with evaluative as well as literal meanings. Like the crowns of kings, the term is a symbol of rule and authority: possession of title gives power, authority and legitimation. To sequester the term 'theory' to refer to the products of one's own activities, and to deny its legitimate use to others lends some authoritative justification, if only in the sense that it lends support and *self*-justification for what one is doing. It is to say, in effect, 'What I do is the only way: mine is the correct (more scientific, most sociologically relevant, or whatever) way of thinking about social reality.' Naturally, and fairly obviously, theory is a notion receiving much of its standing from the pace and standards set by the natural sciences and their success in interpreting and explaining the universe. It would, however, be wrong to see all claims to theory as simply evaluative, or as positions taken in inter-disciplinary warfare. The practices of theorizing do have varied implications for the strategy and tactics of research, and ultimately for the character of sociology.

The first types of theory practice have already been mentioned, and consist of elaborating basic ontological and epistemological postulates which serve, one way or another, to define an area of study or domain of inquiry. There are a number of convenient labels that can be used in referring to this kind of theorizing at its high level of abstraction and its relative remoteness from detailed empirical inquiry. Occasionally such theories have a normative emphasis in the sense of asserting that something, or some state of affairs, should or ought to be the case.

Examples of this kind of theoretical practice are fairly plentiful in sociology, and they range from the elaboration of conceptual distinctions to questions about what this or that thinker really meant. Empirical material is often used for illustration rather than for systematically grounding the theory in any detailed empirical work. It is this which often forms the focus of criticism of this mode of theorizing. One such comment is C. Wright Mills's remark that 'grand theory' involves a 'seemingly arbitrary and certainly endless elaboration of distinctions which neither enlarge our understandings nor make our experience more sensible'.[15] Certainly, it is often difficult to see how the abstractions relate to experience or to data collected in an attempt to answer particular questions.[16]

However, though these criticisms about the remoteness of this type of theorizing for empirical analysis is well taken with respect to some examples, it would be quite wrong to dismiss the practice as entirely misguided or valueless. Earlier, when speaking of ontological postulates and the intellectual-conceptual structuring of reality, it was suggested that these high-level statements are implicit in any perspective or theory about that reality. They are the fundamental conceptual distinctions which make lower-level types of theory possible. 'What is the nature of social reality?' 'What is the social act?' These and similar questions all require answers at a high level of abstraction. And even though they are often left implicit, they are fundamental to the process of more detailed inquiry. In Kuhnian terms, answers to such questions seem to delineate a paradigm, a set of issues which, when developed, form 'puzzle-setters' to the researcher: set subsidiary questions which more particular research tries to solve within the general ontological framework established by this high-level theorizing.[17] So, for example, the contention that sociologists must take account of actors' meanings is not only an assertion about the nature of social reality, but also a guide to the kind of things the researchers must look at and include in any analysis of social phenomena. It is an attempt to assert what should be the proper province of sociological inquiry. Similarly, the position attributed to Durkheim that social behaviour is caused by factors 'external' to the individual is of much the same status, and much of the activity in this type of theorizing is elucidating similarities and differences between different ontological positions or theories.

Nonetheless, though questions and issues raised at this level are ultimately important, it must be admitted (to return to an earlier point) that such theories are often too remote from day-to-day empirical concerns and, for the more empirically inclined, offer little guide for systematic measurement and the development of empirically relevant theory. Certainly within the terms of positivist paradigms this is a well-directed point. To the positivist and others, this form of theorizing is just so much over-elaboration of concepts, almost to the wilful exclusion of any empirical import.

A second style of theorizing stems in large part from the kind of criticism of 'grand theory' briefly cited earlier—namely, that it is too remote from the 'basic stuff' of empirical research. The alternative style and strategy of theorizing argues that building theory cannot be satisfactorily achieved in the armchair: instead, theoretical formulations must (or ought?) to be firmly rooted in the problems of explanation that arise from trying to interpret a specific set of data. As Merton stated some years ago, '. . . *sociological theory* refers to logically interconnected conceptions which are limited and modest in scope, rather than all-embracing and grandiose'.[18] He went on to make the point that sociologists should concentrate on 'theories intermediate to the minor working hypotheses evolved in abundance during the day-to-day routines of research, and the all-inclusive speculations comprising a master conceptual scheme from which it is hoped to derive a very large number of empirically observed uniformities of social behaviour'.[19]

The reason, according to Merton and others, is that sociology is simply not yet ready for the creation of large-scale theories, but should instead concentrate effort on smaller-ranging theories limited to fairly narrow problems, such as, say, voting behaviour, group dynamics, white-collar crime or bureaucracy. A good example of this kind of theoretical strategy is Merton's own work developing Durkheim's anomie theory, and the many case studies, surveys and such like which form the bulk of empirical activity in sociology. A classic example of this kind of theorizing is Michels's study, in the two first decades of this century, of the German Social Democratic Party, in which he argued that oligarchic tendencies would operate in spite of democratic forms of government. The theory was developed on the basis of a few cases at a particular point in time, but it led on to other research inspired by his ideas of an organization which seemed to contradict the theory, but which added a little more to our knowledge about the conditions under which oligarchies are likely to form.[20] Such theorizing involves developing theories narrower in scope than the 'grand theories' as they deal with relatively small-scale issues limited in time and scope, but leading on to the gradual accumulation of theoretical ideas grounded in 'hard' empirical research. They do not claim to answer questions about the nature of social man or society, but about the factors, say, which enter into the act of voting in the United States, the oligopolistic tendencies in democratic organizations, and so on.

Though it has yet to be assessed how well this practice of theorizing avoids the major criticism of 'grand theories' in binding closer together empirical research and theory building, there remains the further problem of developing theoretical statements which go beyond the confines of narrow problem sectors. There are examples where theories developed in one problem area have been used with profit in other areas, and Merton's use of a somewhat modified version of Durkheim's anomie theory of suicide to look at the class differentials in criminal activity is a case in point. However, as a general rule, such 'middle-range' theorizing tends to stay within the area in which it originates.

The third type of theoretical practice is rather odd since it is accused of being a theoretical and is what C. Wright Mills termed 'abstracted empiricism' : studies 'not based upon any new conception of the nature of society or of man or upon any particular fact about them'.[21] In terms of practical examples, Mills was attacking public opinion polls and other studies which displayed an inordinate amount of effort and sophistication, usually statistical, and a dearth of adequate theory. This approach emphasizes the collection of 'factual' data as accurately as possible rather in the tradition of 'letting the facts speak for themselves'.

This kind of practice is included as a *theoretical* practice because, whatever claims are made to the contrary, some kind of theory is being used. 'Any descriptive utterance, any observation statement is already a hypothesis; and . . . every such hypothesis already carries with it a matrix of relevance which guides us to engage in those tests of experience which we take to support or to fail to support this hypothesis.'[22] What facts are collected, and what are conceived to be facts, depend on an implicit ontological scheme. A fact is a fact because it is part of some meaning system, whether or not this is stated explicitly or left implicit. Popper accuses the naïve empiricist of thinking 'that we begin by collecting and arranging our experiences. . . . But if I am ordered : "Record what you are now experiencing", I shall hardly know how to obey this ambiguous order. Am I to report that I am writing; that I hear a bell ringing; a newsboy shouting, a loudspeaker droning, or am I to report, perhaps, that these noises irritate me?'[23]

Though this point should be obvious from what has been said before, it is worth emphasis. For example, to know that 65 per cent of the working class in Britain vote Labour is only a fact when put in context of a meaning system, whether this be related to party machines trying to estimate relative likelihoods of winning the next election, or to the various bodies of sociological theories about, say, social change, effects of social location on political beliefs, strategies of political behaviour, particular ontologies and so on.

The notion of an isolated fact is difficult to conceive of even in the abstract. To repeat again : a fact is a fact because it is defined as a datum within some meaning system which provides it with a certain ontological status. So, even though 'raw empiricism' might eschew theorizing of any abstraction and claim that it is content simply to gather facts, it cannot escape being involved in theorizing, and the danger is that this theorizing is left implicit and unrelated to other bodies of theory within sociology.

These, then, are the main styles of theorizing fairly typical within the sociological trade, and they represent, if you like, intellectual styles of the way in which sociology as a body of ideas should develop. But, of course, theories can be discussed in terms of many other dimensions: scope, content, degree of formalization, and so forth, and to look at some of these more fully it is necessary to examine fairly carefully the notion of theory.

Deductive Structure of Theory

Classically, a theory of a phenomenon is an explanation of it by means of a deductive system of argument in which the relationship to be explained is a concluding proposition derived from premises, at least one of which is of a law-like character. That is, the general structure of a theory must be deductive in form so that the conclusion—those statements describing a phenomena, event or relationship—are logically derivable from certain premises, some of which are theoretical statements.[24] To take a classical example from sociology, that of Durkheim's explanation of the suicide rate in Spain, the theory set out more or less formally looks like this :

1. In any social grouping, the suicide rate varies directly with the degree of individualism (egoism).
2. The degree of individualism varies with the incidence of Protestantism.

3. Therefore, the suicide rate varies with the incidence of Protestantism.
4. The incidence of Protestantism in Spain is low.
5. Therefore, the suicide rate in Spain is low.[25]

Notice the structural features of the theory. First, statements 3 and 5, by the canons of simple logic, are true (although they may not be true empirically as descriptions of the world). Logic provides a calculus whereby deductions can be made from general statements (statements 1 and 2) to more particular statements. This is what is meant by a deductive schema: the conclusion must, as a matter of logic, follow from the premises. Now, although the conclusion may be logically true in the sense that it is arrived at by a valid logical procedure, it need not be factually true. In short, logic is fine, but since a theory purports to explain features of the empirical world, then the theory must contain some reference to this empirical world: which brings us to the second feature of the example used above. Statements 2 and 4 (perhaps also statement 1, but more of this later) operate as descriptions of the empirical world, contingent in the sense that experience is relevant to their truth, and in conjunction they provide the prediction about the rate of suicide in Spain. Suppose we were to go out and observe the suicide rate in Spain, our observations would then constitute a test of the theory. But, though this particular observation may give some corroborative evidence for the theory (or, if the prediction is not confirmed, a refutation of it), no amount of confirmed observations would conclusively prove the theory to be true. For one thing, there may be other theories which could explain the same observation. Equally, there could be other theories, again, which would imply the opposite observation, that is, that the suicide rate in Spain is high. So, if the suicide rate in Spain is found to be low, the observation at least disconfirms alternative theories which would have led to a different prediction. More formally, and more generally, this point can be stated as follows: for any observation O which is deducted from theory T, the alternative theories which imply not-O will be falsified. In other words, the researcher is faced with fewer alternative theories. As Stinchcombe says, the 'basic logical process of science is the elimination of alternative theories . . . by investigating as many of the empirical consequences of each theory as is practical, always trying for the greatest possible variety in implications tested . . .'.[26]

But, of course, in practice no theory is accepted or even totally rejected on the basis of one observation. On the contrary, theories are held with remarkable tenacity before being cast aside as wrong or inadequate. More probably the existing theory will be amended in some degree to make it fit the disconfirming observations better. This process can go only so far until a new theory displaces the older one.[27] However, before this stage is reached the theory is usually tested on a number of observations, and this once again stresses the importance of the deductive structure of theories. For, consistent with the premises of the theory, are a number of observations which could equally serve as tests of the theory. In the example of suicide, the propositions could be replaced by others, such as, say, 'The incidence of Protestantism in Holland is high.' And the conclusion in proposition 5 would become, 'Therefore, the suicide rate in Holland is high'; a conclusion entirely consistent with the theory of suicide contained in the premises, and a further test. This process of generating crucial observations is made easier and more systematic if the deductive structure is made explicit and more formal: a rarity in sociological theorizing. The use of mathematical models as expressions of theories and analyses of their logical implications is one way of making theory more systematic.[28]

Explanation

A further and very important issue is how the theory *explains*. At the beginning of this chapter, the assertion was made that a theory is intended to explain features of the world. Unfortunately, attempting to elucidate with any firmness the notion of explanation is to enter a thicket of issues and problems not easily penetrable.

The orthodox account of explanation has already virtually been offered when speaking of the deductive structure of theories. This is known as the 'hypothetico-deductive' theory of explanation, which states 'that explanations require the adducing of general laws, with the status of empirical hypotheses about the natural order, from which, in conjunction with statements of initial conditions, we can deductively infer statements about empirical consequences'.[29]

In short, the *explanandum*, the thing to be explained, must be entailed by the *explanans*, the law-like statements and initial conditions stated in the premises. As a form of argument, it works from the general to the particular. If, in addition, the premise is taken to be a general causal law, e.g. 'In any social grouping, the suicide rate varies directly with the degree of individualism', then with the statement of initial conditions, the conclusions, the observational statements, must follow, and hence be shown to be necessary consequences of the causal generalization. So, wedding the power of deductive logic to notions of cause and effect, we have given an explanation of the events we wish to explain.

A point to remember is that a deductive explanation is a fusion of two elements: the logic of deductive arguments and the interpretation of these formal elements in terms of generalizations considered to have causal efficiency. As far as logic is concerned, it does not matter what the premises contain in terms of categories supposed to describe the world. Thus, 'All three legged men walk on their second and third legs' is as useful as 'All metals when heated expand.' But, in applying these premises and the structure of deductive logic to the explanation of events in the 'real world', it is of the utmost concern that the premises be well corroborated generalizations about the world—if the explanation is to be considered as true, adequate or plausible. In other words, the terms or concepts which enter into the explanation need to be derived from a meaning system intended to make sense of the empirical world. Hempel and Oppenheim cite the following conditions for a successful explanation. First, the formal requirement that the logical structure of the explanation should be deductive in that the concluding statement is implied by the premises consisting of law-like generalizations and initial conditions. Secondly, that the statements forming the premises should be factually true or, preferably, well-corroborated. Finally, that the *explanans* should be empirically testable.[30]

These, then, are the conditions set up as requirements for scientific explanation. Of course, in practice, things often look a little different. For one thing, and this is specially true in sociology, explanations are rarely set out as explicitly as implied, but instead generally take a more discursive, more literary form. Indeed, some authors regard *induction* as of rather more *practical* importance in theory building than the testing of deductively derived hypotheses. This means that the aim in sociology should be to gain as much theoretical mileage as possible from any given set of data.[31] Nonetheless, while this is valuable as a statement about what inquiry should aim for, on this view, the logic of explanation set out would still be implicit.

Suppose, for example, that we are explaining why a revolution occurred in Russia in 1917. We might talk about the events that preceded the actual event, mentioning the conditions of the Russian working class, the peasantry, the indifference of the Russian nobility, the First World War and its disastrous effect on the morale of the

Russian Army, maybe even the pernicious influence of Rasputin. Although a great many factors and events might be listed as causal precursors of the events of 1917, for them to count as explanations they must be subsumable under appropriate generalizations. Thus, for the condition of the working class in Russia to be accepted as a causal factor, we are also committed to accepting a generalization to the effect that when conditions within a group are such-and-such, they are likely to behave in so-and-so ways. Diagrammatically, the logic of the explanatory schema would look something like Figure 1. Where T_1 to T_6 are time points; E_1 to E_6 are sequences of

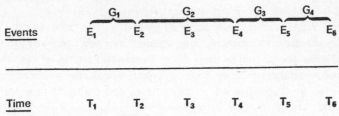

Figure 1. Explanatory sequence.

events considered to be important (e.g. in terms of the example used, T_6 would be 1917 and E_6 the Revolution at that time), and G_1 to G_4 are the generalizations forming the causal sequence.

In examples of this sort of historical analysis, these generalizations would be mostly implicit. Moreover, their content could vary, sometimes referring to general social conditions (e.g. the effect of prolonged economic decline on groups within a society), at other times to more specific linkages, and sometimes to psychological dispositions of key individuals. But, and this is the point, the explanation of the sequence of events still conforms to the logic of explanation set out earlier. In other words, the tradition of historical analysis, sometimes known as *nomothetic analysis*, is a special form of what is taken as the general structure of scientific explanation.[32]

Generalizations

Another set of issues concerns the nature of the generalizations used as premises in the deductive argument. It has already been pointed out that to be used in scientific explanation generalizations must be seen to have causal efficiency: that is, they must be statements taken to refer to processes in the 'real world'. However, generalizations can take a number of forms. One type, frequently found within sociology, is the enumerative generalization. Take the statement, 'All the men in this pub are over 21.' Such statements can be shown to be true by exhaustive enumeration: listing all the men in the pub and seeing whether their ages are over 21. The statement amounts to a string of singular statements ('This man is over twenty-one years old') and the assertion that these cover the case.[33]

One feature of these types of generalization is that 'counter-factual' statements—hypothetical statements about what would have been the case had some non-actual possibility been realized—are not permitted. This amounts to saying that they cannot be employed as law-like statements in arguments about what would have happened in cases other than the present one. So, it cannot be inferred from, 'All the men in this pub are over 21,' that, had another man come into the pub he also would have been over 21. In contrast, take the assertion that 'For all individuals, if an individual desires to attain, or maintain, an intimate relationship with others, he or she must identify with the opinions and values of those others, and the rate of friendly interaction will be highest in those groups where the members exhibit a greater conformity of opinions and views.' This can be tested against experience. We can set up any number of experiments, or look at any number of groups, to see if, and under what conditions, the generalization holds.[34] In other words, a causal generalization, as opposed to an enumerative one, will license future and counter-factual statements. 'License' is an important word to use here since we are talking less about the form of the statement and more about the 'rules' governing its use. Thus, in an enumeration generalization, we have simply counted the number of cases of X's which are also Y's within a specified time and specified place. But, in the case of a causal generalization, the statement is intended to have wider temporal and spatial reference, and, occasionally, reference to 'counter-factual' situations; situations which have not actually existed.

Conceptual Schemes

A third feature of the theory example used earlier is that a conceptual scheme is assumed: 'social grouping', 'suicide', 'individualism', 'Protestantism' and so on must be defined both nominally and operationally. Including these considerations, the explicit and implicit structure of the theory taken together becomes very complex indeed. The point has already been made that a theory needs to contain at least some terms which have reference to observations. 'Movements on a meter needle', 'responses to a questionnaire', 'the rate of eye blink', are examples: terms referred to at various times and places as 'concreta', 'empirical terms', 'descriptive terms', 'variables' and the like. Though these and other terms might seem varied enough, their major feature is that there is a consensus about their factual nature: they are more or less accepted as firmly rooted in our commonsense experience. Of course, our acceptance of their facticity is a matter of degree: an important degree in certain cases. Other terms in the theory are likely to have a rather more indirect reference to commonsense experience. These are more hypothetical in nature. Their existence is inferred from more observable events or things. Many such hypotheticals, like gravity, are very much part of the furniture of our everyday world and are more or less taken for granted: the ontology to which they belong is widely accepted. In other cases, however, the status of a hypothetical construct may be more tentative, depending on the degree to which we accept the reasons or justifications for the inference from the observables to the construct.[35]

These types of concept have more to do with the theory itself than with whatever connection the theory has with the empirical world. They are 'theoretical terms', which, even in principle, cannot be fully defined in terms of observables. They belong more to the explanatory side of a theory rather than to the theory's empirical component: '. . . observations do not give meaning to the theoretical term but rather mark the occasions for its application. Its meaning derives from the part that it plays in the whole theory in which it is embedded, and from the role of the theory itself.'[36] Kaplan goes on to mention terms such as 'castration complex', 'marginal utility' and 'Protestant ethic' as meaningless if dissociated from the theories that contain them. A theoretic term has systemic meaning deriving its sense from the structure and content of the theory as a whole.

The line between observational terms and theoretic ones is difficult to draw in practice. Even observational terms assume the truth of some theory as a warrant for inference, from the 'naked sense data' to all that is involved in the concept, even though this theory may be so much a part of our commonsense understanding that we are unaware of its content. A clock tells the time by pointing to figures arranged in a circle around two pointers. Yet the relationship between the pointer readings and 'time' depends upon the acceptance of a whole series of mechanical, mathematical, engineering and philosophical principles. In this sense, as will be seen in more detail later, inferences are involved in all observational terms, whether direct or indirect. The difference between observational and theoretic terms is even more problematic, especially since, in time, many theoretical concepts become part of our everyday observational experience or, at least, part of the observational repertoire of the scientist. It is not so much that different kinds of entity are referred to by observational and theoretic terms as that they perform different functions within the process of inquiry.[37] In short, the status we assign to terms depends upon their use within a specific context of inquiry.

Theoretic terms may have partial interpretation by means of observational terms, but no set of observational terms can fully stand for a theoretic term since the range of application of a theory, as well as the way it is applied in particular contexts, cannot be fully specified beforehand. In short, theoretic terms have an 'openness of meaning'. As the theory is used for purposes both practical and inquiring, the meaning of the terms becomes progressively more fixed, while still allowing that degree of openness. Each sentential occurrence gives only a partial meaning, and, to be fully understood, the theoretic term needs to be placed in the context of the whole theoretical or meaning system of which the term is only a part. In other words, the theory as a whole is needed to give meaning to the parts, rather like the postulates of geometry which define a 'point' and not alternative lexical formulations such as 'position without extent'.[38] A 'point' is to be understood by what it does within the context of geometry and cannot be fully grasped by definition outside this context. Scientific theories are not quite like the theorems of geometry, yet the point is the same: the openness of the theoretic concept is a result of the theory never being complete in the sense that all of its propositions can be enumerated.

A theory is not valuable simply because it offers an explanation of things studied, but because there is always the possibility of its application to new areas, or to new lines of inquiry enriching the theory further. 'No single specification of meaning suffices for a theoretical term, precisely because no single context of application exhausts its significance for the scientist using it.'[39] Meanings change with new experiences, new evidence, further data, necessitating changes in the theory and the elements of which it is composed. In addition, theoretical terms often suffer from the normal ambiguity and vagaries of ordinary language. Problems of fixing classificatory lines, the contagion of verbal usage and the generally morphogenic capacity of words, all beset theoretical terms as they do ordinary language.

Theoretical terms, unlike observational or descriptive terms, whose meanings can be stipulated or fixed more firmly to observed and felt experiences, have an openness of meaning necessary to their work within scientific investigation. They perform a creative function not possible at a purely descriptive level since they not only solve problems of explanation but also point to further issues and problems, further contexts in which the theory could be placed. This is their role, and this is their importance.

Data and Theory Languages

Within the theory are other terms which connect at some point with what is going to be called a 'data language', and the following is a summary illustration of theory and data languages:

Theory Language	Data Language(s)
1. In any social grouping, the suicide rate varies directly with the degree of individualism.	Within any category of individuals conforming to XYZ, where XYZ are criteria defining a 'social group', the number of suicides per 1,000 will be correlated with the degree of individualism.
2. The degree of individualism varies with the degree of Protestantism.	The degree of individualism = proportion of Protestants in group.
3. Therefore, the suicide rate varies with the Protestantism.	The proportion of Protestants in social group conforming to XYZ will show a high direct correlation with suicides per 1,000 members of same group.
4. The incidence of Protestantism in Spain is low.	The proportion of Protestants in Spain is low compared with other countries.
5. Therefore, the suicide rate in Spain is low.	The suicide rate in Spain is low compared with other countries which have a higher proportion of Protestants.

The data language translates at least some of the theoretical language into a form with more operational connection with the empirical world, or how the empirical world is conceived to be. In the example, some terms have been given an equivalence in both

the theory and the data language, others not so. 'Individualism' is
a case in point. Here the term is given purely an operational meaning, but, in the theory language, it is an important step in the
deductive argument, depending, of course, on other auxiliary
theories connecting Protestantism with certain sets of beliefs which
lead to a lessened sense of corporate belongingness and more of a
sense of individual responsibility for one's fate.

The use of the term 'language' is deliberate. The theory contains
a structure—a grammar—in which certain words have meanings
and there are rules for the manipulation of the words to create
other meanings or link sets of meanings with others. Part of this
grammar is, of course, the rules of ordinary language, but other
parts may belong to more specialized and precise grammars of deductive logic and mathematics. Similarly there is a structure in
what has been termed the data language: sets of all kinds of rules
linking one set of meanings with other sets. Once again, some of
these rules are the rules of ordinary language, or the rules implicit
in ordinary language, while others are more precise rules of mathematics or statistics, or those of a measurement system.

Quite obviously it would be tedious in every piece of research to
spell out all the rules involved in detail. Most are and can be left
implicit.

Another very important set of rules are those defining the correspondence between the theory language and the data language:
those stipulating the equivalences in the 'vocabularies', 'grammar'
and 'syntax' of the two languages. These are not so obvious as
might at first appear. Just because the same word or term appears
in both the theory language and the data language, it does not
imply that they mean quite the same thing. For one thing, the
data language terms are usually much more restricted than those
contained in the theory language. Moreover, the structure of each
language may not, in any given case, be quite equivalent. These are
important points, and it will be necessary to go into them in some
detail.

As has already been pointed out, concepts and theories carve out
particular realities: they define and put a structure on the world
of our experience. In doing so they are dependent upon the kind of
ontological assumptions spoken about earlier. But, though theories
reach up to these kinds of 'world hypothesis', they also have some
autonomy of their own in that they are open to the criterion of
verifiability or testability. As mentioned before, they need to contain experientially relevant statements: they need, in short, data

to attest to their truth or falsity. The data itself is a product of the theory. The theory tells the researcher what to look for, what experiences are relevant, and how the experiences should be processed to test the theory. The data is not simply 'raw experience', unadulterated by human hand, eye or brain. As Sjoberg and Nett put it: '. . . the sociologist's theoretical assumptions or premises concerning the nature of social reality or of human nature commit him to particular kinds of procedures when he collects and analyses his data. So, too, because certain techniques are more compatible with some theoretical assumptions than with others, the scientist, simply by selecting a given set of research methods, necessarily assumes a particular theoretical stance.'[40] The structuring of reality by the initial theoretical language has made sure of this. But, in addition, the techniques used to produce the data and process it for the theory also 'put' a structure on reality. In the suicide example (page 47), statement 1 contained the proposition, 'The suicide rate varies directly with the degree of individualism.' In the theoretical language, we have more than a grasp of what this means: one increases as the other increases. In the data language, it means much the same sort of thing—so that there is an isomorphism at least—except that in the data language the matter can become a little more complicated. For example, we have to make decisions about what experiences are going to count as con-

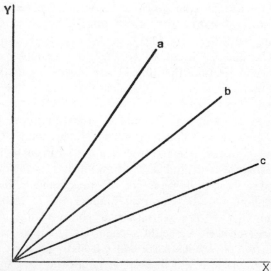

Figure 2. Linear relationships.

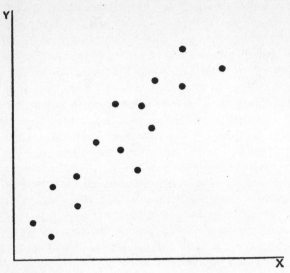

Figure 3. Scatterplot.

forming to the proposition. This is where the operational rules come in.

'Take 'suicide rate' as operationally defined as 'the number of people in any one group defined as having taken their own lives expressed as a rate per 1,000 per year on the members of the group'. 'Individualism' can also be given an operational meaning as 'the proportion of Protestants in a social group'. What about 'varies with'? Mathematically, the idea can be expressed simply as in Figure 2. The lines a, b, and c are just three examples of the infinite number of relationships that satisfy the description; X varies with Y. So, if X were to be the 'suicide rate' and Y 'the degree of individualism', the statement, 'The suicide rate varies directly with the degree of individualism', would be consistently described by any line such as these, depending on the values found. Of course, in any kind of social research we would be fortunate indeed, or positively astonished, to find data fitting such a neat curve. More likely, because of manifold errors of measurement, faulty data collection and so on, the empirical findings would be better described as in Figure 3: a scattering of points fitting no obvious straight line. However, we could assume that this scattering is produced by errors of various sorts and go on to say that the 'true' relationship is the line which 'best' describes the data spread with a minimum of error. This means that we have to decide on criteria for deciding the 'best' straight line, what a 'minimum of error' is, and so on. In other words, we have to develop a whole new meaning system pertaining to the structure of the data. Just as in the theory we are making assumptions about the nature of the world, so in the data structures we are assuming something about the world. In a way, this is to become involved in another set of theories about how the data is produced. In the example and elsewhere we have already mentioned some of them; for example, how suicide is recorded. To take the proportion of Protestants in a population as an index of the degree of invidualism is to name another theory about the relationship between the Protestant religion and a tendency to produce an individualistic ethic in its adherents. It is also to assume something about the nature of social reality. For one thing, it offers a deterministic model in which people are assumed to be moved to do things because of certain 'causes' operating in their environment and the way these causes operate, i.e. in a simple linear fashion. Moreover, those theories contained in the data language must be assumed to be true (if there is no alternative verification of them) so that the data can be used to test the theory.

In short, implicit within the data language are theories and onto-logical assumptions necessary for the data to qualify as data. This is important to grasp, since the data is produced and worked upon by the researcher, and this production may not be as clear or as obvious as might be thought. For example, in the data language, one interpretation of 'varies directly with', is that known as correlation and regression analysis in which the relationship between the suicide rate and individualism is seen as something which should approximate to a straight line described in terms of two co-efficients, one specifying a value for the slope of the line, the other a value for its intercept point. In terms of these conditions, any point not falling on that line is treated as an 'error' due to measurement weaknesses, or the effects of unique factors operating in particular cases. In other words, the technique of analysis assumes that, 'in the world', the 'true' relationship is a linear one. (Of course, if the error should be so great that no straight line could plausibly 'fit' the data, then the theory is falsified, or at least so far as this kind of test is concerned.) This assumption is essential if we are to use this form of analysis. But what if the 'true' relationship were curvilinear, as suggested in Figure 4. There would then seem to be a threshold where the variable 'degree of individualism' has to reach a certain point before it has a marked effect on the suicide rate. This would clearly have important implications for the theory, for

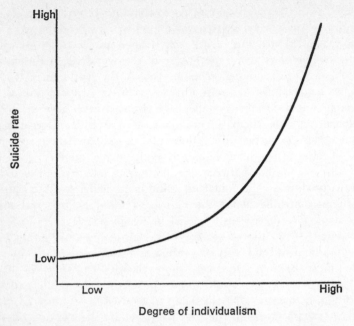

Figure 4. Curvilinear relationship.

as the theory stands it is only approximately 'true' as a description of this segment of the world (from our privileged standpoint of being able to say what the world is).

Thus, the relationship between the theory language and the data language is not as simple as might be hoped. In discussing this problem, Blalock points out that the gap between 'main or general' theories (the 'theoretical language in which we do our thinking') and the 'auxiliary theories' (the 'operational language involving explicit instructions for classifying or measuring'), cannot be bridged by logic alone. Instead, correspondences between the two languages must be established by 'common agreement or a priori assumption'.[41] In short, the data language comes to be accepted as a legitimate interpretation of the theory language by common consent among researchers.

Something else is assumed. In the example used, which is reasonably typical, the concepts contained in the theory are translated into variables which are then given empirical import, or, at least, the concepts are connected with other variables which have empirical import. Part of the operationalization of some of these concepts involves defining them quantitatively. 'Suicide', for example, is expressed as a variable defined as the number of self-administered deaths per 1,000 of the population. Similarly, the degree of individualism is measured as an index constructed as the proportion of the Protestants in an area. Since each of these concepts has been made equivalent to some variable that can be expressed numerically, all kinds of mathematical operation can be performed: regression, correlation, means, standard deviations, and so on. We can use, in other words, the logic of mathematics as part of the data language so as to manipulate the variables in ways we think important. To see what this involves is the topic of Chapter 3.

Exercises

These exercises are intended to give you the opportunity of working with and explicating concepts as a step towards understanding the roles they play within sociological theory and empirical research. The first exercise asks you to start from the theory language and to try to construct an appropriate data language. The second reverses this and presents some data out of which you have to make theoretical sense.

1. Take one of the major concepts used in sociology, e.g. 'social structure', 'social class', 'stratification', 'alienation', 'cohesion', 'social change', and so on. Select one with which you are familiar, not necessarily relying on those just mentioned. If you are not confident of your knowledge about what the concept means, read it up. Remember what a concept does: it offers a grid, a way of marking out particular aspects of the reality in which we happen to be interested. In other words, no concept stands alone, but is related to others within some theoretical model. Depending on the concept you have chosen, the particular theoretical model(s) involved—the same concept may be involved in more than one model —may be very general, referring to the whole of social life, while other, more particular models may apply only to certain aspects of social life. No matter; the task you have to do will be the same. Look in some detail at the role which the concept you have selected plays within your model. Explicate it, showing how it relates to other concepts in the model. For example, the concept of 'social structure' draws attention to certain aspects of society. What are they? What other concepts does it relate to? Try 'norm', 'culture', 'institution' and so on, in this example. Think about why it might be important for the sociologist to use the concept you have selected,

and what model of man and society it suggests. Try to sketch out the major definitions and propositions within your theoretical model, showing how each concept relates to the others. Do not worry too much about being able to cast your model into deductive form.

2. Think about an appropriate data language for your theoretical sketch. In other words, try to devise indicators for at least some of the terms in the model. Remember that some of the theoretical terms will not refer directly to observables. Nonetheless, such terms will link either definitionally or by implication with other terms in the theory language, which are able to generate appropriate indicators in the data language. Thus, 'social structure' is an abstract concept drawing attention to certain recurrent features of social life. Explication of this concept, and relating it to other concepts, should suggest appropriate indicators, not necessarily by direct measurement, but by showing how the indicator is generated by the theory of which the original concept is a part. Make these auxiliary theories as explicit as you can. (Note: although the examples used in the text were statistical, yours need not be.) The important thing is to realize some of the problems and issues which arise when working between theory and data.

Notes and References

1. H. Blumer, 'Science without Concepts', *American Journal of Sociology*, 36, 1931, p. 515.

2. A. Kaplan, *The Conduct of Enquiry*, Chandler Publishing, San Francisco, 1964, p. 46.

3. See, on this point, C. G. Hempel, 'Fundamentals of Concept Formation in Empirical Science', *International Encyclopedia of Unified Science*, Vol. 2, No. 7, University of Chicago Press, Chicago, 1952; R. Bierstedt, 'Nominal and Real Definition in Sociological Theory', in L. Gross (ed.), *Symposium on Sociological Theory*, Harper & Row, New York, 1959, pp. 121–44.

4. H. V. Wiseman, *Political Systems*, Routledge & Kegan Paul, London, 1966, p. 72. I am not claiming any special status for this particular definition. The volume came easiest to hand.

5. See, for comments on this and related points, G. J. Direnzo, 'Concept Definition in the Behavioural Sciences', in Direnzo (ed.), *Concepts, Theory and Explanation in the Behavioural Sciences*, Random House, New York, 1966, pp. 3–18.

6. It should be pointed out that this study was a magnificent failure in that a great deal was learned from it.

7. H. Blumer, 'What is Wrong with Social Theory?', *American Sociological Review*, 19, 1954, p. 9; also, Hemple, 'Fundamentals of Concept Formation', loc. cit., p. 47.

8. E. Durkheim, *Suicide*, Routledge & Kegan Paul, London, 1952, translated by J. A. Spaulding and G. Simpson.

9. See J. Maxwell Atkinson, 'On the Sociology of Suicide', *Sociological Review*, 16, 1968, pp. 83–92; and, for a fuller statement, J. D. Douglas, *The Social Meanings of Suicide*, Princeton University Press, Princeton, 1967; and 'The Sociological Analysis of the Social Meanings of Suicide', *European Journal of Sociology*, 1, 1966, pp. 249–98. For a general discussion of the use of official statistics, see A. V. Cicourel, *Method and Measurement in Sociology*, The Free Press, New York, 1964, esp. p. 27; and B. Hindess, *The Use of Official Statistics in Sociology*, Macmillan, London, 1973.

10. See M. V. Quine, *Word and Object*, MIT Press, Cambridge, Mass., 1964, p. 127, for an illuminating discussion of the importance of vagueness in language.

11. J. D. Douglas, *American Social Order*, The Free Press, New York, 1971, pp. 131–2.

12. Quoted in Kaplan, *The Conduct of Enquiry*, p. 41. See also, H. M. Blalock, 'The Measurement Problem: A Gap Between the Languages of Theory and Research', in H. M. Blalock and A. Blalock (eds.), *Methodology in Social Research*, McGraw-Hill, New York, 1968, pp. 7–12.

13. This example is taken from W. R. Catton, *From Animistic to Naturalistic Sociology*, McGraw-Hill, New York, 1966, pp. 126–7.

14. In this sense, the example is a bad one, as will be seen later, since the link between values and behaviour is too often taken as unproblematic.

15. C. Wright Mills, *The Sociological Imagination*, Oxford University Press, New York, 1959, p. 33. The kind of theoretician Mills is attacking is best illustrated by Talcott Parsons. See Parsons, *The Social System*, Tavistock Publications, London, 1952, for an example.

16. See M. Phillipson, 'Theory, Methodology and Conceptualization', in P. Filmer *et al.*, *New Directions in Sociological Theory*, Collier-Macmillan, London, 1972, p. 77, where he states very forcibly, '. . . the linguistic architects of sociology have constructed vast edifices which bear unknown relationships to the social world. . . . Certainly these constructions provide shelter for verbose sociologists but, from the point of view of men engaged in practical activities in the world, they are more likely to appear as esoteric retreats whose doors are barred except to the converted.' See also Blumer,

'Science without Concepts', *American Journal of Sociology*, 36, 1931, p. 515.

17. T. S. Kuhn, *The Structure of Scientific Revolutions*, University of Chicago Press, Chicago, 1962.

18. R. K. Merton, *Social Theory and Social Structure*, The Free Press, Glencoe, 1957 p. 5 (italics in the original). In the same spirit, B. G. Glaser and A. Strauss, *The Discovery of Grounded Theory*, Aldine, Chicago, 1967, where they argue the case for 'grounded theory' generated from 'data systematically obtained from social research', p.2. For other comments on Merton's notion of 'middle-range theory', see W. Wallace, *The Logic of Science in Sociology*, Aldine Atherton, Chicago, 1971, pp. 110–12.

19. Merton, *Social Theory and Social Structure*, pp. 5–6.

20. See ibid. for Merton's studies on anomie, reference groups, mass media effects and so on. The Michels study is in *Political Parties*, Collier Books, New York, 1962, and the other study mentioned is in S. M. Lipset *et al.*, *Union Democracy*, The Free Press, Glencoe, 1956.

21. Mills, *The Sociological Imagination*, p. 55.

22. M. W. Wartofsky, *Conceptual Foundations of Scientific Thought*, Macmillan, New York, 1968, p. 182.

23. K. Popper, *The Logic of Scientific Discovery*, Science Edition, New York, 1961, p. 106.

24. See R. B. Braithwaite, *Scientific Explanation*, Cambridge University Press, Cambridge, 1953, and E. Nagel, *The Structure of Science*, Routledge & Kegan Paul, London, 1961, for classic statements on the deductive nature of theory. And, applied to sociological theory, see G. C. Homans, 'Contemporary Theory in Sociology', in R. E. Faris (ed.), *Handbook of Modern Sociology*, Rand-McNally, New York, 1964, pp. 951–9, and A. Stinchcombe, *Constructing Social Theories*, Harcourt, Brace & World, New York, 1968, esp. pp. 15–24.

25. This particular example is culled from Homans, 'Contemporary Theory', loc. cit. Stinchcombe, *Constructing Social Theories*, contains a similar example, as do other books on theory construction, which attests, in some way, to the durability of Durkheim's ideas!

26. ibid., p. 22. See also, D. T. Campbell, 'Prospective: Artifact and Control', in R. Rosenthal and R. L. Rosnow (eds.), *Artifact in Behavioural Research*, Academic Press, New York, 1969.

27. Kuhn, *The Structure of Scientific Revolutions*.

28. See, on this, K. C. Land, 'Formal Theory', in H. L. Costner (ed.), *Sociological Methodology*, 1971, Jossey-Bass, San Francisco, 1971, pp. 175–220.

29. A. Ryan, *The Philosophy of the Social Sciences*, Macmillan, London, 1970, p. 46; C. G. Hempel and P. Oppenheim, 'Studies in the Logic of Explanation', *Philosophy of Science*, 1948, pp. 135–79; and J. O. Wisdom, *Foundations of Inference in Natural Science*, Methuen, London, 1952.

30. Hempel and Oppenheim, 'Studies in the Logic of Explanation', loc. cit.

31. Glaser and Strauss, *The Discovery of Grounded Theory*.

32. See E. H. Carr, *What is History?*, Penguin Books, Harmondsworth, 1964.

33. Ryan, *The Philosophy of the Social Sciences*, p. 85.

34. This generalization is taken from E. Katz and P. F. Lazarsfeld, *Personal Influence*, The Free Press, Glencoe, 1955.

35. Relevant in this connection is the 'empiricist theory of knowledge', which tends to be the prevailing account of knowledge in social science. See R. Carnap, *The Logical Structure of the World*, Routledge & Kegan Paul, London, 1967.

36. Kaplan, *The Conduct of Enquiry*, pp. 54–5.

37. ibid., p. 56.

38. ibid., p. 63.

39. ibid., p. 64.

40. G. Sjoberg and R. Nett, *A Methodology for Social Research*, Harper & Row, New York, 1968, pp. 3–4.

41. See H. M. and A. Blalock, *Methodology in Social Research*, pp. 23–4; and H. M. Blalock, *Theory Construction*, Prentice-Hall, Englewood Cliffs, 1969, pp. 151–4.

3
Measurement

Generally speaking, measurement is 'the assignment of numerals to objects or events according to rules'.[1] That is to say, numerals, simply a set of symbols such as '1', '2', '3', and so on, are mapped on to events, objects or properties according to rules which enable one to operate with the numerals as representations of a numbers system.[2] It is important to realize the distinction between numerals and numbers. The former are simply symbols: conventional marks on paper. The latter, however, imply a set of rules in a logico-mathematical system which define numbers and their relationship with each other.

The distinction can be illustrated as follows. Suppose, in a room full of people, we were to give everyone a numeral. Joe was given '1', Fred '2', Sandy '3' and so on. However, if we wanted to indicate something more than a simple labelling or naming process by attaching numerals, we would have to map the numerals on to some number system. If, say, we wanted to indicate the tallest in the room, then the second tallest, and so on down to the shortest, the numerals would have to be allocated in such a way that the distribution of the property 'tallness' would be satisfactorily reflected. Thus, if Sandy was the tallest, she might be given the numeral '1'. If Joe was the second tallest, he would be given '2', and so on, through the remainder of the group. However, in this case the numerals mean something more than names or labels. For one thing, they are being employed to indicate an order. If Sandy was the tallest, Joe the second tallest, Fred the third tallest, the numerals would have to be assigned in the order, '1', '2', '3' respectively, not '1', '3', '2', or '2', '1', '3'. The reason is that the numerals have been given a correspondence to a number system in which order is denoted by the sequence 1, 2, 3, etc. Of course, the relationship between the numerals and the number system is a matter of convention, but nonetheless, once the convention has been chosen, consistency requires that the rules be adhered to. The numerals 1, 2, and 3 could be given another meaning, but this would mean altering the marks or signs which indicate or stand for an ordinal number system: the marks may be changed, but not the ordinal properties of the number system.

Measurement, then, is about employing a number system so as to manipulate the events, objects and properties which constitute the data. To measure is to bring into the data language a set of rules by which the data can be operated upon in a quantitative manner. The normal justification for measurement is that it enables the researcher to state more exactly the theoretical relationships in which he is interested. Measurement is thus not only a tool for more accurate description, but also a tool for achieving more effective theory. The rules involved in a measurement system give unequivocal, non-subjective guides for bringing data to bear on research questions. What is happening is that an uninterpreted axiomatic system, the mathematics of number, having no reference to the empirical world, is interpreted: that is, such purely logical terms as 'or', 'and' 'not' are used in connection with terms that have descriptive and empirical import, and the rules of the axiomatic system then become the rules for manipulating these descriptive terms.

Levels of Measurement

Let us look in more detail at some of the rules for manipulating a number system. Four classes of rules are normally distinguished, each corresponding to a level of measurement: nominal, ordinal, interval and ratio.

Nominal Measurement

The first, nominal measurement, is the most basic and simple operation in any form of inquiry, and is that of classification. Classification is fundamental to any science, and all succeeding levels of measurement involve classification as the first essential operation. As Wartofsky points out, 'Once concept formation and language attain to the ideas of *thing* and *same* and *different*, discourse already exhibits the notion of *class* as an ordering concept . . . measurement already has its roots, in the process of identification, comparison, and classification. . . .'[3]

An example has already been given of this kind of measurement when the people in the hypothetical room were given numerals as labels or names. As long as the names are attached unambiguously in the sense that no object or event is given the same name/ numeral (unless it belongs to the same class) as another object or event to which it is dissimilar, then the criterion of nominal measurement is satisfied. Formally, the nominal level of measurement possesses the properties of symmetry and transitivity. A relation between A and B is symmetric if the relation also holds between B and A. Thus, A is B's cousin is symmetric in that B is also A's cousin. Simply, if an event or object, A, is in the same set as B, then B is in the same set as A. Transitivity means that if A is equal to B, and B is equal to C, then A is also equal to C. So, if A and B are in the same set and B and C are in the same set, then A and C are in the same set.

So, at the nominal level of measurement, in assigning numbers to objects the only rule is that the same number must be aplied to the same objects. In the example using numbers as labels for people in a room, no number was used twice because, for the presumed purposes at hand, the numbers were used to identify different people. This is fairly pointless in practice, since names would serve equally as well, and more familiarly. However, if we wish to use numbers to refer to the sex of the person according to the rule: 'To males assign the number 1, and to females assign the number 2' (as we might in coding questionnaires for machine processing), then any number of people may be assigned the same number, providing they belong to the same class, male or female. In this rather trivial example, all males would be assigned the number 1 and all females the number 2, in accordance with the rule. In these terms, one can perhaps better see the properties of symmetry and transitivity.

But, though numbers can be assigned in nominal measurement, nothing mathematical in the way of addition, subtraction, multiplication or division can be done with them. The function of the number in this case, as said before, is simply that of naming or denoting categories. It would not make sense, for instance, to add the street numbers of houses, or the numbers assigned to hotel rooms.[4] So the nominal level of measurement, though crucial and fundamental to the whole measurement process, is difficult to regard as true measurement since none of the standard mathematical operations can be performed on the numbers. Yet it is a process which is a necessary first step in the construction of higher-order measurement systems. However, though it may seem a relatively simple process to assign a nominal scale to a set of objects or events or properties, awkward problems can occur in practice and attach to classificatory procedures in general, irrespective of whether or not we wish to assign numbers to the classes.

One such problem is associated with the attempt to give the quality of uniqueness possessed by numbers to a given property or variable. Take the example of classifying people according to which political party they prefer, as one might do in a questionnaire or interview analysis. If we insist that they give only one party as an answer, this may seriously misrepresent their 'true' position. They may have leanings towards different elements of all parties (a not uncommon situation), preferring, say, the economic policies of one party and the social welfare policies of another. To force them into one category would seem to do rather arbitrary violence to their actual position. This kind of problem occurs in most similar situations. Sociology is full of classifications—folk/urban, primitive/advanced, sacred/secular, pre-industrial/industrial—which involve difficulties over borderline cases. In some situations we are relatively safe from the arbitrariness of assignment of cases to categories, sex being a case in point. The difficulty is that the nominal scale is insensitive to fine gradations within characteristics, and it would seem preferable to use a scale more finely tuned to this kind of problem.

Ordinal Measurement

To return to the example of people in a room, at one stage, numbers were assigned according to how tall a person was, giving 1 to the tallest, 2 to the next tallest, and so on. In this case, the numbers served another purpose besides labelling exclusive categories: they indicated an order with respect to the property 'tallness'. We may imagine a continuum of the characteristic along which individuals are ordered, the numbers indicating relative location on that continuum. Apart from having the formal properties of nominal scales, ordinal scales such as this are symmetric in that certain relationships may hold between A and B which do not hold for B and A. The relationship 'greater than' ($>$) is asymmetric in the sense that if $A > B$, B cannot at the same time be greater than A. Transitivity still holds in that if $A > B$, $B > C$, then $A > C$. It is precisely these properties which enable us to place objects being measured along a single continuum.

An ordinal level of measurement, however, does not give any indication of the magnitude between any of the points on the scale. We may know that A is greater than B, but not by how much A is greater than B. Similarly, we cannot say that the difference between A and B is greater or lesser than the difference between other points on the scale, say C and D. This being the case, as with nominal scales, we cannot add or subtract, multiply or divide, the numbers, except in a very restricted sense. For example, if there were the following points along a continuum:

$$
\begin{array}{cccc}
| \quad | & & | & | \\
A \quad B & & C & D
\end{array}
$$

we can say,

$$AD = AB + BC + CD.$$

What we cannot do is compare the distances AB and CD at the ordinal level.[5]

Many relationships in sociology are of this ordinal character. The ranking of people on any continuum involves, at least, ordinal measurement; i.e. social status, prestige, educational attainment, attitudes towards any object, person or event, and so on. But, as with nominal measurement, it is crucial to recognize that ordinal measurement does not allow us to use numbers in the ways specified by the mathematical operations of addition, subtraction, multiplication and division. Unlike nominal measurement, however, we can make judgements in terms of more or less, greater or lesser, and such like, but not by how much. Nonetheless it is a gain in respect of a problem noted in nominal scaling. A nominal scale is often too crude to plausibly represent fine divisions within a variable. In the case of assigning a person to a political party of his or her choice, one could, rather than asking him or her to name one party, ask to what extent does he or she support X or Y party? A slightly different method is, rather than conceiving categories as 'either-or' choices, to see them as continua. Thus, instead of societies being either folk or urban, they are conceived of as being more or less folk, more or less urban, so that the polar types fall to either end of the continuum or series of continua.

Such refinement does not, of course, guarantee that the data will have any more systematic import than less precise nominal scale concepts, but transforming a variable into an ordinal scale does markedly improve precision and avoid the more infelicitous categorization that sometimes occurs.

A second difficulty is that, in any practical research situation, it may prove difficult to argue that a characteristic, property or relationship invariably meets the axioms of an ordinal scale, especially when, at first glance, it might seem to conform obviously to these axioms. To take the transitivity axiom, if $A > B$,

B>C, then A>C. It might appear that there are any number of characteristics in social life which satisfy this axiom: prestige, authority, educational attainment and so forth. However, care must be taken. 'Power', to take one instance, might seem to satisfy the axiom admirably in that, if A is more powerful than B, and B is more powerful than C, then A must be more powerful than C; but this will not necessarily be so. In other words, it is an empirical matter rather than a logical one. Think of a situation. A wife may be more powerful than her husband, her husband more powerful than her child, but it does not necessarily follow that the wife is powerful in regard to the child. It may or may not be the case. Concepts like these have to be carefully considered before they are taken as obviously ordinal.

Interval and Ratio Measurement

In a restricted sense, the term 'measurement' is normally not only reserved for procedures whereby we can assign numbers to variables, objects, properties or events as labelling or ranking devices, but also to indicate the precise distances between the ranks: that is, 'measurement' is often reserved for those situations where an exact numerical meaning can be given to the intervals between the numbered points. If this can be achieved, then we have an interval scale of measurement. It implies that we have an agreed upon unit of measurement which acts as a common standard and is invariant with repeated usage: the scale can be used over and over again and will give the same results. Feet and inches, centimetres and millimetres, degrees and seconds, pounds and ounces, are all familiar units of measurement which have this property. Given such a unit, it is possible to determine precisely the difference between any two or more points on a scale. It can be said, for example, that one building is three times as high as another building, that this basket of fruit is only half the weight of that bag of flour, and so forth. In short, we are able to use the standard mathematical operations of addition, subtraction, multiplication and division. Thus, if we had a unit of measurement to represent 'authority', we could say that a person A has, say, 60 units of authority more than person Y, who, in turn, has 20 units more than person Z.[6] Or that the difference between an IQ of 40 and one of 80 was the same as the difference between an IQ of 80 and another of 120.

There are not many cases in sociology where this level of interval measurement can be used. 'Income' is one fairly common example, except that its relevance to the sociological concepts for which it is supposed to stand, such as life-style, is often not as direct as it is convenient. Nonetheless, there are cases where interval levels of measurement are often casually assumed, as in the case of IQ. Yet careful consideration would suggest that such usages are strictly, illegitimate. As Blalock points out, it makes sense to add the incomes of husband and wife, but not their IQ scores.[7]

A ratio scale is achieved when an absolute or non-arbitrary zero point is locatable on the scale. This kind of measure has an additional property in that it is meaningful to compute a ratio of two scale values. For instance, we can say that one score is twice as high as another. If the zero point is arbitrary, as in the case of Fahrenheit and Centigrade temperature scales, this would not have been legitimate. We cannot legitimately assert that 60° F, is twice as hot as 30° F, though we can say that the difference *between* these temperatures is the same as that between 60° F and 90° F. (However, it is arguable that the distinction between interval and ratio scales is purely academic. In practice, it is always possible to conceive of zero units.)[8]

These, then, are the types of scales normally identified, though intermediates and sub-variants are occasionally distinguished. In the case of the ordinal scale, for example, a partial ordering is sometimes distinguished. This happens when, among the objects or properties being ordered, more than one object or property receives the same rank order because there is no detectable difference between them. In the case of ranking a group of people according to their height, two or more people may be of the same height and so, under the symmetric rule, would receive the same rank number. In other words, a unique ordering does not result only a partial ordering. When attitude scales are used on large populations, the resultant ordering is, for most of the time, a partial ordering.

Choice of Measurement Level

However, having identified the various levels of measurement, the problem is to decide which to employ in any given case. There are clear advantages of precision in choosing an order of measurement as high as possible, say the interval, since, at this level, it is possible to make use of more powerful mathematics in the description and analysis of the data. In an earlier example, that describing a possible way of setting out the relationship between the suicide rate and the degree of individualism, use was made of powerful statistical techniques known as regression and correlation analysis. In terms of the positivistic approach to sociological research, regression analysis, for instance, enables the researcher to describe the nature of the relationship between two or more variables with such precision that the value of one variable can be predicted from the value of the other variable. Hence, from knowledge of the degree of individualism in a population, the suicide rate can be predicted with some accuracy. (This cannot be done at the present time. Some would argue that it could never be achieved, even in principle. Nonetheless, I hope the reader can appreciate the scientific importance of being able to do this kind of thing—for the moment, assuming our example is possible.) To achieve this, the technique makes use of the mathematics for describing the properties of straight lines.

To draw a straight line to describe the relationship between any two variables, all we need to know, as a minimum, are two sets of values: the intercept point and the slope of the line. Call the intercept point 'a' and the slope 'b', and using the formula $Y = a + bX$ we can represent the regression of Y on X. Now if, instead of talking about X and Y, we talk about 'degree of individualism' and the suicide rate, we can see how a straight line could be drawn which would enable us to predict the value of one variable from knowledge of the value of the other variable. We can go further than this by giving a value to the strength of the association between the two variables: a measure known as the *correlation coefficient*.

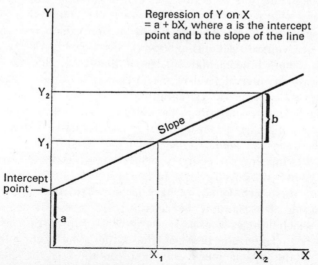

Figure 5. A regression line of Y on X.

As stated when discussing this example previously, few relationships in social research are likely to follow a perfect straight line. However, by various techniques, of which the least-squares estimator is the most common, a straight line can be drawn which best fits the data according to the criteria of minimizing the errors around the line. But there would not be much point in having a line to predict X from Y unless the relationship were strong, or else, when predicting one from the other, we would have to deal with a great deal of error. The correlation coefficient (r) varies from $+1\cdot0$ to $-1\cdot0$. If all the points fell exactly on the line, the measure would take the value of $+1\cdot0$ or $-1\cdot0$, depending upon whether the relationship was positive or negative. If, on the other hand, the data were scattered widely around a possible line, the correlation measure would take a zero value. The better the fit of the data around the line, the higher the value of r.

It is, I hope, possible to grasp the power and elegance of this form of analysis. It gives the researcher a tremendous tool by which to describe, analyse and explore relationships in the data and provides him with better guides to formulate and test his theories. Unfortunately, and here is the crux of this section, there are a number of assumptions about the level of measurement involved before techniques such as these can be used. One of them has already been mentioned. These techniques assume that the data, excluding measurement errors and the like, is related in a linear fashion. It may not be. Thus, if $r = 0$, this does not mean that there is no relationship whatsoever between the variables, only that the relationship is not linear. Though r may be zero, there may well be a strong curvilinear relationship between the variables.

Perhaps a more fundamental problem is that the techniques require at least an interval level of measurement. If we are describing, in regression terms, a relationship between two variables, we have to be able to assume that the scales on which the variables are mapped are under a constant linear transformation; that the distance between the points is describable in terms of a unit of measurement. Imagine the contrary, where the unit changes from point to point: no possible straight line can be constructed. So, when using these techniques, we have to be certain that what we are measuring may plausibly be described in interval terms.

All of which brings us back to the problem already discussed, namely, the relationship between the assumptions and understandings in the data language and those contained in the theory language, and our notions of social reality. Can the world, meaning the social world, plausibly be conceived in interval terms without distortion? Take a simple case, that of income. Income measured in monetary terms is an interval, indeed a ratio, scale: £200 is twice £100, £50 is half of £100, a quarter of £200, and so on. If, however, income is being used as an index of wealth, does it make sense to use this property? Of course, it makes *some* sense, except that one or two awkward questions arise. One such is whether an income of, say, £2,000 is 'really' only half as wealthy as an income of £4,000. In other words, it raises the question as to what is meant by 'wealth' in the theory language and its equivalence in the data language. A similar example would be the differences between IQ scores. If we assume they are interval, then the difference between an IQ of 80 and one of 100 would be the same as the difference between scores of 100 and 120, 120 and 140, and so on. This is hardly credible, since there are important qualitative shifts in performance between the same 'distance' on IQ scales. In other words, assumptions and understandings made within the data language may be implausible, unwarranted or misleading if carried over to the theory language.

Foundations of Measurement in Sociology

Ultimately all this boils down to a serious issue concerning the foundation for measurement in sociology. Mathematical systems, including the number systems sketched here, are abstract, uninterpreted axiomatic systems with no substantive content or reference to experience. This is the power of mathematics: the fact that it can be applied to diverse experiences because of its uninterpreted nature. However, in the more developed sciences, such as physics, the axioms of the mathematical system and deductive theory are isomorphic with each other; that is, the laws of the explicit theory can be translated into the axioms of the mathematical system so that there is a one-to-one correspondence with the terms of the two systems and the logical connections between the laws and the axioms are preserved.[9] In other words, it is not always the case that the distinction I have drawn between a theory language and a data language is so obvious or so distinct. In fact, in some cases the two languages are almost identical because of their isomorphic correspondence with one another. However, the question is whether such isomorphism can be assumed within sociology. It is claimed that most measurement in sociology is measurement by fiat that 'depends on *presumed* relationships between observations and the concept of interest'.[10] The criticism is that the sociologist maps his data on to a measurement system which he thinks is relevant rather than seeing whether his data satisfies any measurement system. The problem is compounded by the impression conveyed by sociological concepts themselves, which often fail to suggest what forms of measurement system would be appropriate for the data under investigation. They fail to generate numerical properties corresponding to existing or constructable measurement systems.[11] The implicit assumption in a great deal of sociological measurement is 'that the events of interest to the sociologist have the same properties mathematically that physical properties have and, therefore, that social events are amenable to the same kinds of measurement theories, if only the "right" combination or derivation of the axioms of arithmetic can be found along with "adequate" data that fit the model'.[12]

According to Cicourel, the difficulties facing the sociologist eager to measure are as follows. First, a point already mentioned, the theoretical concepts may not be sufficiently precise to suggest what forms of measurement system may be adequate for measuring them. Secondly, it may be that the very measurement devices employed are inappropriate by nature of their construction and so lead to measurement by fiat rather than literal measurement.[13] These objections are based on a general point made before. The sociologist, in beginning to analyse social reality, begins by classifying that reality in different ways: by delineating categories of, for example, social class, of political preferences, of friendship choices, of types of organization and so on. And, as said before, the major principle of classification is that if any object, event or property is equivalent to any other object, event or property, then it belongs to the same class (or, alternatively, if any object, event or property is not equivalent to any other object, event or property, then it belongs to a different class). Hence, if we are using numbers to denote some property, then these numbers should be given in accordance with this principle. Thus, if we are constructing a scale of violence in which certain types of event are classed as more or less violent and given numbers to reflect this property, we might end up with a scale something like the following:

Peaceful demonstrations = 1
Riots   = 2
Political assassinations = 3
Civil war   = 4

In many ways, a scale constructed in this (or a more sophisticated) manner could be extremely useful. For one thing, we could compare states in terms of their rates of political violence and, in turn, correlate these rates with other measures to see what kind of factors are associated with high and low degrees of violence.[14] But, from the point of understanding social reality, the assumption necessary for measurement, namely, that all categories—peaceful demonstrations for example—are equivalent and therefore receive the same numerical value, may not be valid from the point of view of the social reality it purports to identify. It may be that peaceful demonstrations in one society may not be equivalent (sociologically) to peaceful demonstrations in another society. In a relatively politically stable society, a peaceful demonstration may be a part and parcel of accepted civil liberties, while the same kind of activity in a less tolerant society may be perceived by the rulers as highly threatening and suppressed with all the force at their command. Yet, in the measurement scale just illustrated, these receive the same number because they belong to the same class even though their meaning within different social contexts may be radically different. What has happened is that the measurement structure itself has imposed an equivalence and not the theoretical concept.[15] All this goes back to issues mentioned earlier, namely, the claim by some sociologists that theoretical concepts must, for the sociologist, begin with the subjects' pre-selected and pre-interpreted cultural meanings and not the arbitrary classifications devised by observers. Indeed, the very attempt to achieve objectivication by use of measurement procedures is doomed to failure because the 'decision procedures for categorizing social phenomena are buried in implicit commonsense assumptions about the actor, concrete persons, and the observer's own views about everyday life'.[16] Moreover, one danger of measurement by fiat is that the measurement scales used assume logical relationships which may not correspond to the implicit theories.

These and other similar points are often taken as reasons for the ultimate impossibility of using the precision of quantitative methods to understand the nature of social reality. It is, so the argument goes, to create 'scientized man', not social man. Whatever the final outcome of this debate, the general point about measurement in research operations is that it should be done carefully and with thought. Care should be given to the question as to what it is that one is intending to measure, and to whether and in what ways any particular measurement will add to the investigation. As will be seen throughout this text, whatever is taken as an index or measure of a phenomenon will involve a theory of instrumentation, that is, a statement about how the index is produced or acted upon by the phenomenon in question; and it is these theories which are at issue in fitting substantive theory and data languages together. As far as measurement is concerned, it means providing good and adequate reasons why the phenomena in question can be measured according to any of the scales discussed earlier.

Exercise

These exercises are designed to provide some experience in constructing measurement devices suitable for sociological research. However, it is important to think about the issues raised in this chapter in your other reading.

1. Assume that you want directly to measure the following concepts: 'income', 'prestige', 'power', 'social class', 'aggression', 'normative deviance', 'attitudes to war and/or peace', 'democracy', 'friendship', and any others as you see fit. Say what level of measurement would be appropriate for each and why. Think about possible operational indicants of each concept and what number system could plausibly be mapped onto them.

2. Below are a list of activities, all, to a degree, illegal. Make a list of them and ask class members individually (or any other accessible group of people) how *serious* they would rate each activity using the following scale:

10 9 8 7 6 5 4 3 2 1

Very serious   Not very serious

Note that the same rating can be applied to more than one activity. In other words, two or more activities could be regarded as equally serious.

Activities

Being drunk and disorderly	Drunken driving
Cruelty to children	Common assault
Breaking and entering	Cruelty to animals
Driving while disqualified	Fraudulent use of credit card
Keeping TV receiver without a licence	Shoplifting
Possession of marijuana	Indecent exposure
Making false tax report	Adultery

Once this stage is complete, for each activity calculate the 'average seriousness', i.e. sum the different numbers awarded to each activity and divide the sum by the total number of attributions. Then rank the activities from least to most serious. What does this show? If you want to extend this exercise, give the rating scale to subjects differentiated according to some socially relevant property, such as 'sex', 'age', 'social class', 'political beliefs' and so on, to see whether the activities are, on average, evaluated differently.

Now think about what it is you have been doing. Do the numbers add anything, and, if so, what? What is being measured here? What assumptions have to be made in order that numbers may be attributed to the different activities? Are these plausible? Here think about the calculation of 'average seriousness'. Is the procedure used warrantable in light of the assumptions necessary for mapping number systems on to properties? Suppose you were going to use the measure of 'average seriousness' to indicate the normative structure of a group, would this be plausible? Here, try to notice whether there is much variation in scores attached to each activity; that is, have the subjects evaluated particular activities in widely different ways, and, if so, what are the implications?

3. If you have time, you might like to ask the subjects who had rated the activities in the preceding exercise whether or not they found their task easy. Probe to see what *they* thought of the operation. You might ask them whether it makes sense to rate the activities in isolation from other considerations. Would their rating have been different depending upon the person who had committed the act? What criteria did they use when awarding a score? Could they use these unambiguously? Think about the implications of these answers for measurement both in regards to this particular exercise and in general. Finally, consider whether, in your opinion, measurement operations such as these aid sociological understanding?

Notes and References

1. S. S. Stevens, 'Mathematics, Measurement, and Psychophysics', in S. S. Stevens (ed.), *Handbook of Experimental Psychology*, John Wiley & Sons, New York, 1951, p. 1.

2. See C. Coombs, 'Theory and Methods of Social Measurement', in L. Festinger and D. Katz (eds.), *Research Methods in the Behavioural Sciences*, Dryden Press, New York, 1953, p. 472; C. W. Churchman and P. Ratoosh, *Measurement*, John Wiley & Sons, New York, 1959.

3. M. W. Wartofsky, *Conceptual Foundations of Scientific Thought*, Macmillan, New York, 1968, pp. 153–4 (italics in original).

4. See H. M. Blalock, *Social Statistics*, McGraw-Hill, New York, 1972, p. 16.

5. ibid., p. 17.

6. For an extensive discussion of this, see Coombs, art. cit., pp. 481–3.

7. Blalock, *Social Statistics*, p. 18.

8. ibid.

9. See A. V. Cicourel, *Method and Measurement in Sociology*, The Free Press, New York, 1964, p. 9.

10. W. Torgerson, *Theory and Methods of Scaling*, John Wiley & Sons, New York, 1958, p. 21 (italics in original).

11. Cicourel, *Method and Measurement in Sociology*, p. 14.

12. ibid., p. 13.

13. ibid., pp. 13–29.

14. See, for example, T. Gurr, *Why Men Rebel*, Princeton University Press, Princeton, 1970. It must be admitted that the indices of violence used in this study are more sophisticated than the example used in the text. Nonetheless, the criticism is still pertinent. See P. Drew, 'Domestic Political Violence: Some Problems of Measurement', *Sociological Review*, 22, 1974, pp. 5–25.

15. Cicourel, *Method and Measurement in Sociology*, p. 28.

16 ibid., p. 21.

4
The Experiment

There are two reasons for taking the experiment as the first case in the more substantive discussion of research methods used in sociology. The first reason is that experimental design is, in many ways, the paradigm of that tradition of scientific inquiry which stems from the natural sciences. The experiment, in which all factors are controlled so that the precise determination of causal relationships and the testing of hypotheses can take place, is often seen as *the* design responsible, in large part, for the prominence of the natural sciences in the acquisition of human knowledge. Though historically incorrect (or at least too simple a view), it has often been claimed that the lack of development in the social sciences is a result of the ethical and practical difficulties involved in experimenting upon human beings. The second and related reason for starting with experiments this early is that the logic of experimental design informs many other kinds of data analysis within sociology, especially multivariate analysis, and it seems as well to introduce these ideas by looking first of all at experimental designs. Although laboratory experiments as such are relatively little used by sociologists, their design raises issues relevant to other modes of research.

Before looking in detail at experimental design and its variants, it is as well to see why the design should be regarded, by some at least, as one of the most powerful research methods available.

It could be said, in very general terms, that what the scientific investigator is trying to do is find what causes what in the universe. Why do things occur in the way they do, and not in other ways? The theories he develops are full of statements asserting that X is associated with, or causes, Y, and the general laws he constructs are explanations as to why the things in the universe happen in such a way. But, as should be fairly clear by now, this is not an entirely haphazard process. Evidence must be produced and good reasons given for a particular belief that an explanation accounts for certain sets of phenomena. In other words, if the assertion 'X causes Y' is made, good reasons must be given for us to take this statement as true or, at least, as plausible. For one thing, we must be fairly certain that Y follows X in temporal sequence, since it would be difficult, if not impossible, to envisage a cause following an effect. And although this rule, 'Every cause precedes an effect,' is predominantly definitional, it forms one of the 'good reasons', a very preliminary one, that must be provided if we are to consider any particular law-like statement as plausible.[1] It must also be established, as far as is possible, that there are no other factors involved in the causation of Y, or, if there are, what effect they have with respect to X. A third assurance that could be sought is to discover the conditions under which X causes Y. There are other and more detailed questions, but the point is that these and others are the kind which might be asked of any assertion to the effect that something causes something else; and, as we shall see, experimental design offers a set of rules by which evidence might be assembled relevant to answering them.

Classic Experimental Design

The design illustrated in Figure 6 is intended to throw into sharp relief the explanatory variable, or cause, X, while observing its effects on another variable, Y, other possible confounding variables being controlled in some way. (The term 'variable' is used to refer to any property or characteristic which can vary. Thus, the variable 'sex' can take, among humans, two values: 'male' and 'female'. The term 'independent variable' refers to that variable taken as the causal factor or stimuli, and 'dependent variable' to the effect. For example, in the statement, 'In Britain, sex is associated with political opinions,' 'sex' is the independent variable and 'political opinion' the dependent one. In some cases, the language of variables is often preferred to a language using the notion of 'cause'.)

In the classical experimental design, two samples—an experimental sample (E) and a control sample (C)—are selected in such a way as to be as nearly alike as possible at time 1 with regard to all factors which might potentially affect the relationship between X and Y, the presumed cause and the presumed effect. The presumed causal factor (X) is administered to the experimental sample, but withheld from the control sample. The dependent variable in the

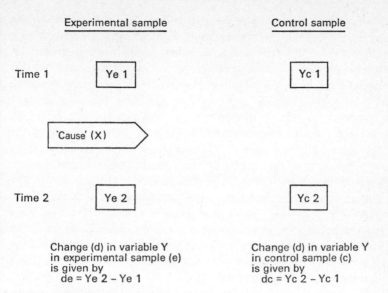

Figure 6. Classical experimental design.

two samples (Ye and Yc) is observed at both time 1 and time 2. The changes which occur in the dependent variable in the experimental sample (de) are then compared with the changes (if any) occurring in the same variable in the control sample (dc), and any difference, if it is significantly larger than de, is then attributed to the causal or independent variable.[2]

In its pure form, the classic experiment is a dynamic study in which time sequence, a necessary (but not sufficient) condition for establishing cause-and-effect relationships, is established. The design systematically controls the variables under study by manipulating both the independent and those other variables which might possibly influence the relationship between the independent and the dependent variables.

The first important feature to note about the design is that it presupposes a very clear idea of what relationship, and possible confounding factors, is to be the subject of the experiment. An example illustrating the importance of this point was mentioned in Chapter 2 (page 36) when speaking of concepts and the Powers experiment on the prevention of delinquency.[3] This study was an attempt to test the hypothesis that 'delinquency might be prevented by an intensive, enduring, personal, friendly relationship' between a social worker, or counsellor, and a potentially delinquent boy.

However, the experimental design used in the study was too rigorous, given the very vague specification of the independent variable —the 'warm and friendly' relationship between a social worker and a delinquent boy. The problem was that 'warm and friendly counsel' embraced a wide variety of activities, so that it was difficult to know what the independent variable was and whether it was applied uniformly throughout the study. 'Each counsellor was left largely to his own resources', and treatment consisted of 'the application of whatever skills each counsellor was capable of applying'.[4] So, even if the results of the experiment had been positive, it would have been difficult for the researchers to know precisely what it was about the 'warm and friendly counsel' that had been responsible. Thus an important condition of a good experiment is that the hypothesis, or relationship being tested, be clearly specified. A well and precisely formulated theoretical model is a precondition for an adequate experiment—not always as easy to achieve as might be supposed.

This requirement tends to put the experiment firmly into the arms of those social scientists who seek intellectual kinship with the natural scientists. Also, it is a design very much concerned with hypothesis-testing kinds of research rather than with more exploratory types of investigation. To study a situation where little is known about possible factors affecting the relationships of interest requires tools and designs of a different order from those provided by the experiment.

The second major feature of note is the use of a control sample which is as like the experimental sample at time 1 as possible, and from which the independent variable is withheld. The importance of this should be clear from the following example. Suppose a group of educational researchers wished to evaluate a new method of teaching on student attainment and used a design diagrammed in Figure 7. In this case, student attainment (Ye1) is measured at time 1, and after the new method of teaching has been administered for a suitable period, attainment is measured (Ye2) once again at time 2. Can the conclusion that any change in attainment (de) is attributable to X, the new method of teaching, be made with any confidence? While the result may be regarded as some sort of evidence, the lack of a control group means that we cannot, with confidence, draw any conclusions about the effects of the new teaching method on student attainment. We must ask the question: What other factors could have resulted in any changes in the dependent variable (a question that needs to be asked of *any* result)? Maybe the

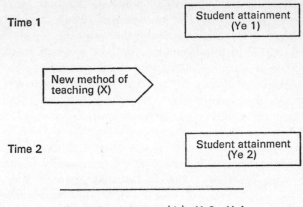

Figure 7. One-shot experimental design.

students would have changed in any case through maturation and other factors quite unconnected with the new teaching method. The point is that, without a matched control group, none of the other possible factors can be accounted for. Of course, not just any old group will do. The control group must be as nearly alike to the experimental group as possible at the outset of the experiment.

The Logic of Experimental Design

To understand precisely what is involved it is necessary to look at the principles embodied in experimental design. One of the rules it incorporates is known as the 'method of agreement' which states that, when two or more cases of a given phenomenon have one and only one condition in common, that condition may be regarded as the cause or the effect of that phenomenon. So, if X is observed in every case that Y is found, then this is taken as part of the grounds for inferring that X and Y are causally related. (Whether X is taken to be the cause of Y, or vice versa, depends upon the temporal priority of X and Y.) But, of course, this principle alone is not sufficient. The possibly apochryphal association between the number of ordained Catholic priests in New York and the high illegitimacy rate might lead all but the scurrilously irreligious to conclude that this principle, taken alone, has certain weaknesses. Fortunately, this is not the end of the story, for another principle is involved: the 'negative canon of agreement' which provides the logic of the control group.

D

This principle states that when non-X is found to be associated with non-Y, then a causal relationship may be suspected between X and Y. Once again, taken by itself, this principle is not sufficient. However, if the two are combined, then a much more powerful rationale appears for attributing cause and effect. This fusion of the method of agreement and its negative (the fusion termed the 'method of difference') goes something like this: if there are two or more cases, and in one of them Y can be observed, while, in the other, it cannot, and, in the case of observation, Y, X is also observed, while in the other X is not, then it can be asserted, with some degree of confidence, that X and Y are causally related. When applied to the experiment, the combination of non-X and non-Y is represented by the control group, while the experimental group represents the combination X and Y.[5]

These procedural rules, if they are to provide a basis for causal inference, must be applied in suitable circumstances; for example, the factors presumed to be causally related must be shown to be unequivocally related. What this means is that there must be no other factors which could possibly account for the relationship. This is the reason for the stress on the similarity of the two groups at the outset of the experimental period. If this is the case, we can be sure that the only difference between the two groups is the causal factor, and hence that the concluding difference, if any, is owing to this factor and this factor alone. However, it must be clear that these rules or procedures provide only a basis for inferring that any variables are related. As will be seen in subsequent discussion, there are many slips to be made between hunch and verification. More of this later. Now it is necessary to discuss how the similarity between the two groups can be achieved.

Matching and Randomization

The similarity is achieved by two major methods: matching and randomization. Matching is a fairly obvious procedure. The subjects to constitute the two groups are paired on all, or all the known, significant factors which might possibly influence the relationship between the independent and the dependent variables. Suppose, as in the previous example, that a researcher was interested in the effect of a new method of teaching on scholastic attainment, it might be felt that the sex of the pupil could have a differential effect on attainment in that girls might be less motivated than boys. So, if the researcher had more girls in the experimental group than in the control group, the results might tend to underestimate changes produced by the new teaching method. In a similar way, if there were more boys in the experimental group, this might tend to over-emphasize any effects of the new method.

A way to overcome this sort of problem is to control the sex variable by excluding it from the experiment and testing the hypothesis on either boys or girls. This is the principle involved in a number of animal experiments where variations in genetic, physiological and other factors is controlled by breeding pure strains for experimental purposes. However, if control by exclusion is not feasible, then a matching procedure becomes appropriate. In the example being discussed, this would require that 'sex', and any other variables needing control, are measured and the subjects paired so that the members of each pair are similar on all relevant variables. Suppose it were felt that 'sex', 'age', 'academic motivation' and 'IQ' were the most likely confounding factors, then each subject would be paired with another subject in the control group with the same value on these variables. However, there is a limit to the extent to which a matching process can be sustained. In the rather simplified example used here, only four variables are being controlled: 'sex', 'age', 'academic motivation' and 'IQ'. It is more than likely that many other variables could be considered as plausible candidates for control, and as the number of variables and the values they can take increases, so the number of subjects required becomes very large indeed.[6] The practical problems of carrying out the experiment increase enormously.

The Powers experiment mentioned earlier displayed considerable care in the matching of subjects. From a main sample of some 782 boys rated as either pre-delinquent or not (on the basis of a series of tests), the researchers attempted to create two similar samples of 325, each containing equal numbers of pre-delinquent and non-delinquent boys. The individual boys were paired according to their similarity on traits considered relevant to the causes of delinquency, such as age, delinquency prediction rating, health, intelligence, educational achievement, personality, family and environmental factors. The objective of this case-by-case matching was to control potentially confounding factors that might be associated with the subjects themselves.

Unfortunately, matching alone can never be sufficient in controlling all possible factors that may be associated with the dependent variable, for many of these may be unknown to the researcher. Further, it is almost impossible to be certain that the experimental and control samples are distributed alike on all potentially confounding factors.[7] So, at this stage, it is necessary to randomize other potential sources of confounding effects. In the Powers study this was achieved by allocating, purely at random, a boy in each pair to either the control or the experimental group, the intention being to remove any systematic bias in the samples by making the influence of extraneous factors random. This avoids, for example, the danger that, in selecting a boy from each pair to be included in the experimental sample, the researcher might unconsciously have selected those boys more likely to improve by the treatment meted out. Random allocation in this way means that unmatched factors are prevented from exerting any *systematic* effect on the outcome of the experiment.

Matching and randomization are thus two important features of the classic experimental design, and are intended to ensure that all confounding factors, suspected and unsuspected, are prevented from exerting any systematic influence on the relationship between the presumed causal factor and its effects. This therefore implies that any difference between the experimental group and the control group can only be a result of the effects of the independent variable and/or chance error. To assess the latter, statistical tests are available to assess the extent to which any differences found between the experimental and the control groups could be owing to chance error. If such tests indicate that the result is unlikely to be owing to chance, then this is taken as evidence that the causal factor is responsible for any differences found between the experimental and the control groups.

Variation in the Classical Design

Random Allocation

There are variations to this classical design. In some cases, where the detailed information required for systematic matching is unavailable, this is often omitted and subjects from the sample pool are allocated randomly to either the experimental or the control groups. In evaluating the new method of teaching, for example, students might be assigned randomly to the experimental and to the control groups. In this way, each of the two groups becomes a random sample of the initial pool of subjects in that each person in the pool has an equal chance of being placed in either the control or the experimental group. Thus, since each student can be placed only in one of the two groups, each has a 50-50 chance of being in either of them. Each group can then be considered to be representative, within certain limits, of the original pool of subjects, and hence will tend to be similar in relevant respects.

The difference between control by randomization and 'precision control' by matching subjects, pair by pair, may be summarized as follows. Matching can only be done with a few variables at a time, whereas randomization controls all variables, within a certain degree: a degree which improves as the size of the group increases. Furthermore, while, in the case of matching, the proportions of subjects between the experimental and the control groups will be equal, it is possible to lose a number of subjects from the initial pool owing to difficulties in finding suitable partners to make the pair. This is serious when the initial pool is intended to be representative of some larger population, for, as cases are lost, it becomes less and less representative.

Two-Control-Group Design

Two other variants of experimental design are worth mentioning. The first is Solomon's Two-Control-Group Design.[8] As the name suggests, this design calls for two control groups besides the experimental group. The reason for this brings to the fore one of the most important effects which needs to be accounted for in any research: the effects of the research itself upon the subjects. In setting up an experiment, the prior measurement of relevant variables may interact with the independent variable. For example, the children being used as subjects for the teaching method evaluation study would quite probably be subjected to a battery of tests prior to the administration of the new method of teaching. It may be that such prior experience will sensitize them to the fact that 'something is going on'. They may put two and two together and get a fairly good notion of what the experiment is about. This may cause them to react in various ways: awkwardness, a refusal to co-operate or an over-enthusiastic participation in the objectives of the experiment. But, whatever the response of the subjects, the point is that it is unaccounted for in the design of the experiment; it will become another uncontrolled factor that may affect the result in unknown ways. The effect produced by sensitizing the subject by 'before' measurements, and the effect of this on 'after' measurements, is known as the 'interaction effect'.

Solomon's solution, to provide for two control groups in addition to the experimental group, means that estimates can be made of both the interaction effect and the effect of the independent variable. One control group is treated exactly as if it were part of a classic design : the members of the group are measured, along with the experimental group, on all relevant characteristics. The other control group is given no pre-test. On the face of it, this seems to violate one of the basic principles of experimental design, namely, that the experimental and the control group should start out as alike as possible. However, the argument contained in this design is that if all the groups are composed of subjects randomly selected from a pool, then it can be expected that the groups will vary on any one factor only to a limited degree. Therefore, if the 'before' measures on both the experimental and the first control group are averaged, this will provide an estimate of the 'before' measures on the subjects in the second control group.

An illustration of the design is to be found in Figure 8, which contains hypothetical data on the effects of a new method of teaching. This hypothetical experiment is designed to determine the effects of a new teaching method on pupil's interest in subject S. The subjects are selected from a pool and randomly allocated to respective groups. The experimental and the first control groups are measured on their interest in subject S before the experiment starts. This is the 'before' measure, and is equivalent to measuring the dependent variable in the classical experimental design prior to the administration of the independent variable. The second control group's interest is estimated from the scores of the other two groups, a procedure justified by the fact that the allocation of subjects to each group was random. Looking at the changes induced by the new method of teaching, we find that the largest change is in the experimental group : a change (d) of 40 per cent. However, this result could be owing to an interaction effect between the experimental variables, i.e. the new method of teaching and the 'before' measures sensitizing the subjects to the objective of the study. In the case of the first control group, the change (d_1) is only 15 per cent, a change entirely resulting from the effects of pre-test sensitization since the new method of teaching was withheld from this group. The change (d_2) in the second control group, a group subjected to the independent variable, is 15 per cent, owing entirely to the effects of the new method of teaching since no 'before' measures were taken. We are now in a position to estimate the effects of the 'before' measures, the experimental variable, and the interaction between the two. The first two effects are already accounted for, and the interaction effect is calculated by separately abstracting the changes which result from the experimental variable, and the 'before' measures from the changes which result from both combined:

$$\begin{aligned}
\text{Interaction effect} &= d-(d_1+d_2)\\
&= 40-(15+15)\\
&= 10
\end{aligned}$$

The conclusion is that there is a small, but detectable, interaction effect besides the separate effects of the 'before' measures and the 'before' measures and the independent variable.

Factorial Design

Other elaborations of experimental design are devoted to the examination of more than one variable within a single design. The factorial design, for example, has two or more independent variables, each varied in two or more ways. This is an important step, for, as Fisher puts it, 'We are usually ignorant which, out of innumerable possible factors, may prove ultimately to be the most important . . . we have usually no knowledge that any one factor will exert its effects independently of all others.'[9] The factorial design is intended to meet some of these problems in ways similar to the Solomon design discussed above. The logic underlying factorial

	Experimental group	1st control group	2nd control group
T1 'Before' measurements (% claiming interest in subject S)	30	30	(30)
	New method of teaching		New method of teaching
T2 'After' measurements (% claiming interest in subject S)	70	45	45
% change	d = 70 – 30 = 40	d1 = 45 – 30 = 15	d2 = 45 – 30 = 15

Figure 8. Illustration of Solomon's Two-Control-Group Design.

designs is set out in Figure 9. In this case, a different experimental group is needed for each possible combination of factors. Suppose a researcher was interested in examining the effects of two methods of teaching, call them X_1 and X_2. The possible combinations of these variables are each by itself and both together. In this way, the joint effects, or interaction, of the two methods can be examined. Again, suppose that the dependent variable is the interest shown in subject S by the pupils. From Figure 9 it appears that X_1 has an effect

	1st group	2nd group	3rd group	4th group
T1 'Before' measurements (% claiming interest in subject S)	20	20	20	20
NEW METHODS OF TEACHING, X1, X2	X1	X2	X1 + X2	
T2 'After' measurements (% claiming interest in subject S)	40	20	65	20
% change	d1 = 20	d2 = 0	d3 = 45	d4 = 0

Figure 9. Illustration of factorial design.

(compare change d with the change in the group with no treatment, d_4), whereas X_2 (d_2 compared with d_1 and d_4) has no effect except in conjunction with X_1. Thus, it appears that the two methods of teaching, X_1 and X_2, interact to produce an increase in the pupil's interest in subject S.[10] This kind of design can be elaborated to explore more complex relations between variables.

Thus, in experimental designs, sociologists have a potentially powerful tool for testing fairly rigorously defined hypotheses. Yet, as with life, nothing is quite as good as it seems. Indeed, there are a number of factors which can inhibit the value of any experiment. These will be discussed in terms of two fundamental problems which need to be considered with regard to any research, experimental or not: internal and external validity.

Internal and External Validity

Internal validity concerns the problem of deciding what conclusions can be drawn about the results in terms of the study itself. It has already been seen how the logic of the classic experimental design is devoted to controlling out the effects of all extraneous variables. Another way of putting it is that the design tries to reduce the variation in the dependent variable resulting from other factors and to isolate the variation resulting from the independent variable. If you accept the premises of experimental logic, then, as a matter of logic, you must accept the result of the experiment.[11] More particularly, if you accept the principles of randomization and of matching, and are satisfied that these have been applied correctly, then it is difficult to reject the results. On the other hand, of course, if we do not accept that the design has been satisfactorily adhered to, then we are in a position to criticize and doubt the validity of the result. It is not simply a matter of whether the result is 'right' or 'wrong' as a description of the world, but rather that we are not able to judge as the criteria, the 'good grounds', for accepting it as a true or false description have not been applied.

External validity concerns the application of any findings to a wider context. Does the result apply to subjects other than those studied? Does it apply in other places at other times? Suppose a researcher had studied the effect of a new teaching method on 14-year-old children, has correctly applied the procedures and obtained a positive result, does this mean that the findings can be taken to apply to 12-year-old children, to 8-year-olds, to adults, and so on? Does it apply equally to children in Glasgow, Tokyo or Calcutta? The issues of external validity are therefore about the grounds we have for inferring that the results apply to populations or situations other than those studied.[12]

Internal Validity

To look at the problems of internal validity first, and to illustrate some of the points which need to be considered in assessing the internal validity of any experiment, take again the 'one-shot' design where the researcher simply applies an experimental treatment to a group of people and observes the result. Suppose our perpetual group of students were subjected to a new teaching method (X) and their performance observed at a later time. There is no control group. Whatever the result of the experiment, could valid conclusions be drawn about the effect of the treatment, X? Remember that validity is about two sorts of things: the criteria by which we judge or assess validity, and whether or not these criteria have been successfully applied. As far as the first is concerned, the 'one-shot' design fails to rule out possible extraneous factors which could account for the result, whatever it might be. Nothing is known about the subjects themselves, so it cannot be discovered to what extent the change in performance, if any, was caused by the experimental variable or by factors inherent in the subjects themselves. If the results had shown an improvement in student performance, we could not know whether this was a result of the supposed new method of teaching or simply the maturation of the subjects; or to especially good teaching on another course, or to a host of other factors left uncontrolled.

'Maturation' is the term used to refer to those processes or changes that occur within the subject because of his or her nature as a human being, regardless of what is done in the experiment. Thus, if research was being carried out on children over a lengthy period, the design would have to include provision for those factors associated with their growth and maturation. 'History', on the other hand, refers to those events or processes in the environment of the subject that might affect the outcome of the study. In terms of the example, a subject who grows up in a family where reading is the norm would be subjected to a historical effect, while reaching an age when the faculties develop to allow a greater concentration in attending to a task would be a maturation effect.[13] Obviously, rigorous attention to the construction of a proper design for the experiment can do a great deal to offset such factors. Matching procedures, a careful selection of cases, randomization and, perhaps above all, comparison with a control group are the obvious design features to take account of these kinds of extraneous factor and to improve the internal validity of the results.

The Hawthorne Effect

However, there are other sets of factors more difficult to account for, which are, the effects of the experiment itself: a series of effects known as 'control effects'. Researchers became alerted to these during a long-term research programme carried out between 1927 and 1932 at the Western Electric Company's Hawthorne plant in Chicago. One aim of the study was to examine the effects of various changes in working conditions on the output of a group of girl workers so that it could be determined which set of conditions were the most satisfactory in creating high output. Six girls were chosen for the experiment. They were chosen as average workers, neither inexperienced nor terribly expert. Their work consisted of the assembly of telephone relays.[14] The girls were taken to a test room divided from the main work area. Care was taken to make sure that the output rate, as something easily measured in terms of units produced, was unaffected by factors extraneous to the experiment. The number of faulty parts, the weather each day, the state of health of the girls and so on were all recorded so that they could be taken into account during analysis. The nature of the experiment was carefully explained to the girls, and every effort was made to allay any of their natural anxieties. Whenever an experimental change was planned, the girls were fully informed and their comments requested—and received. Throughout the study, they were repeatedly told not to strain themselves unduly, but to continue working at a pace they felt comfortable. For a two-week period prior to entering the test room, the output of each girl was measured, without her knowledge, while she was working in the regular production setting. For five weeks after the girls had entered the test room, no change was made in the working conditions. In this way, the investigators hoped to notice any changes in output attributable to transfer from the regular asembly room to the test room. A third period involved a change in the method of payment. Some eight weeks later, two rest periods of five minutes each were introduced. Six five-minute periods were established in the next experimental period. Other changes introduced at various stages were light lunches at company expense, earlier clocking-off, and a five-day working week, each change lasting some weeks.

The results, in terms of the output curve, were somewhat surprising. Throughout the period of the experiment, the output curve had risen slowly but steadily. Even when weekly output fell on the introduction of a five-day week, daily output still increased. The researchers, trying to find a control, for a twelve-week period returned conditions to what they had been originally. Output rose higher than ever !

The conclusion forced on the researchers was that, in this case at least, output did not seem to depend upon working conditions, otherwise returning to the original conditions of work should have caused output to decline to its original level. Certain other conditions were also repeated, and in no case did the output from identical conditions remain the same. Indeed, the only apparent uniformity was the increase in output through each successive experimental period. The experimenters concluded that the increase in the output curve was reflecting something other than the responses of the group to the experimental stimuli. But what? Many possible factors were ruled out. There were no errors caused by inadequate matching, since the group functioned, as was thought, as its own control. History was ruled out, since the girls were working in a contrived setting under isolated and carefully controlled conditions and because various supplementary records indicated otherwise.

After ruling out other possible explanations, with a certain inevitability the researchers concluded that the experiment itself was confounding the intended aim of their study. Questioning the girls afterwards, the researchers discovered that each girl knew she was producing more than when she was working in the regular assembly shop. It seemed easier, it seemed fun, and they were able to work in a relaxed atmosphere away from the normal supervisory control. In addition, the girls knew they were taking part in an important and interesting experiment, the results of which could, in some way, lead to an improvement in working conditions in the plant as a whole. The researchers had, from the beginning, taken pains to acquaint the girls with what was going on, to reassure them and, very different from their normal work routine, to consult them. In short, the very act of research had generated processes in the group so that output was recording not the physical conditions of the work setting, but the social development of the group itself. Over the period of the experiment, the group of girls developed a cohesion and a pattern of relationships, including leadership roles, friendship bonds (which often continued after hours) and reciprocal ties, none of which had been particularly apparent before the girls became subjects in the experiment. In a way, the members of the group developed common purposes, and soon after the inception of the study had committed themselves to a continuous increase in output.

The importance of these developments for experiments in general is that they are not the traditional kind of coincidental changes which could have occurred apart from the conditions imposed by the research, but were a result of the research itself. By isolating the girls, and by heightening their awareness that they were under study, thereby enhancing their sense of importance, the researchers changed the very action they wanted to study. Interestingly, this discovery of the relationship between the development of an informal group structure and group productivity was to become one of the major findings of the research and was the start of a massive reorientation in the study of work group dynamics. But, in addition, the interest for methodology is that it alerted researchers to one important factor which could influence the results of research : the research itself.

External Validity

Turning now, for a moment, to problems of external validity, the issue here is to what extent can inferences be drawn from a particular experiment to a wider context? Can the results be generalized beyond the data of a specific study? There are a number of types of relevant generalizability. First, there is the generalizability of the independent variable. In the case of a new teaching method, is it a method which can be used by all teachers, or does it depend upon particular teacher abilities? Is the method limited to a particular subject-matter, or is it generally applicable? In short, how flexible is the variable?

The second type of generalizability is concerned with the measures used for the experimental variable. To what extent is the result owing to the application of a particular form of measurement system? If a variable has been measured by an eleven-point verbal scale, would the results have been different if other methods had been used—say, a sentence-completion test, or whatever?

Thirdly, to what extent are the results applicable to persons other than those used in the experiment? Is, say, the new method of teaching applicable at all age levels, all ability levels, in different types of school in different countries, and so on? It is this latter type of issue which causes much critical comment about psychological research in that it tends to show too great a readiness to use college students as subjects—a somewhat small minority and an untypical section of the population.

There are no simple or easy recipes to help us find answers. Internal validity is by itself no necessary guide to external validity. An optimal research design should include both types of validity, though sometimes attempts to secure one can interfere with the other; excessive concern to obtain internal validity is often incompatible with external validity. Consider what would be required to generalize the results of an experiment to a wider population. For one thing, we would have to be sure that the subjects chosen for the experiment were representative of some wider domain. Yet, the use of control samples in experiments creates special requirements for the sampling procedure, which has to give two samples as nearly alike as possible so that the relationship between the variables in which the researcher is interested can be analysed. This is an attempt to meet internal validity, but, in so doing, the researcher runs the risk of drawing a sample unrepresentative of the population of theoretical concern. In the case of the perpetual example, in an attempt to highlight the relationship between a new teaching method and the interest shown by the pupils in a subject, the researcher may well select children who are unrepresentative of the total population of school children. To take another obvious example, to examine the relationship between certain personality traits and behaviour in a laboratory experiment, controlling out all extraneous factors might seem odd, especially if it is argued that one of the major sets of factors determining behaviour is the situation or context in which the behaviour takes place. If this is the case, presumably behaviour would be seen as an interaction between personality and situation; and if the situations are controlled out, then it would be difficult to generalize from the experiment to the 'real world'.[15]

Additional constraints upon the representativeness of the findings are the limitations set by the experimental arrangements. This is a fairly familiar objection in disguise, namely, that one cannot study people in a laboratory, and, whatever the ultimate answer, it does raise a very fair point in that the experimental situation is somewhat 'artificial' in at least two senses. First, though the experimenter takes great pains to control all possible extraneous variables so that he can explore one or two relationships, it may be that, in the 'real world', it is precisely these controlled variables which are important in determining the relationships under scrutiny. While it is true, as indicated earlier, that there are experimental designs which try to look at more than one variable at a time, in practice they represent only a marginal improvement in getting at 'real-world-multi-causal-situations'. Thus the experiment, as a design which selectively focuses on a few variables at a time, may fail to include those factors crucial in the area of theoretical concern.

Of course, these are objections not in principle but of practice, and certainly not everything to do with human behaviour is beyond experiment. Physiological factors, for example, which vary little between individuals, are obvious candidates for experimental work. Also, we can take note of Festinger's advice to work continually between 'real life' and experimental situations.[16] Nonetheless, the objection here probably lies behind sociologists' occasional use of field experiments, like the Powers study discussed earlier. Here the intention is to use the power of experimental design to test relationships between variables without 'over-controlling' other variables which may be important in 'real-life' situations. As might be expected, all the factors which detract from the power of the experiment tend to be magnified when actually used in the field.

Pursuing these ideas further, it may be argued that what is being studied in the experimental situation is how people react to such situations, as is suggested by the Hawthorne study. Even though the experimenter may take great care in the design, and in the selection of subjects, once they are in the experimental situation, it cannot always be assumed, though it often is, that the subject's behaviour results entirely from the operation of the experimental factors. This point has been made before, but since it is important to a great deal that follows, is worth discussing at length.

The Experiment as a Social Setting

In research, particularly in social research, the causal or independent variable is often more complex than is supposed. This was certainly the case in the Powers experiment, where the independent variable, 'warm and friendly counsel', was interpreted by the counsellors in numerous ways, so preventing the invariant application of the variable to the subjects: a necessary requirement of experimental procedure. Similarly, a set of factors which can cloud the original purity of the variables used are the additions, both conscious and unconscious, provided by the subjects themselves. Edwin Boring cites a neat example to illustrate:

> 'Bring me that rattlesnake,' says the experimenter of a live coiled rattlesnake behind invisible glass, and the subject complies until prevented by the glass. Would he have done so had there been no glass? Perhaps, but the 'demand' made upon him . . . was more than the verbal instruction. It included the knowledge that this was an experiment, that you do not get truly injured in an experiment, that there is an experimenter and a university looking out for you.[17]

In other words, a subject taking part in an experiment is not shorn of experiences gained outside, but he or she brings them into the laboratory situation. Similarly, the experimenter, though indubitably a high priest in the church of objectivity, is also human and, as such, is liable to err on the side of advantage. Certainly what evidence there is suggests that when errors of observation do occur, they tend to be in the direction of the researcher's hypothesis rather than against it.[18] Though errors of observation ('seeing the facts') might appear serious enough, imagine the greater margin of error when it comes to the interpretation of the results. It is difficult enough to state accurately and unequivocally any rules for observation, but even more difficult to state similar rules for that essentially private process, interpretation. Imagine the latitude for errors of interpretation in the average experiment: the subtle categorization of doubtful cases in favour of the hypothesis, the sly and inadvertent communication of the experimenter's intent to his subjects, and so on. But this is not exactly a new problem. The stress in the scientific culture on publicity of method and results and the replication of findings (this latter a rule, in sociology, more honoured in the breach than in obedience) are intended to exert at least some long-term normative control over such tendencies.

But errors, if such they can be called, do not all originate with the experimenter. The subject's characteristics and his response to the experimental situation also intrude into the objectivity of the experiment. In one study, the interaction between experimenter and subjects was recorded on film and in sound. Only 12 per cent of the experimenters ever smiled to their male subjects, while 70 per cent smiled at their female ones. This, in itself, sounds rather obvious and harmless, even quaint, had it not also been found that smiling on the part of the experimenter affected the subjects' responses. Further evidence on this point suggests that female subjects tend to be more protectively treated by experimenters.[19] The point need not be laboured, except to say that there is a considerable body of work which shows large variations resulting from the subtle interactions of experimenter and subject characteristics. Hence the almost inevitable conclusion that the experimental situation has many of the hallmarks of fairly typical social situations in which behaviour can be seen as a complex interplay of personal and social characteristics conveyed by all the media of human communication, and in which participants, both experimenter and subject, mutually react in non-reflective ways. The fact that the research is conducted in a laboratory by men and women in white coats who ask a subject to do unusual things, calls into play echoes from the 'outside' culture about science and research. What these beliefs are, and how they react on the experimental situation, is an important and crucial question. It might be, for example, that since scientific activity has a relatively enhanced but mysterious status so far as the lay public is concerned, subjects may unwittingly play the role of 'subjects' rather than representations of a social category or variable that is the object of study. It all points towards seeing the information-gathering setting as also a behaviour setting worthy of study in its own right.

These interpersonal effects are not confined to the laboratory experiment, for such effects operate in most, if not all, sociological data-collecting contexts. An illustrative case, apart from the Hawthorne study, is a study of low socio-economic-status children. All the children in an elementary school were given an intelligence test, disguised as a test to predict intellectual 'blooming'. Each of the six grade or year levels contained three classrooms: above-average ability, average ability and below-average ability children, respectively. In each of the eighteen classrooms, about 20 per cent of the children were chosen at random to form the experimental group, and each teacher was given the names of the children from their class who were in the experimental group. The teacher was told that these children had scored high on the test for intellectual 'blooming', and that they would show remarkable gains in intellectual ability during the next eight months. Thus the only difference between the experimental and the control group was in the minds of the teachers.

After eight months, all the children were retested with the same IQ test used originally. For the school as a whole, the children in the experimental group showed only a slightly greater gain in verbal intelligence than did the control-group children. But, in total IQ and in abstract reasoning, the experimental children had gained appreciably more than the control-group children. Interestingly, children of the highest level of achievement showed as great a gain as did the children of the lowest level of achievement.[20] Moreover, the teachers described those children from whom they were led to expect intellectual growth as having a better chance of becoming successful in the future, as more interesting, curious and happy, as more appealing, better adjusted and needing less social approval. In short, the interpersonal expectations occur, in different ways, outside the laboratory, and the unintended (or, as in the above example, the intended) effect of the investigator's research hypothesis must be regarded as a potentially damaging artifact.

To summarize, the following problems have been identified as the main possible confounding effects of the experimental setting. First, are the experimenter's intentions, expectations and hopes for the outcome of the study. Then a second group of factors, termed by Orne 'experimental demands' of the research setting,[21] are the result of actors entering the experimental setting with certain kinds of expectation.

Confounding Factors as Rival Explanations

It all begins to look as if the sociologists, even one positivistically inclined, must disregard the experiment as a tool of analysis. Yet it is important to remember that, historically, the use of control groups was devised to meet more or less the same kinds of problem. E. G. Boring suggests that the control group, a feature now taken as axiomatic to experimental design, was invented specifically to control for plausible rival hypotheses in psychology, namely, that pre-tests would produce gains in subject performance even in the absence of experimental treatments.[22] In other words, it was a realization that some other theory could account for the results that led to the development of control-group design so as to rule out, or control out, this possible rival explanation. As Campbell points out, '. . . it is not a failure-to-control in general that bothers us, but only those failures of control which permit *truly plausible* rival hypotheses, laws with a degree of scientific establishment comparable or exceeding that of the law our experiment is designed to test'.[23] In short, the control-group idea is not a logical dispensation, but a very practical empirical achievement based on certain well-known theories—truly plausible rival hypotheses—about the effects of measurement and experimentation on the performance of experimental subjects. Interestingly, the control group is missing from most of the nineteenth-century physics, chemistry and physiology from which certain trends in sociology took their methodological models.

In other words, methodology is not revealed truth, but has 'an empirical component and its constituents have the status of empirical discoveries'.[24] Far from invalidating experimental procedures the kind of findings just discussed suggests the need for new control groups to allow for previously ignored factors such as the unintended interaction of experimenter and subject and other types of artifact. The volunteer subject, for example, has always worried the experimenter in that he will, as likely as not, behave in ways different from subjects who do not volunteer. But, rather than regarding this as an argument for rejecting the whole basis and philosophy of experimentation, it is necessary to rethink the choice of subjects and the detailed design of the experiment concerned.[25] For example, one strategy for controlling 'experimental demand' is to use hypothetical actors: a group of people who are given a description of the experiment and asked how they think most actors would behave in such conditions. The extent to which actors only hypothetically involved can accurately predict how actors in a real experimental situation would behave is a guide to the extent to which experimental results can be attributed to the experimental treatment.

So, those features which are 'instrumental incidentals' of the experiment—aspects of the experimental treatment itself, and inevitably irrelevant to the theoretical variable that is the subject of the experiment—should be treated as potentially rival explanations of the experimental result.[26]

It must be said that many of the criticisms of the experiment reflect an over-idealized and impractical view of the method of scientific investigation and the production of knowledge. The criticism that experimental settings are artificial and not representative of the 'real world' is an important and well-taken point. However, one counter-view is that this criticism, if taken too far, becomes ridiculously misleading about the process of acquiring knowledge. To take the issue of representativeness of experimental subjects, in an important sense it is unreasonable to ask for a representative sample from some universe of theoretical relevance since, in social science, this is in practice, and possibly in principle, impossible to specify in all dimensions. Time is one such dimension which may be used to illustrate this point. 'In the physical sciences, the presumption that there are no interactions with time (except those of daily, lunar, seasonal and other cycles) has proved to be a reasonable one. But for the social sciences, a consideration of the potentially relevant population characteristics shows that changes over time (e.g. a thirty-year comparison of college students) produce differences fully as large as synchronous social class and sub-cultural differences.'[27] To sample a universe of generalization representatively would also require representative sampling in time—a matter of considerable difficulty. But, once again, this is not a matter for despair. Campbell goes on to quote the case of Nicholson and Carlisle, who, in 1800, took a very 'parochial' sample of Soho water, inserted into it a very biased sample of copper wire through which flowed a very local electric current. At one electrode, oxygen was given off, at the other hydrogen. In spite of the 'unrepresentative' elements used in the experiment, they went on to generalize to all water, past, present and future. This was a hypothetical generalization rather than 'proven fact', and subsequent studies of hydrolysis have demonstrated the effects of impurities. But the point remains that limitations to generalization such as these emerge from testing and checking them in a variety of contexts.

One lesson from this is that no experiment stands alone. Controlling for every possible factor in an experiment is impossible. What can be achieved more reasonably is the devising of experimental designs to control out, or enable one to account for, the most plausible rival hypotheses. What these may be cannot always be decided in advance of the problem, and perhaps all one can say, in the spirit of the Hawthorne researchers, is that what is a nuisance for one researcher may be interesting and potentially important for another. To give Campbell a final word:

> The logic of scientific inference indicates that experiments cannot prove theories, but only probe them. For every theory-corroborating experimental result there are an infinity of rival explanations potentially available. . . . A major class of those plausible rival hypotheses are methodological artifacts introduced through irrelevant vehicular aspects of the experimental treatment. . . .
>
> Control can never be complete in ruling out all plausible rival hypotheses in advance. As a rule, research must seek out ways of controlling each artifact as it is developing, through means that are specific to each combination of artifact hypothesis and theoretical variable.[23]

Quasi-Experiments

Although these have been mentioned briefly, they deserve special attention since they are an interesting incursion of experimental thinking into contexts typically considered non-experimental. From the previous discussion, it could forgivably be thought that experiments can, by and large, only be carried out with reasonable success in the laboratory. However, the logic of quasi-experiments suggests that some elements of experimental thinking can be applied to problems of a societal scale. Societal 'experimentation' is a continuous process in modern societies, sometimes initiated by governments, businesses or other organizations, and at other times by natural forces. Examples of the former would be laws passed by governments, the introduction of a new marketing strategy, warnings against cigarette smoking, or the establishment of a new school system. Examples of natural forces' 'experiments' could include the devastation of an area by a tornado, a change in climate and so on. To the extent that such changes also introduce changes in patterns of behaviour, they may be regarded as equivalent to experimental treatments and analysed as such.[29] An example is Campbell and Ross's study of the effects of a crackdown on speeding in Connecticut.[30]

The occasion of this study was the effort by the state authorities in Connecticut, in 1955, to do something about the rising road-death toll by instituting much stricter enforcements of speed violations. Much stricter law enforcement led, in the succeeding six months, to a decline in the death toll and the number of speed violations. It was hailed as a great achievement. Campbell and Ross's problem was to evaluate the extent to which the more rigorous law enforcement was responsible for the decline in fatalities and violations: a type of problem typical in social science where change must be evaluated in non-randomly selected groups where systematic controls are impossible. Their general methodological stance was that the lack of control and randomization are only damaging to inferences about cause and effect to the extent that a systematic consideration of alternative explanations reveals that some are plausible.

From the graph (Figure 10), the result of the crackdown looks impressive enough as measured in terms of the decline in traffic fatalities. But such displays can be misleading. Looking at the data

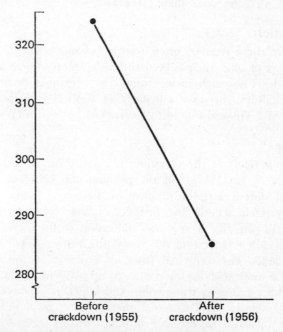

Figure 10. Connecticut traffic fatalities, 1955–6.

as a quasi-experiment and using the 1955 figures as the 'pre-test', the crackdown as the experimental treatment, and the 1956 figures as the 'post-test' data, and applying the technique of looking for plausible rival explanations, the effects of the 'experimental treatment' can be assessed. In other words, the hypothesis that the crackdown caused the decline can be held, provided that consideration is given to other plausible explanations of the decline in traffic fatalities. This means looking for, and if possible eliminating, those factors not controlled for in the design. And this means looking for the following kinds of factor, as in the normal experiment.

History

That is, those specific events other than the experimental treatment which occur between the pre-test and the post-test and which might also account for the change. It might be, for example, that the winter of 1955–6 was particularly dry with fewer accidents from rain or snow. There might have been a dramatic improvement of the safety features of 1956-model cars. Elimination of these and similar factors as rival explanations must be attempted by checking suitable data; for example, that the winter concerned was not unusual, that new cars were no safer than previously.

Maturation

These are those regular, often routine, changes which recur with the passage of time, such as becoming older, more experienced and so on. In this case, such factors might be a general decline in road traffic fatalities, increased efficiency of medical care, better roads, and the like. These also need to be checked against suitable evidence.

Testing

This factor refers to the variation in a measuring instrument independently of any change in the phenomenon being measured. Instrument shift is a classic problem in the use of public records for social research where, for instance, better recording by public authorities can give a spurious indication of an increase in, say, crime. In earlier versions of this study, the death rate per 100 million vehicle miles was computed from an estimate of the number of gallons of fuel sold in the state. A decrease in the actual miles obtained per gallon by using engines of larger horsepower or driving at higher speeds could thus masquerade as a lower mileage death rate by inflating the estimate of miles driven. Conversely, if the crackdown had resulted in lower vehicle speeds, this could have increased miles per gallon leading to an under-estimate of mileage driven in the post-crackdown period and an over-estimate of the fatality rate during the period in question.

Instability

If the drop in fatalities had occurred in a small township, it would have seemed less impresive since small size can make for greater instability in the measures involved. In field situations of this sort, the size of the relevant population is only one of the many sources of instability.

Regression

Where a group having an extreme score on a variable is selected for study, it can be said that, on average, the post-test measurements will be less extreme than the pre-test ones. This is a possibility in this case since a crackdown could be expected in those states with an exceptionally high casualty rate and applied at a time in which fatalities were exceptionally high. Thus regression might at least in part account for less extreme 1956 figures.

Campbell and Ross go on to test out some of these rival explanations, and conclude that while the crackdown did have some effect, no unequivocal case can be made that the decline in fatalities was owing entirely to its influence. Not all of these sets of rival hypotheses need apply with equal force in all studies of this type, but nonetheless they do represent factors which must be ruled out before the original hypothesis can be accepted with confidence. Quasi-experiments mark a kind of mid-way position between those who regard no result as valid unless it is derived from a design conforming as strictly as possible to the canons of control and randomization, and those, at the other extreme, for whom attribution of cause may be made without much consideration of any other plausible rival explanations. They do, however, allow to some degree a translation of experimental thinking into situations normally felt to be beyond experimental analysis.

Conclusions: Experimental Design and Sociological Research

In trying to place the experiment in some methodological context, perhaps the simplest starting point is to suggest that the experiment constitutes a set of procedures, or rules, designed to achieve a particular sort of knowledge, i.e. knowledge of general causal propositions asserting that a causal relationship exists between two or more variables. The particular feature of the experiment is that a relationship is as far as possible examined in circumstances where other possible confounding factors have been eliminated by matching or randomization.

However, there are, even in this brief characterization, a number of the problems already mentioned which reach up to the arguments and perspectives about the nature of the sociological enterprise itself. The threats both to internal and external validity discussed earlier have been taken as a reason for neglecting the experiment as a way of gathering useful sociological knowledge. Yet this particular objection can be met by designing better experiments and using more circumspection when drawing inferences from the results.

A more serious objection is associated with the position which says that whatever else sociologists should be doing, they should not be concerned with the establishment of cause-and-effect relationships: a rather definite feature of the experiment. Certainly the hypothesis-testing approach of the experiment, with its attempts to control variation and exclude rival explanations, would seem to place it as a research design fairly firmly in the camp of those who entertain some affinity between the natural and the social sciences. If this is so, it would seem necessary for the sociological experimenter to accept, tacitly or otherwise, that it is acceptable to talk of human behaviour as subject to 'laws of nature', whatever these may turn out to be. Thus, the kind of facts produced by experiments are generalizations about the effects of certain variables, singly or in combination, on human behaviour. Whether one finds this an acceptable position depends upon many things. It involves accepting that the behaviour of special interest to the sociologist is interpretable in terms of cause and effect. This is a point going back to the arguments made in Chapter 1. But even if it is accepted that social behaviour is understandable in these terms, it does not follow that the experiment is the ideal way to go about producing this knowledge. Arguments about the artificiality of the experimental setting, and the difficulties of generalizing from the setting to the 'outside' world, are all relevant. However, the irrelevance or otherwise of experimental laboratory work to the 'outside' must not be assumed; its irrelevance or otherwise is an empirical matter. There are many subtle and important variations possible, even in a laboratory, to detract from the artificiality of the setting.[31] In short, unless it is a matter of ruling out the experiment by fiat, then these objections are really suggestions for further thinking. After all, no experiment stands alone, but is part of the whole process by which knowledge is produced.

There are besides some further and more general points deriving from this discussion of experiments and experimental designs which have relevance, as will be seen, to other research techniques used in sociology. It was suggested that many of the artifacts which enter into the experimental situation point towards treating the experiment as a behaviour setting in its own right. That is, in so far as the experiment itself has a social and psychological dimension, this must be taken into account as one of the sets of plausible rival hypotheses concerning how the results turned out. Generalizing this idea, we have the principle that any results, derived by whatever method, need to be evaluated in terms of possible theories of instrumentation which could account for them. It would not be too venturesome to suggest that, since most modes of sociological research can at some stage also be regarded not just as techniques but also as social processes in themselves, then it means taking seriously the possible theories of instrumentation implied by each method. These ideas will be discussed at length in the remaining chapters, but it is as well to note three possible major consequences. First, since many theories of instrumentation will also be substantive sociological theories, there is a closer marriage of method and theory. Secondly, it will be possible to increase the scope of serendipity, finding the unexpected element so important in theoretical creativity. Thirdly, it could result in an improved research strategy.

Exercises

Mounting a full-scale experiment is often an involved business. However, the 'risky shift' phenomenon is relatively easy to study, administer and modify. Some studies (see R. Brown, *Social Psychology*, Collier-Macmillan, London, 1965, Chapter 13, for a discussion of them) found that when subjects are presented with descriptions of social situations in which the central character is faced with a dilemma, they tend to recommend riskier choices when acting as members of a group than when choosing individually. The following story is an example of the kind that could be used.

J.G. is the manager of a football club due to play an important cup-tie against a tough opposing team. One member of the club is a gifted but temperamental striker. On his best days he is capable of penetrating the best defences in the league to get goals. Unfortunately, his heart has not been in the game just recently and his exceptional performances have become fewer. When this happens the rest of the team become frustrated and dispirited. The manager is faced with the choice. To play a striker and run the risk of him being off form, or to play a reserve and hope that the rest of the team will be settled enough to play well.

Imagine that you are advising the team manager. Listed below are several probabilities or odds of the striker being on form. Please indicate the *lowest* probability that you would accept before recommending that the player should be selected.

_____ The chances are 1 in 10 that the player will be on form.
_____ The chances are 3 in 10 that the player will be on form.
_____ The chances are 5 in 10 that the player will be on form.
_____ The chances are 7 in 10 that the player will be on form.
_____ The chances are 9 in 10 that the player will be on form.
_____ The player should not be selected, no matter what the chances.

Other stories with reference to a variety of situations could be constructed on these lines. Typical ones used in past studies have included investment choices, changing jobs, choice of career, political and moral choices. No matter what subject matter is chosen, the central character should be faced with a choice between two alternatives, one more risky than the other. The subjects are then asked to act as advisers and recommend the lowest probability of the riskier alternative being successful before recommending that choice.

In general, studies have shown, though not always consistently, that group discussion tends to produce a 'shift to risk'; i.e. subjects asked to participate in group discussion concerning the advice they would offer tend, on the whole, to recommend riskier choices than subjects choosing singly.

What you are asked to do in this exercise is design and carry out an experiment to test this finding. Write out about six or seven stories of the type illustrated. Then design your experiment so that subjects have to read and make choices in all cases. Think about the nature of the controls you will need to employ. Do not necessarily limit yourself to one control. For example, you might

like to divide your subjects randomly into those who will participate in groups of four or five persons (depending upon the size of
the class) the remainder making their choices singly. Alternatively,
you might ask all subjects to make their individual choices one
week, participate in a group discussion the next, and so on. Whatever you do, make sure your design has a chance of answering the
questions you want to ask. One point about group decisions: previous studies have varied the manner in which subjects involved in
group discussion complete their advice forms. In most cases, the
groups were asked to reach a unanimous decision within a specific
time period, or, if unanimity was impossible, a majority decision.
However, in other cases, group members were asked, after discussion, to record their own personal choices in addition to the one
reached by the group as a whole. Why do you think this was done?
The experiment can be modified or made more sophisticated, as you
think fit. For example, you might use different types of subject to
see whether this affects the choice of probabilities: Do women
make less risky choices than men? Is age and experience a factor?
And so on. In addition, you might consider the following kinds of
question:

Are group decisions generally riskier than individual ones? If so,
why? What theories could you advance to account for any
findings? Are there any other variables which could affect the
responses? What about the nature of the risks? It may be that
the advice given to characters facing employment choices is, on
the whole, less risky, than to those confronted with the dilemma
in a sporting situation.

As far as the experiment itself is concerned, can you think of any
possible reactive effects? Are decisions made early in the experiment more or less risky on average than those made later? Could
this be due to the fact that the subjects have become sensitized?
Does the artificiality of the experimental setting detract from its
validity?

What modifications would you introduce to control for any
alternative hypothesis which might explain the results, including
those to do with the experiment as a behaviour setting.

Notes and References

1.   Teleological explanations would seem to violate this rule. However,
     the end-goal is not a cause following an effect (the behaviour to
     seek the end); rather, the *intention* to seek the end is the prior

cause. Most so-called teleological explanations can be restated in traditional cause-and-effect terms.

2. For a discussion of experimental design, see S. Stouffer, 'Some Observations on Study Design', *American Journal of Sociology*, 55, 1950, pp. 355–61; D. T. Campbell and J. C. Stanley, *Experimental and Quasi-Experimental Designs for Research*, Rand McNally, Chicago, 1963; J. Ross and P. Smith, 'Orthodox Experimental Designs', in H. M. and A. Blalock (eds.), *Methodology in Social Research*, McGraw-Hill, New York, 1968, pp. 334–89.

3. E. Powers, 'An Experiment in the Prevention of Delinquency', *Annals of the American Academy of Political and Social Science*, 261, 1949, and selections reprinted in M. W. Riley, *Sociological Research: A Case Approach*, Harcourt, Brace & World, New York, 1963, pp. 572–80.

4. Quoted in ibid., p. 622. This volume contains a very thorough discussion of the Powers study.

5. For a discussion of these principles, see J. S. Mill, A *System of Logic*, first published 1843.

6. Simply multiply together the number of values a variable can take, and multiply this total by two to obtain the number of subjects required to form pairs matched for any possible combination of values.

7. See R. A. Fisher, *The Design of Experiments*, Oliver & Boyd, Edinburgh, 1937, p. 21.

8. R. L. Solomon, 'Extension of Control Group Design', *Psychological Bulletin*, XLVI, 1949, pp. 137–50.

9. Fisher, *The Design of Experiments*, p. 101.

10. For a fuller treatment of factorial designs, see A. L. Edwards, *Experimental Design in Psychological Research*, Holt, Rinehart & Winston, New York, 1950; and J. L. Myers, *Fundamentals of Experimental Design*, Allyn & Bacon, 1972, 2nd edition.

11. Remember this is a matter of logic. You need not accept the premises. There are other theories of knowledge.

12. Campbell and Stanley, *Experimental and Quasi-Experimental Designs for Research*.

13. See P. J. Runkel and J. E. McGrath, *Research on Human Behaviour*, Holt, Rinehart & Winston, New York, 1972, p. 38; and Riley, *Sociological Research*, p. 616.

14. For further details and comment on these now famous experiments, see F. J. Roethlisberger and W. J. Dickson, *Management and the Worker*, Harvard University Press, Cambridge, Mass., 1940; J.

Madge, *The Origins of Scientific Sociology*, Tavistock Publications, London, 1963.

15. For arguments for and against this, see T. E. Drabble and E. J. Haas, 'Realism in Laboratory Simulation: Myth or Method', *Social Forces*, 45, 1967, pp. 337–46.

16. L. Festinger, 'Laboratory Experiments', in L. Festinger and D. Katz (eds.), *Research Methods in the Behavioural Sciences*, Dryden Press, New York, 1953, pp. 169–70.

17. E. G. Boring, 'Perspective: Artifact and Control', in R. Rosenthal and R. L. Rosnow (eds.), *Artifact in Behavioural Research*, Academic Press, New York, 1969, p. 8. Apparently even animals respond to experimenters' gestures and anticipations; see N. J. Friedman, *The Social Nature of Psychological Research*, Basic Books, New York, 1967.

18. See, for example, R. Rosenthal, *Experimenter Effects in Behavioural Research*, Appleton-Century-Crofts, New York, 1966. Incidentally, Phillips notes that psychologists have been much more alert to the relevance of 'definitions of the situation' for empirical research than have sociologists. Sociologists know that an individual's attitudes, opinions, and behaviour are influenced by the interpersonal situations in which he finds himself, yet take little cognisance of this fact and how it effects their research instruments. D. L. Phillips, *Knowledge From What?*, Rand McNally, Chicago, 1971.

19. R. Rosenthal, 'Interpersonal Expectations', in Rosenthal and Rosnow (eds.), *Artifact in Behavioural Research*, p. 186.

20. R. Rosenthal and L. Jacobson, *Pygmalion in the Classroom: Teacher Expectation and Pupils' Intellectual Development*, Holt, Rinehart & Winston, New York, 1968.

21. M. T. Orne, 'On the Social Psychology of the Psychological Experiment', *American Psychologist*, 17, 1962, pp. 776–83.

22. E. G. Boring, 'The Nature and History of Experimental Control', *American Journal of Psychology*, 67, 1954, pp. 573–89.

23. D. T. Campbell, 'Prospective: Artifact and Control', in Rosenthal and Rosnow (eds.), *Artifact in Behavioural Research*, p. 356.

24. D. T. Campbell and H. L. Ross, 'The Connecticut Crackdown on Speeding: Time Series Data in Quasi-Experimental Analysis', in E. R. Tufte (ed.), *The Quantitative Analysis of Social Problems*, Addison-Wesley, Reading, Mass., 1970, p. 123.

25. R. Rosenthal and R. L. Rosnow, 'The Volunteer Subject', in Rosenthal and Rosnow (eds.), *Artifact in Behavioural Research*, pp. 59–118.

26. Campbell, 'Prospective: Artifact and Control', loc. cit.

27. ibid., p. 361.

28. ibid., p. 378.

29. For a discussion of quasi-experimental analysis, see Campbell and Stanley, *Experimental and Quasi-Experimental Designs for Research*. Also, D. Bushell and R. L. Burgess, *Behavioural Sociology: The Experimental Analysis of the Social Process*, Columbia University Press, New York, 1969.

30. Campbell and Ross, 'The Connecticut Crackdown on Speeding', loc. cit.

31. See D. Mixom, 'Behaviour Analysis Treating Subjects as Actors Rather than Organisms', *Journal of the Theory of Social Behaviour*, 1 1970, pp. 19–31.

5
Getting Involved

It is appropriate to follow a discussion of experiments with a style or strategy of sociological research taken by many to be the direct antithesis of the relatively formalized procedures involved in experimental designs. Such methods represent a departure from the experimental method in that the researcher is required to become intentionally involved, in some way, in the ongoing, day-to-day world of the persons he is studying. In other words, it is a research strategy which argues, among other things, for the study of social behaviour in natural settings not disturbed or distorted by the artificiality of the experimental situation.[1] In addition, the strategy usually involves a commitment to the idea that full and adequate knowledge of human social behaviour cannot be fully grasped until the researcher has 'understood' the symbolic world in which his subjects live. To achieve this requires that the sociologist must adopt, as far as is possible, the perspective of those he would study. This position, then, argues that social behaviour is, essentially, meaningful behaviour motivated, guided or based upon the 'meanings' actors use to make their worlds intelligible. As a result, the actor's social world cannot be fully or even partially understood by methods such as the experiment and others based upon positivistic methodologies that 'scientize' or 'objectify' or 'externalize' the actor's world. What is required instead are methods of acquiring knowledge of the actor's day-to-day world and the meanings he uses to make sense of it.

As already indicated, this perspective reacts strongly against the physical science stance in its approach to sociological problems and issues. The claim is that the natural science model of inquiry creates a view of human behaviour that is both artificial and unrelated to the social worlds in which people live.[2] Implied by this is a criticism of the emphasis which many sociologists place on narrow technical methodological issues—an activity felt to be even further removed from social reality than most sociological theories! Although, no doubt, this view overvalues and distorts the enemy it purports to attack, it does nonetheless point to a number of rather crucial issues about the nature of sociological inquiry.

The Rationale of Participant Methods

The perspective takes as its starting point the assertion that man has both an 'inner' and an 'outer' life, and that, to account fully for human behaviour or conduct, knowledge of the 'inner' life is essential. Stress is laid, in other words, on the human ability to know oneself, and hence to know and understand others through processes that have been variously characterized as 'sympathetic introspection', 'imaginative reconstruction', 'verstehen' or 'empathy'. Man, being a symbol manipulator, can only be understood through an understanding of those symbols which he manipulates as part of his situation. Social reality is made up of the meanings which actors give to their actions and situations.[3] Society is ordered by social actors who produce that order in terms of *their own* constructs, not those of a detached sociologist. Thus the sociologist must understand and interpret human behaviour at a greater depth through the social construction of meanings than the 'outer' perspective, associated with positivistic methods, can allow. In short, it specifies that the researcher must try to picture the social world as it exists for those under investigation. Weber articulated this view when he offered a definition of sociology as attempting 'the interpretative understanding of social action in order thereby to arrive at a causal explanation of its course and events. In "action" is included all human behaviour when and in so far as the acting individual attaches a subjective meaning to it. . . . Action is social in so far as, by virtue of the subjective meaning attached to it by the acting individual (or individuals), it takes account of the behaviour of others and is thereby oriented in its course.'[4]

Although at first blush this perspective might seem anti-positivistic in its stress on the subjective world of man, it does not always eschew the necessity of theory-building, predictions, and explanations of social behaviour. Rather, it seeks to place these activities on a surer footing by basing them on the 'real stuff' of sociological inquiry: knowledge of the actor's inter-subjective world. However, it does tend to de-emphasize the role of the 'objective observer'. As Blumer puts it:

To try and catch the interpretative process by remaining aloof as a so-called 'objective' observer and refusing to take the role of the acting unit is to risk the worst kind of subjectivism—the objective observer is likely to fill in the process of interpretation with his own surmises in place of catching the process as it occurs in the experience of the acting unit which uses it.[5]

Though, as we shall see, this raises problems, it also stresses the need for the sociologist to become involved in the situations he is claiming to study. Only in this way can he obtain his basic material : knowledge of the situation as seen and understood by the actors themselves. How is this to be achieved? Briefly, by using those methods which allow the researcher to become, as far as possible, part and parcel of the action under study : methods known, in general, as *participant observation*.

The Process of Participation

To be a participant observer requires the investigator to become part of an interaction or situation. The methods involve a number of separate techniques—questioning, watching, listening and acting—all done in an attempt to understand a particular organization, group, sequence of action or whatever. Unlike the experiment, the methods involve a relatively unstructured research design and are often claimed to be more suitable in research situations where the aim is discovery rather than the rigorous testing of hypotheses. The researcher tries to share as intimately as possible in the life and activities of the people he is studying. This is the classic approach of the anthropologist, who will spend long periods with a tribe or in a village attempting to discover the distinctive features of its social and cultural life. This quotation from Malinowski conveys very well the flavour and spirit of the anthropologist's approach :

Living in the village with no other business but to follow native life, one sees the customs, ceremonies and transactions over and over again, one has examples of their beliefs as they are actually lived through and the full body and flesh of actual native life fills out soon the skeleton of abstract constructions. That is why, working under conditions as previously described, the Ethnographer is enabled to add something essential to the bare outline of tribal constitution, and to supplement it by all the details of behaviour, setting and small incident. He is able in each case to state whether an act is public or private; how a public assembly behaves and what it looks like; he can judge whether an event is ordinary or an exciting and singular one; whether natives bring to it a great deal of sincere and earnest spirit, or perform it in fun; whether they do it in a perfunctory manner, or with zeal and deliberation.

In other words there is a series of phenomena of great importance which cannot possibly be recorded by questioning or compiling documents but have to be observed in their full actuality.[6]

The methods, of course, have been employed in rather less exotic situations, as in studies of medical students, hospital patients, drug addicts, prisoners, military trainees, dock workers and so on in almost endless variety. All are examples of studies where the investigator has become part of a daily round, learning languages and meanings, rules of interpersonal relations and work patterns, and, in short, living the life of the people under study.

While the participation of the researcher in the social and symbolic world of those he is studying sounds dramatic and exciting, it is by no means easy. Even the relatively simple matter of learning a new language, if this is necessary, takes time. Also, more seriously, learning a language is not simply a matter of learning the grammar and vocabulary, but also a matter of learning conversational, colloquial and technical forms. Certain terms, for example, may have no literal equivalent in the researcher's parent language. Yet there is no short cut to learning the language in which so much of the content of the understandings and meanings the investigator is seeking to uncover is embedded.

These practical considerations are only a start. Becoming involved, learning and sharing the meanings used in others' worlds, creates problems for the participant observer in that one of his tasks is to make his knowledge part of the sociological tradition, and yet, by becoming involved, he runs the risk of adopting the perspective of those he is studying. The observer may find himself no longer observing, but simply 'taking the view', the values and attitudes of those he has set out to study—a process succinctly called 'going native'. Accordingly, participant observation requires that the observer, though a participant, must also maintain his detachment. Again, while the participant observer seeks to study a group undisturbed as an ongoing process in its natural setting, few natural settings allow for the role of observer, and his coming may be regarded as an intrusion. So, while gaining entry to a group may or may not be easy, it is uncertain to what degree an observer will by his presence 'distort' the normal and routine interaction. Whyte, for example, in his study of a street gang in an Italian-American slum district, reports a remark made by one of his informant friends, Doc: 'You've slowed me up plenty since you've been down here. Now when I do something, I have to think what Bill Whyte would want me to know about it and how I can explain it. . . . Before I used to do these things by instinct.'[7] The implications of this comment are fairly obvious: a loss of spontaneity and an increase in self-reflection on the part of the actor concerning what he is doing and why, which may detract from the 'natural-ness' which the observer wishes to study.

Participant Observer Roles

These and other problems can be posed in terms of participant observer roles, of which four are usually identified.[8] All represent different combinations of the dilemma of balancing the role of observer with the requirements of involvement to secure relevant knowledge.

The first role is that of 'complete participant', whose role as an observer is concealed by his becoming a fully-fledged member of the group he is studying. Such an observer, for instance, may work as a normal wage earner in a factory to learn about informal group interaction. One such investigation was an inquiry into the motivations, attitudes and behaviour of US Air Force personnel during training. The observer was to take part in the full training programme under the guise of a conventional recruit. For nine months, the would-be participant went through a prior training programme to provide him with a plausible identity and one through which he might achieve a maximum of rapport with other trainees. Dress, speech, mannerisms, interests, attitudes and general appearance were carefully coached and the process rounded off with minor surgery and considerable weight reduction. An entire life history was invented so effectively that the recruiting sergeant in the town where the observer was to 'enlist' recommended he be turned down because, to all appearances, the candidate was a juvenile delinquent. So successful was the transformation that a USAF psychologist recommended the observer be reclassified because of his feelings of mild anxiety over 'killing' his father.[9] Of course, not all complete participant roles involve such an intensive degree of preparation.

A major feature of the complete participant observer role is its large degree of pretence.

> The complete participant realizes that he, and he alone, knows
> that in reality he is other than the person he pretends to be. He
> must pretend that his real self is represented by the role, or
> roles, he plays in and out of the . . . situation in relationships
> with people who, to him, are but informants. . . . He must bind
> the mask of pretence to himself or stand the risk of exposure
> and research failure.[10]

This pretence can create very real dilemmas for the observer who
adopts the role of complete participant. Can he be sure that he is
being 'natural'? Has his cover been broken? How would the kind
of person whose role he is playing *really* react in such-and-such a
situation? These are constant questions and tensions which may
arise in this type of research role. Clearly, if the observer's cover
is broken, not only is his role as an observer jeopardized, but he
may also evoke annoyance in the other members of the group at his
duplicity.[11] In sum, the complete participant has to face two
potential problems: (a) becoming so self-conscious about revealing
his real identity that his observation is handicapped by his attempts
to give a convincing performance; or (b) becoming so immersed in
the participant role that he 'goes native'. Either way, the difficulties
of detached observation are increased. Interestingly, in the military
training study mentioned earlier, it was felt necessary for the participant observer to have frequent meetings with the research team
who helped to detach him from his participant role so that he could
reflect and report his findings. These meetings were 'important in
reassuring the observer and helping him regain his objectivity'.[12]

The second role, the 'participant-as-observer', differs from the complete participation in that both researcher and informants are aware
that theirs is a field-work relationship. A typical example of this
sort of observer role is provided by the many community studies
in which the observer develops contacts and relatively enduring
relationships with certain individuals in the community. This particular observer role often involves the use of a number of data-
collecting techniques ranging from informal contacts to relatively
formalized interviewing. One danger of this role, as with the complete participant, is that the observer's relationships with informants may move beyond that of a detached observer into friendship,
personal commitment or intimacy. In this way, the researcher may
lose perspective. A second danger is that informants themselves
may become so identified with the researcher that their effectiveness
as informants is jeopardized.

The third observer role is that of 'observer-as-participant'. This role is characteristic of one-visit interviews with informants and need not be detailed here since it is the subject of Chapter 6. The only point to be made at this stage is that while it is a role which minimizes the risk of too great an involvement with the people under study, it runs the opposite danger of too little involvement so that the perspective of the informant is too rarely appreciated.

The fourth and final role is the 'complete observer', who is insulated from any social contact with the people under study. Here a field worker attempts to observe in ways which makes it unnecessary for the subjects to take him into account in any way. This role is rarely used, except in cases where a preliminary reconnaisance of the area is required.[13] The obvious difficulty is that the researcher has little basis for 'understanding' or appreciating the perspective of the subjects he wishes to study.

Problems of Objectivity

What all these role characterizations suggest is the intricate balance that the participant observer must maintain between the requirements of his observer role and those of his participant persona. These must be balanced for the social-symbolic world of the actor to be observed with appropriate 'scientific detachment'. Too much either way will destroy the utility of the methods for sociological research. Unfortunately, there are no clear criteria for objectivity as in, say, the experiment (even though the criteria there are hardly unproblematic!). The claim for participant observer methods, however, is not that they necessarily produce objective knowledge of the kind sought by such 'hard' methods as the experiment; rather, they are seen as exploratory techniques: methods of discovery not proof. This comes out forcefully in Becker's comment that analysis of participant observation data is carried out 'sequentially', or while the researcher is still gathering his data. Further data gathering takes its direction from provisional analyses as the investigation proceeds.[14]

Nonetheless, to the positivistically inclined the methods of participant observation would seem to fall short of the objectivity required by a scientific discipline. Some of the criticisms in this regard have already been mentioned. One major limitation is that, by taking a role, the researcher may affect the structure of the interaction he intends to study. This sort of 'error' is known as 'control effect': a change in the action being studied brought about by the research process itself. This reactive effect is common, of course, even in the more systematic of such research designs as the experiment. The problem arises when it is an unintentional and unforseen or un-accountable feature of the research. An interesting example occurs in a study of a religious cult by a group of researchers who pre-sented themselves as committed believers. The cult had predicted the imminent end of the world, and the entry of the disguised believers may well have served to reinforce the cult's belief in the correctness of the prophecy.[15] But, the question arises, what might the response of the cult members have been if the researchers had been more sceptical and less enthusiastic about the prophecy? The point about control effects is that they often go unrecognized. To guard against this, field workers are urged to make full field notes, noticing especially any effects that their presence might have on the society or group being studied.

Another limitation arising from the observer taking a role is that it tends to impose certain restrictions upon his understanding of the situation. If the researcher plays only one role, he will, likely as not, perceive only those aspects of the situation apparent from that role. Moreover, as he matures into the role, this effectively begins to structure his interaction, so cutting him off, as it were, from information that might be available through other sources. One of the features of Whyte's role was that he was able to play it in a way which did not force him to take sides or to form alliances with particular members of the gang to the exclusion of others. A role which it is often claimed can offset the limitations imposed by play-ing a role within a previously defined and structured interaction is that of the 'outsider' or 'stranger'. The 'stranger' role arguably offers to the members of a society or group the opportunity to talk, uninhibited by the expectations and opinions of other members of the group. As Merton remarks, '. . . informants will not hesitate to make certain private views known to a disinterested outside observer—views which would not be expressed were it thought that they would get back. . . . The outsider has "stranger" value.'[16] An excellent example of this is Trice's study of the differences between alcoholics who had successfully been through Alcoholics Anonymous and those who had failed. Initially, the researchers experienced con-siderable resistance from both groups. However, the research was rescued once the investigators adopted 'outsider' roles, stressing their neutrality and dependence upon the subjects for informed and valuable information.[17] Of course, it should go without saying that the adoption of this sort of role is not always an option open to the would-be participant observer. A great deal depends upon both the type of research and the nature of the group being studied.

Strategy and Tactics of Participant Methods

Both these sources of error are fairly obvious to appreciate, though rather less easy to control in practice. This is not to say, however, that the methods of participant observation are useless or unimportant, even in terms of some positivistic paradigm. To understand this, it is necessary to look closely at the typical ways in which knowledge is produced by these methods. We saw earlier how the participant observer analyses his data sequentially, while the data gathering is still in progress. The first stage of the research strategy is, fairly obviously, some conception of a problem and its importance within some body of theory or theoretical tradition. This initial conception is very much affected by the researcher's own interests and motivations. It might be, as in Whyte's case, a desire to refute what are felt to be misconceptions of traditional theory. Whyte spent time studying a slum district largely because he felt that existing concepts of slum areas as disorganized were wrong. Rather, he suspected that they possessed a pattern of social organization as durable and meaningful as, if rather different from, the pattern of life regarded as typical in more prosperous suburbs.

Once a choice of situ and focus of investigation has been chosen, the next problem is to become part of the social life, learning the language, roles, cultural prescriptions and definitions that make a person a member of a particular group. It means that the researcher has to select events, phenomena, observables and so on which give clues to making apparent 'what is going on'. At this stage, much of the data will consist of very simple notes to the effect that such-and-such an event took place, that so-and-so said something, and that saying something seemed to be associated with such-and-such an event. The researcher may notice that certain words are uttered whenever a person of the group meets another for the first time during the day. He may make the immediate inference that this sequence of words forms part of a greeting procedure. Repeated observations of different people in different contexts may reinforce this inference as against other possible interpretations, such as that the words were names, passwords, insults or whatever. Though this is perhaps an over-simple example, it illustrates the process involved in drawing conclusions and testing them against further observations: the generalization 'the words are part of a greeting procedure' serves to direct observations towards other relevant instances.[18]

Becker gives a more sophisticated illustration of the process. An observer participating in a hospital may note: 'Medical student X referred to one of his patients as a "crock".' He may proceed to interpret this observation in terms of some sociological theory to the effect that the members of one social category in an institution classify members of other categories by criteria derived from the kinds of problem those persons raise in relationships between members of the categories concerned. This combination of observed fact and theory directs the observer to look for the problems in medical student-patient interaction signified by use of the term 'crock'. Further, by discovering specifically what students have in mind when using this term, the investigator may develop more specific hypotheses about the nature and meaning of the social relationship of student and patient.[19] Of course, and this is an important caveat, these further observations may force the researcher to abandon his initial inference, which, in any case, should only be treated as a provisional hypothesis.

Here comes another problem. How does the investigator decide that his first provisional hypothesis is false, or, at least, unsound? After all, it is not as if he is dealing with the kind of data on which statistical tests can be used. What kind of canons, then, can be applied to particular items of evidence for them to count as evidence? Becker suggests the following. First, many items of information will consist of statements by individual members of the group under study, about themselves, about other members, or about the world in general. However, these should neither be taken at face value nor dismissed as valueless until the credibility of the informants has been adequately assessed. The researcher needs to ask whether the informant has reason to lie or conceal the truth. Has prejudice lead him or her to distort a state of affairs? Was the informant alone with the observer when the disclosure was made, and so perhaps more willing to say things counter to prevailing group norms? Did the informant actually witness the events about which he claims knowledge? These are all the kinds of question a detective or historian might ask of personal testimony or personal documents.[20] Secondly, a statement volunteered could, though this is arguable, be regarded as better, surer evidence than a response to a question put by the observer. Third, relevant to the inference drawn from an utterance is the situation or context in which the utterance was made. To use Becker's example, students in their clinical years may express idealistic sentiments about medicine when alone with a researcher, but with fellow students will speak in a more cynical manner. So, the number of participants, the number of others present when observations are made or questions asked, are all relevant to the interpretation of observed utterances and actions, and 'the rules of etiquette . . . the categories of participants who interact in them, and the varieties of action that transpire within them . . .' should all be noted and evaluated.[21]

However, it is not always a question of deciding upon the truth or falsity of an observed statement. Rather, it is a matter of choosing the conclusion to be drawn from the datum about the members and their interactions. At this point, the researcher cannot avoid some commitment to some theory or other which makes sense of the observations. Take the example about the 'idealistic' *versus* 'cynical' tones used by medical students when talking about their medical careers. One might regard the observation of the two styles of talking as a problem about which is the more 'correct', 'truer' or a more 'faithful' reflection of the students' feelings. In other words, what do the students *really* think? Are they idealistic or are they cynical? Is the idealistic tone merely a front for the public and their real feelings far more cynically instrumental? Alternatively, the researcher might conclude that the medical students are basically idealistic, but that group norms prevent the expression of these ideals among fellow students. Whichever the conclusion, each answer will guide the investigator to further observations for or against the inference.

Also important in this process of drawing inferences from observations is how members of the group react to the presence of the observer in whatever role he has chosen. If he is known to be a researcher, part of the evidence relevant to the adequacy of the inferences drawn from the data will be how he is defined by the group members and whether or not they 'slant' the information they provide.

This process of formulating ideas, pursuing them and drawing conclusions from them gradually begins to focus around an interpretation that begins to look more promising than others. By looking at the relative frequency of certain activities, by checking and rechecking interpretations, an understanding of the social action under observation begins to emerge and become clarified as an account of 'what is going on'. This final stage of analysis in the field consists in bringing together the individual findings into some generalized model of the social system being studied.

The kind of conclusions likely to emerge at this stage, according to Becker, include fairly complex statements about the necessary and sufficient conditions for some pattern of action or for the existence of some phenomena. For example, a conclusion that medical students develop a consensus about limiting the amount of work they do could be attributed to the fact that they face large work loads, that they engage in activities which create channels of communication between all members of their class and face a common danger in the form of examinations set by the medical faculty. Or, as Whyte found, the structure of the corner gang arises out of the habitual association of the members from early childhood. A second kind of conclusion which could emerge at this stage are statements that some phenomena are 'important' or 'basic' to the social action under study; that is, that some phenomena exercise a persistent influence on what may be very diverse events. To use a Becker example once again, the ambition to become a general practitioner is 'important' in the medical school because particular judgements and choices are made by students in terms of this aim and many features of the medical school's organization take account of it. A type of statement which may form the third kind of conclusion to emerge are those indentifying a situation as an instance of an event, phenomenon or process described in more abstract terms in some sociological theory; that is, an observation is to count as an instance of a more general relationship. For example, the observation that the leader of Whyte's corner gang spent more money on his followers than they spent on him is an instance of the necessary independence of leadership roles from the obligations of those of lower status in the group.

Once conclusions such as these have been formulated, the next task is to test the ideas further by subjecting them to confirming and disconfirming observations. This means refining the model by making its conclusions more precise, reformulating them or whatever is necessary to produce a more plausible picture of the social system being studied. The important point here is that this assembly of conclusions and models is a process that is very much an integral part of the field-work. The observer, in short, does not simply wait until 'facts' reveal themselves, but explores ideas and conclusions in a manner intimately associated with finding out what the 'facts' are.

The final refinement takes place after completion of the field-work. Material is systematically assembled and final refinements made to conclusions, models and theories. Field notes are structured and negative or disconfirming observations searched for and fed back into conclusions already tentatively formulated. At this stage, the work becomes more formally structured than perhaps was possible previously. Hypotheses may be stated, since these often make the search for negative cases more deliberate and less haphazard. Typologies may be developed and further conceptualizations arrived at until the researcher is satisfied.

One important question remains: how should the results be presented? Unlike statistical and other kinds of quantitative data, material acquired by participant observation cannot be presented so summarily or systematically.[22] The use to which any observation is put, and the conclusions drawn from it, are the subject of much thought and argument not easily presented in shorthand ways. Yet it is impossible to report everything. Becker's own recommendation argues for a 'natural history' method of reporting, involving description of the form the data takes at every stage of the research, noting significant exceptions, and presenting clearly the case for any inference drawn from the data. In this way 'evidence is assessed as the substantive analysis is presented' so that the reader is able to 'follow details of the analysis and to see how and on what basis any conclusion is reached'.[23]

Problems of Validity

Meanwhile, a fuller justification for the cogency of the analysis must pay attention to the familiar problems of internal validity. 'History', for one thing—those events or processes occurring before the observation was undertaken or between the first and the final stages of the research—could be very relevant to the validity of the analysis. Similarly, both subjects and observer could be influenced by 'maturation' factors. Both these problems require the observations to be supplemented by information relevant to such processes and their effects evaluated. Subject maturation has already been mentioned (page 120), but now needs a little more consideration. The persons studied by the participant observer will be of two major types: the respondent and the informant.[24] An informant has rather a special relationship with the researcher, as Doc in Whyte's study trusts him, gives information freely and frankly attempts to explain what is going on and why, even to the risk of his position within his group. Such an informant, in short, is an intimate. The respondent, on the other hand, does not have this sort of relationship. Normally, there will be no special trust, no privileged information imparted, and he will answer questions only when asked.

In effect, the informant acts as an observer for the researcher, giving an insider's view of the group under investigation, providing access and generally acting as a kind of research colleague. The nature of this relationship is crucial to assessing the validity of the information the informant provides, and the researcher needs to be sensitive to the dual role the informant plays: as a member of the group and as a sociologist-in-the-field, as it were. It could be, for example, that the informant develops too deep a commitment to the researcher and keys his information to maintaining this personal bond. Once again, there is no simple answer, except that changes in attitudes of both informants and respondents, and of the investigator, should be noted as the relationship matures.

Other problems of internal validity, such as subject bias and subject mortality, also require the observer to supplement his record with relevant evidence. Another matter, already mentioned, is the reactive effects of the research on the social system being observed. The introduction of a participant observer into a field role, whether as researcher or as a fully-fledged member of the group, must inevitably result in some reactivity. Once again, the investigator needs to be sensitive to these effects and to evaluate them as best he can. The converse side is the effects of the research on the observer himself. He or she may 'go native', so losing the 'outsider' perspective which, in unison with the participant perspective, is claimed to be the special strength of participant observer methods.

Analytic Induction

This method of approach as a strategy for making appropriate inferences is known more formally as *analytic induction*: a strategy which calls for the investigator to search deliberately for instances that negate his hypothesis and, using these, to refine the hypothesis further. As Lindesmith, the most explicit user of the logic of analytic induction, says: 'The principle which governs the selection of cases to test a theory is that the chances of discovering a negative case should be maximized. . . . This involves going out of one's way to look for negating evidence.'[25] In practice, the process of analytic induction proceeds by formulating a rather vague generalization and then revising it in the light of contrary evidence, so that there is a continual process of redefinition, hypothesis testing and a search for negative cases until a point is reached where a universal relationship can with some confidence be established.

One basic assumption of analytic induction is that causal propositions can be stated as universals which apply to all cases of the problem under analysis. Thus the researcher must formulate his theories in such a way as to indicate crucial tests of the theory by the explicit search for negative cases. Also, it is a strategy that as it were tests a theoretical proposition once and for all, and while involving the use of sensitizing concepts in the initial stages, the procedure results in a tighter formulation of the theory.

One feature of analytic induction which needs to be noted is its reliance on theoretical sampling rather than on statistical sampling models. This point will be developed further later, so suffice it to say here that the strategy involves sampling cases in a continual effort to search out those which might possibly invalidate the theory. This implies that the theory is complete to the extent that negative cases are not identified by the researcher. It is a sampling strategy which is devoted less to obtaining a description of the overall distribution of a phenomenon in some universe than to discovering crucial observations which might falsify the theory.

Validity

The time has come to present some general assessment of participant observation methods, and the issue of sampling is a convenient starting-point. One major criticism levelled at these methods is that they are normally involved in the study of one case, one instance of a phenomenon, group or process. This presents, at first glance, a rather serious drawback for the external validity of the method. How can the observer be sure that the case he has studied, whether a military training programme, a street-corner gang, a group of workers in a factory or whatever are representative of the population about which the inferences are made? It may be that the group studied is relatively unique, is unusual at the time studied or is not the same as other groups in other areas. As Denzin points out, 'The participant observer will . . . have to know intimately the social and personal characteristics of his subjects, and be sensitive to any biasing features they possess. His investigations will also typically reveal characteristics of the cases studied that are not universally shared.'[27] This would seem to require some knowledge about the population of cases in question, their relative distribution and their typical features.

It will be remembered that one of the major claims for participant observation methods was that the social actor and his behaviour could not be viewed wholly from the perspective of the outsider. Action can only be fully understood from the actor's point of view, the meanings he gives to his acts and the understandings he has of what is going on and why. This derives from the belief that social action is caused not by factors external to the individual, but rather that the individual, constructs a meaningful universe which mediates interaction with others.[28] Positivistic-style methodologies, however, cannot perceive this inter-subjective world, partly because they rely on prior definitions suited to the mechanics of analysis rather than to the world in which the people they are studying live. The most favoured target for the anti-positivistic viewpoint being elaborated here is official statistics which are the end result of meaning negotiations that have more to do with the practical day-to-day problems of the collectors of those statistics than they have to do with the 'real world' they are supposed to indicate or measure.[29] Thus, whether a man is defined as a criminal and appears in the statistical record as such depends a great deal upon how the policeman coped with the practical situation of deciding whether or not the man had done a criminal act. The interpretative procedures employed by the policeman (in some ways, the starting point of criminal statistics) to solve his practical problem of what to do, are very relevant to the understanding of criminal statistical data. The data may say more about the aggregate culmination of policemen's interpretative procedures than it does about the 'real' distribution of crime. Though this example may seem somewhat terse, hopefully it shows up one of the grounds for looking at meanings employed by actors-in-the-situation as *the crucial* element in sociological theory and analysis-using methods which do not assume away the very stuff of social life. And yet, more appropriate methods, such as participant observation, while giving the researcher possible access to meanings, rarely fulfil the criteria of measurement, reproducibility and rigorous inference so beloved by positivistic epistemologies. This point has been put very forcibly by Blum when comparing survey types of research with observational studies:

. . . it is no trick to produce rigorous, relatively 'behaviourized' descriptions of human activities (i.e. descriptions that can be reproduced by colleagues doing a minimum of interpretative work which draws upon knowledge extraneous to the event under study), but it *is* difficult to demonstrate the sensible character of such descriptions (i.e. the extent to which the descriptions are oriented to by members as constraints upon their activities and as possible products of those selfsame activities). Similarly, it is no feat to produce descriptions from members' point of view (i.e.

sensible and relevant descriptions) as long as such descriptions do not have to be reproduced with reference to observable affairs. The problem is one of creating sensible (theoretically relevant) descriptions that are objective (reproducible).[30]

The ideal of objectivity is one of the most strongly held tenets in sociology. Intuitively, we all have some idea of what 'objectivity' means: conclusions drawn independently of race, colour, creed, occupation, nationality, sex, moral or political preferences, and so on; views independent of any subjective considerations attaching to the formulator, and accordingly reproducible in that other researchers using the same methods would arrive at the same conclusions. It has already been pointed out that a great deal of methodological work is devoted to improving the objectivity (removing the bias) of research and its conclusions. Such is the normative stress on the repeatability of results, the publicity of the research process, the formalization of the logic of the research design, the standardization of measures, and so on. In a similar vein, the procedures, if this is not too strong a word, involved in participant observation are often designed to achieve the same end. Formalization of the logic of inference in terms of analytic induction is an example of such justificatory procedures which serve to increase the validity of the conclusions by controlling possible biases on the part of the investigator. Nonetheless, despite such tactics, in participant observation (as in any method of research) a great deal of 'interpretative work' is necessary on the part of the researcher to bring conclusions out of his data: work which is not part of any explicitly formalized process of inference and which could be regarded as a potential source of error. The reporting of 'facts', for example, the very stuff and matter of research, is, as was noted earlier, implicitly allied with judgements of value. In Sudnow's study of 'dying' as a socially relevant phenomenon in a hospital, he notes, in the course of his observations, that on public wards 'sheets are not carefully drawn to conceal examinations of patient's "private parts". . . . [But] formulating that fact as a "lack of concern for privacy" involves a significant judgemental jump.' In other words, from the perspective of a middle-class observer more used to privacy, the public ward of a hospital appears very public indeed, but this does not mean that this feature is seen as such by the patients being observed.[31] Of course, other observations could have been made to reassure any conclusion, but there is a practical limitation to the extent to which this can be done, and the prob-

lem remains as a general issue, for our knowledge is always the
result of both observation and inference, never of observation alone.

Discovering Meanings

This observation leads on to what might seem to be a serious
problem concerning not only the method of observation but also the
sort of theory underlying its use as a research technique. If we are
interested in exploring the meanings used by actors in a situation
so as to truly experience the actor's world, we need to become one
of the actors. As Blumer says, 'Since action is forged by the actor
out of what he perceives, interprets, and judges, one would have to
see the operating situation as the actor sees it, perceive objects as
the actor perceives them, ascertain their meaning in terms of the
meaning they have for the actor, and follow the actor's line of
conduct as the actor organizes it. . . .' The possibility of this depends upon how strongly the word 'become' is interpreted. At one
extreme, there is a clear impossibility of 'becoming' one of the
persons being studied, possessing, as it were, his or her history,
experiences, outlook and frame of reference: a logically impossible
task. Unfortunately, if a weaker sense of 'becoming' is allowed,
equivalent to something like 'imagining one is that person', then
there enters the possibility of bias and interpretation mediated by
the observers' 'uncleansed' experiences which he must inevitably
bring to the research setting.

This kind of methodological problem should be familiar since it is
a perpetual feature of our everyday life. The force of the logical
impossibility of literally 'being someone else' not only has relevance
in a research situation, but is a constant feature of daily, quite
ordinary interaction. And yet none of this means that we do not
understand each other or do not act towards each other in sensible
ways—at least, for most of the time. The difference between
everyday life and the research situation is that, in the latter, the
investigator is involved in settings which are not part of his everyday life whereas normally he will have established or constructed
a set of understandings which allow his interaction with others.
Instead, what he must try to do is penetrate the understandings
of those persons he is studying. How is he to be sure this has been
achieved? Whatever the answer, it would seem to argue for the
involved observer rather than one detached in some way.

For only by becoming involved in what we are studying can
we fix upon the thing itself, become aware of it, experience it,

and obtain 'knowledge of' as well as 'knowledge about' it. Certainly if we sociologists are really interested in process and interaction . . . and if we wish to study the construction of meanings and of social relations, we can only do so from more active involvement and participation.[32]

There still remains the problem of how to get at the meanings used by the actors being studied. One source from which the researcher can derive an understanding is his own experience. As Tiryakian says, 'Since the observer is a human being studying other human beings, he has access to the inner world of experience. This direct access is "sympathetic understanding" and "intuition" by which the observer can view cultural phenomena "from within".'[33] In other words, by becoming involved in a piece of action, the researcher begins to share in the commonsense world of the actors and, by doing so, gains access to his own personal experience as a participant.

The major objection to this introspective knowledge is that its productions are not public, as is the case with, say, overt acts, and hence it might be regarded as less than valid. However, it can be argued in return that though the process of introspective observation is private, the information gained and the conclusions drawn are not. If, for example, we were to relate the results of our introspections to each other and understood them, then, to some degree, the criterion of publicity of report is satisfied. Phillips, for one, believes that sociologists should explicitly use their own personal experiences far more than they do, for, quoting Gouldner in support, 'men may be led to truth no less than to falsehood by their socially shaped personal experiences in the world'.[34]

Even though introspection and personal involvement may be allowed as sources of sociological data, as ways of achieving understanding, there still remains the problem of how other sociologists will recognize that such understanding has been achieved. How is the observer's understanding to be verified as accurate? One answer to this question depends upon the acceptance of the view that what is distinctive about human behaviour is that it depends or involves the following of rules. In any relationship, what matters is that the actors know the rules. Understanding is achieved when the researcher has learned the rules of the action he is studying. Thus, if we were to say, as Phillips does by way of example, 'X helped Y because they are friends,' we are merely saying that the notion of friendship involves conducting oneself according to certain rules pertaining to friendship in the particular group concerned.[35] The sociologist's task is to elucidate these rules so that they are intelligible both to the actors and to fellow sociologists. Accordingly, to verify the conclusions and the data produced by observational methods, the researcher should be able to provide other potential participant observers with a set of instructions on how to put themselves in the same situation so as to have the same or similar experiences. The principle of verifiability offered, then, is two-fold: understanding is achieved when the sociologist knows the rules and can communicate them to both actors and colleagues in such a way that if a colleague were to follow them, he could also become a member of the actor's group.

As is to be expected, there are one or two queries raised against this argument. One is that inter-subjectively confirmable truth can still be subject to collective ignorance. There is little that one can reply to this objection, except to make the general assertion that we must always leave the door open to further inquiry and new approaches. A second query is that the situation can never be the same for another person as it was for the first. Reasons for this are fairly obvious. The historical, biographical and situationally varying aspects of each context make it very unlikely that the same situation will be precisely repeated. It has been argued, for example, that the general economic position of Americans had important consequences for the field research reported in Whyte's study, and so, for this reason alone, subsequent participant research would be unlikely to reproduce the findings exactly.[36]

However, the difficulties concerning the ability of methods of participant observation to achieve a satisfactory measure of objectivity represent a serious disjunction in the method and its methodological warrant. A great deal of the justification of participant observation rests on the claim that it can get at the facts better than other methods. As an example, Becker and Geer, in a paper comparing the interview method with participant observation, claim that:

> The participant observer is both more aware of problems of inference and more equipped to deal with them because he operates, when gathering data, in a social context rich in cues and information of all kinds. Because he sees and hears the people he studies in many situations of the kind that normally occur for them . . . he builds an ever-growing fund of impressions, many of them at the subliminal level, which give him an extensive base for the interpretation and analytic use of any particular datum.

This wealth of information and impression sensitizes him to subtleties . . . and forces him to raise continually new and different questions, which he brings to and tries to answer in succeeding observations.[37]

In other words, there seems to be an assumption that participant observation is more objective than other methods since, not only does it observe people in situations in which they act (unlike the experiment), but also provides the researcher with access to richer sources of data so that he can construct a 'truer' account. To the extent that researchers using this method agree with this, then they begin to have an affinity with the paradigm discussed in Chapter 2, stressing the role of research as seeking causes and explanations, rather like (though with different subject-matter) the natural scientist, even though the claim is that participant observation belongs to the humanistic tradition of sociological inquiry.[38] Thus, although everyday life and the meanings employed by actors in the situations being studied are taken to be the initial source of all sociological knowledge, there is a significant tendency then to employ the rules of procedure and justification familiar to more positivistically inclined sociologists, which proceeds thereby to 'impose ordering concepts and hypothetical form of reasoning upon the everyday world, rather than seeking to describe and analyse the ordering concepts and form of reasoning of the social actors'.[39] This represents an interesting *impasse* in participant observation. On the one hand, the observer needs to obtain a grasp of the commonsense constructs used in the everyday life of those he is studying, yet, on the other, he must also retain sufficient detachment to interpret what he sees scientifically.[40] He needs to know whether his description is based on his own constructs as a participant actor, or whether they are based upon some scientific theory and whether these possible sources are compatible.[41]

Unfortunately, along with a lack of clear criteria to decide these issues, there is a dearth of information from participant observers on how they have actually gone about establishing rapport with actors, making judgements on what is to count as data, continuing and eventually terminating their activities, and so on. In short, there is a lack of knowledge about the researcher *as* researcher and his interaction with his subjects—knowledge useful in its own right as an understanding of the principles of social action.

The point at issue is a subtly important one. A participant observer has a unique opportunity to present reflective evidence on very basic questions concerning the properties of social life. For example, before an observer approaches a group, he needs to evaluate his position relative to the actors, the means of access he will use and how his presence will affect the group's members. Accordingly, the question of how one presents oneself before others becomes basic and relevant to an evaluation of any research product.[42]

This sort of question is part of the sociological search for the basic principles of social interaction: a search which could be enhanced by the field worker's reflections on his own interactions with the people he is studying. He can do this by treating the principles of social interaction as problematic and using his model of the actor as a guide for entering and managing the relationships he seeks to develop for purposes of research. In other words, the research act itself can be important as a source of knowledge if the researcher's own commonsense procedures can be made explicit. This argument parallels one made earlier in connection with the experiment, namely, that the research situation should be looked at as a behaviour setting in its own right, since, hopefully, this will help to make explicit some of the almost subliminal theories which are part of the researcher's frame of reference and which do more than merely influence the interpretation of data. Indeed, the observer's own behaviour will be representative of a number of theories of social action. His or her interpretation of 'what goes on', such as judgements about an actor's behaviour as, say, 'cynical', 'show-offish', 'spinning a line', 'truthful' or whatever, will be seen to depend upon implicit theories about how people show categories of behaviour. Indeed, participant observation, more than any other method of sociological research, is closer to the methods employed by actors to make sense of their 'everyday' world. After all, in our everyday life we regularly act as participant observers, and the methods we employ to discover 'what is going on' are interesting case-studies of the ways in which commonsense reality is constructed. However, the implications of this seem to force a radical revision of the traditional ways in which problems of inference, proof, objectivity and validity are considered. This revision is suggested by recent thinking which offers a model of the actor in which sense of the social world is achieved through a process of 'documentary interpretation'.

Documentary Interpretation

'Documentary interpretation' is a process of identifying an 'underlying pattern behind a series of appearances such that each appearance is seen as referring to, an expression of, or a "document of", the underlying pattern'.[43] Yet, since the underlying pattern is identified through its concrete appearance, so the appearances reflecting the pattern and the pattern itself virtually determine one another. In the same way, we know a 'part' only, or at the same time, as we know a 'whole'. Further, an important feature of appearances is that later ones may force a revision of the perceived underlying pattern, which, in turn, compels a reinterpretation of what previous appearances 'really were'. The same applies to the present interpretation of appearances by projecting the underlying pattern into future unfolding of events; an unfolding necessary to understand what present appearances mean.[44] The consequences of this for understanding social action is that what the situation 'really was', and what the actors 'really did' on a particular occasion, remains continually open-ended, a subject for redefinition and reappraisal. Accordingly, 'definitions of situations and actions are not explicitly or implicitly assumed to be settled once and for all by literal application of pre-existing, culturally established system of symbols. Rather, the meanings of situations and actions are interpretations formulated on particular occasions by the participants in the interaction and are subject to reformation on subsequent occasions.'[45] If this view of the process of interpretation is correct, and if it is also accepted that essential to sociological knowledge is knowledge of actors' meanings, then the researcher can only gain access to the actions by going through the same documentary interpretation that the actor uses. And, to the extent that the investigator must rely on these documentary accounts, his own analysis will also be a documentary interpretation.

There are for traditional methodology two rather serious implications of this model. One concerns the unsuitability of deductive forms of explanation in the context of participant observation materials, owing to the argued impossibility of providing literal descriptions of events, actions or motives. In the deductive form of explanation, events, facts and phenomena are explained by showing how they may be logically deduced from theoretical premises and stated empirical conditions. But this is only possible if the descriptions entering into the propositions of the explanation are independent of the occasions of their use; that is, have stable meanings and are independent of the circumstances producing them. This problem of obtaining equivalence in the use of concepts was discussed earlier as a necessary requirement of measurement, objectivity and validity (page 76). The literal description of a phenomenon is based on perceived features that the phenomenon displays to the observer, and on the basis of these features it is assumed that the phenomenon has some clearly designated property, or logically belongs to some particular and well-defined class of phenomena. So, if social inter-action is regarded as, essentially, an interpretative process, then des-criptions of interactions must also be interpretative not literal. 'In describing interaction interpretatively, the observer necessarily im-putes an underlying pattern that serves as the essential context for see-ing what the situations and actions are, while these same situations and actions are a necessary resource for seeing what the context is . . . a context that gets its meaning partly through the very action it is being used to interpret.'[46] This mutual determination of event and context means that accounts of 'what is going on', or 'what went on', are always subject to continual revision in the light of further events, information or thought.

The second implication concerns the status of the criteria of objectivity, truth, validity and so on. Although accounts are con-tinually subject to revision, is there no point at which we can finally say that this is a definitive account? The answer would seem to be in the negative. The view of the social process as a product of inter-pretative processes means that objectivity, truth, validity and so on are established, for both sociologists and laymen, through these interpretative processes rather than simply by reference to a set of given, culturally independent and common standards. It means treating seriously the idea that the production of knowledge is a social enterprise, and depends upon the same sort of procedures typical of the everyday. This argument could be applied with equal force to the natural as well as the social sciences. Take the case of literal description and its relationship to deductive forms of ex-planation. It is not that the natural scientist is more able to provide such descriptions, but simply that the social organization of natural science depends upon commonsense, taken-for-granted knowledge on the part of his scientific community. No researcher, for example, can give a complete account of his research activities, but must rely on commonsense understandings taken for granted by all 'competent' members of his community. 'Thus, scientific research is a practical activity, which is embedded, as is any practical activity, in a con-text of implicit commonsense knowledge and is carried on by members of a particular scientific community for the purpose of developing descriptions that can serve as the basis for essential theoretical understanding.'[47] As a consequence, social research, from this point of view and as a practical activity, is both a method and a resource from which to obtain an understanding of the basic principles of human social interaction; but it is an understanding difficult to judge in terms of the prescriptions of positivistic epistemologies.

Conclusions

It is difficult to present final conclusions on the methods of participant observation, especially since its intellectual underpinnings vitally depend on models of the social actor which are seriously challenged. Nonetheless, in their traditional form, the methods stand in contrast to the experiment, which is regarded by its champions as the paradigm of all scientific inquiry. The supporters of participant observation methods claim, however, that it is the only method which can get at the 'stuff' of social life, the meanings and processes the actors use to make sense out of their social worlds. The methods do, however, raise some awkward questions about the principles of validity and objectivity: questions which require a re-examination of the models of the social actor presumed by the methods.

Exercises

Since participant observation normally requires a long and enduring commitment in some ongoing situation which few students can give because of the pressures of other courses, the first exercise is simply observation without participation.

1. Choose a situation in, say, a bar, a café or a restaurant, in the Public Library at the check-out desk or in a shop or doctor's waiting-room, and so on. Whatever it is, try to make sure that the events which take place are of relatively short duration and can be unobtrusively observed. (If necessary, obtain permission to observe from the relevant authorities. Remember: in all social research the anonymity of the subjects must always be preserved.) Pick a situation which is relatively self-contained and does not involve chasing all over the place. It is an idea for class members to choose situations which have some comparability with each other, e.g. customer-vendor behaviour as revealed in the contexts of a bar, a grocery store, a supermarket, a bookshop, and so on; each member of the class picking a different context.

Once the observational situation has been chosen, spend a few moments orientating yourself to the general features of the particular interaction you are to observe. Make sure that you are in a good, but not too obtrusive, position to observe. Then, once you are comfortable, start to note down what you see and hear. Record any gestures, talk, movements that occur. At this stage, just record 'basic' observational data with as little inference as possible. Be as complete as you can. Do this for as long as is feasible, but do not gather so much material that it will take months to analyse.

When you come to analyse the material collected, look at your record and try to see what categories and concepts are suggested. Try to bring out the sociological features of what it was you observed. If, for example, you have been observing customer-vendor relations, try to reconstruct the rules that seem to govern this type of interaction, and illustrate them from your data. Notice any departures from these 'rules', and what might account for them. Describe, according to your data, the roles of the different participants to the relationships. Throughout the analysis, use your data to support your theoretical ideas.

2. A variant of Exercise 1 is to have two or three observers (no more) watching and recording the same situation or event simultaneously. Recording and analysis should be done without consultation. Once these are complete, it will be interesting to compare both the recordings and the analysis to see how far they differ from each other. This raises questions of the reliability of observational data.

3. If time, resources and inclination permit, you might like to undertake a more sustained effort at *participant* observation. In this case, your records will be much fuller and will need to take account of the problems posed by participant roles.

With all these exercises, you should consider some or all of the problems raised in the chapter. Be critical, but not destructive. As always, the aim is to give you experience in creating and using sociological data as well as evaluating it methodologically. The observations you make are for a purpose, i.e. to find out 'what is going on', or, more formally, to illustrate some processes identified in various sociological theories. Methodologically, one of the important issues concerns the step from observations to instancing them as a process of phenomena identified by a sociological theory. Think of the bases for making such inferences.

Notes and References

1. This is not to argue that there is a historical dimension to this in that participant observation methods developed in response to anxieties about the experimental method. This history of participant observation is possibly older than that of the experiment.

2. I. Deutscher, 'Words and Deeds: Social Science and Social Policy', reprinted in W. J. Filstead (ed.), *Qualitative Methodology*, Markham Publishing, Chicago, 1970, pp. 27–51.

3. See ibid., Introduction. This contains a fuller discussion of some of the substantive sociological theories which consitute this perspective. See also, G. H. Mead, *Mind, Self, and Society*, University of Chicago Press, Chicago, 1936; H. Blumer, *Symbolic Interactionism*, Prentice-Hall, Englewood Cliffs,1969.

4. M. Weber, *The Theory of Social and Economic Organization*, translated by T. Parsons, Oxford University Press, New York, 1947, p. 88.

5. H. Blumer, 'Society as Symbolic Interaction', in A. Rose (ed.), *Human Behaviour and Social Processes*, Houghton, Mifflin, Boston, 1962, p. 188.

6. B. Malinowski, *Argonaughts of the Western Pacific*, Routledge & Kegan Paul, London, 1922, pp. 18–19. Chapter 1 of this book makes an excellent case for participant observation. Another classic study in this vein is W. F. Whyte, *Street Corner Society*, University of Chicago Press, Chicago, 1955, 2nd edition.

7. ibid. Apparently, Whyte was over six feet tall and well-built with it, which may explain something about his remarkable achievement in getting involved with the gang.

8. R. L. Gold, 'Roles in Sociological Field Observations', *Social Forces*, 36, 1958, pp. 217–23. Gans emphasizes three roles for the field worker: the total participant, the research participant and the total researcher. See 'The Participant Observer as a Human Being: Observations on the Personal Aspects of Field Work', in H. S. Becker *et al.* (eds.), *Institutions and the Person*, Aldine Press, Chicago, 1968, pp. 300–17.

9. M. A. Sullivan *et al.*, 'Participant Observation as Employed in the Study of a Military Training Program', reprinted in Filstead (ed.), *Qualitative Methodology*, pp. 91–100.

10. Gold, 'Roles in Sociological Field Observations', loc. cit.

11. On this and other ethical issues involved, see K. T. Erikson, 'A Comment on Disguised Observations in Sociology', *Social Problems*, 14, 1965, pp. 366–73.

12. Sullivan *et al.*, 'Participant Observation', loc. cit.

13. This does not refer to observational techniques as used in the laboratory, e.g. by R. F. Bales, *Interaction Process Analysis*, Addison-Wesley, Cambridge, Mass., 1950.

14. H. S. Becker, 'Problems of Inference and Proof in Participant Observation', *American Sociological Review*, 23, 1958, pp. 652–60.

15. L. Festinger *et al.*, *When Prophecy Fails*, Harper & Row, New York, 1956.

16. R. K. Merton, 'Selected Problems of Field Work in a Planned Community', *American Sociological Review*, 12, 1947, pp. 304–12.

17. H. M. Trice, 'The "Outsider's" Role in Field Studies', in Filstead (ed.), *Quantitative Methodology*, pp. 77–82.

18. It is not a bad idea to think oneself into a stranger role in one's everyday life—if only for a minute or two—and note how much knowledge is presumed in doing the most mundane of activities. This social knowledge is the sort that the participant observer must discover.

19. Becker, 'Problems of Inference', loc. cit.; and H. S. Becker and B. Geer, 'Participant Observation and Interviewing: A Comparison', in Filstead (ed.), *Qualitative Methodology*, pp. 133–42.

20. See, in this style, W. B. Saunders (ed.), *The Sociologist as Detective*, Praeger, New York, 1974.

21. N. K. Denzin, *The Research Act*, Aldine, Chicago, 1970, p. 204; H. S. Becker and B. Geer, 'Participant Observation: The Analysis of Qualitative Data', in R. N. Adams and J. D. Priess (eds.), *Human Organization Research*, Dorsey, Homewood, Ill., 1960, pp. 267–89.

22. This is not to say that quantitative presentations are impossible. See H. S. Becker *et al.*, *Boys in White*, University of Chicago Press, Chicago, 1961.

23. H. S. Becker, 'Problems of Inference and Proof in Participant Observation', *American Sociological Review*, 23, 1958, pp. 652–60.

24. Denzin, *The Research Act*, p. 202; also M. Dalton, 'Preconceptions and Methods in "Men Who Manage"', in P. E. Hammond (ed.), *Sociologists at Work*, Basic Books, New York, 1964, pp. 50–95.

25. A. R. Lindesmith, 'Comment on W. S. Robinson's "The Logical Structure of Analytic Induction"', *American Sociological Review*, 17, 1952, p. 492. (Robinson's original article appeared in *American Sociological Review*, 16, 1951, pp. 812–18.) Denzin, *The Research Act*, contains a full discussion of analytic induction.

26. A. R. Lindesmith, *Opiate Addiction*, Principia Press, Bloomington, 1947; *Addiction and Opiates*, Aldine Press, Chicago, 1968.

27. Denzin, *The Research Act*, p. 200.

28. Reference has already been made to some of this literature in Chapter 2.

29. Excellent on this is J. D. Douglas, *American Social Order*, The Free Press, New York, 1971.

30. A. F. Blum, 'Methods for the Study of Social Problems', unpublished MS. quoted in Phillips, *Knowledge from What?*, Rand McNally, Chicago, 1971.

31. D. Sudnow, *Passing On*, Prentice-Hall, Englewood Cliffs, 1967, p. 176.

32. Phillips, *Knowledge from What?*, p. 152. An interesting and possibly vital point in this regard is that the distinction between 'knowledge of' and 'knowledge about', represented in French by *'connaître'* and *'savoir'*, in German by *'kennen'* and *'wissen'* and in Spanish by *'conocer'* and *'saber'*, is not easily grasped in English, which employs the single verb, 'to know'. Thus, the distinction important in sociological theory and methodology and to the debate between positivistic and anti-positivistic epistemologies, between 'subjective understanding' and 'objective cognisance', may be culturally difficult for English speakers to understand. See I. Deutscher, 'Asking Questions Cross-culturally : Some Problems of Linguistic Comparability', in H. Becker *et al.* (eds.), *Institutions and the Person*, p. 326.

33. E. A. Tiryakian, 'Existential Phenomenology and the Sociological Tradition', *American Sociological Review*, 30, 1965, p. 678.

34. Phillips, *Knowledge from What?*, p. 159.

35. ibid., p. 162.

36. J. D. Douglas (ed.), *Understanding Everyday Life*, Aldine, Chicago, 1970, p. 31.

37. Becker and Geer, 'Participant Observation and Interviewing', loc. cit.

38. Not all of those committed to the methods being discussed would necessarily accept this characterization of them. Like most 'schools', they contain considerable variety of viewpoint. Nonetheless, I do maintain that this disjunction between humanistic ideals and justifications in terms familiarly positivistic is identifiable. So does Douglas (ed.), *Understanding Everyday Life*, who calls the strand I am talking about 'behavioural interactionism', as opposed to 'phenomenological interactionism', the latter school not subscribing to the positivistic paradigm.

39. ibid., p. 17.

40. See A. Schutz, 'Commonsense and Scientific Interpretation of Human Action', *Philosophy and Phenomenological Research*, 14, 1953, pp. 1–38.

41. A. V. Cicourel, *Method and Measurement in Sociology*, The Free Press, Glencoe, 1964, p. 52.

42. ibid., p. 59.

43. T. P. Wilson, 'Normative and Interpretative Paradigms in Sociology', in Douglas (ed.), *Understanding Everyday Life*, p. 68.

44. See H. Garfinkel and H. Sacks, 'On Formal Structures of Practical Actions', in J. McKinney and E. A. Tiryakian (eds.), *Theoretical Sociology*, Appleton-Century-Crofts, New York, 1970, pp. 338–66.

45. Wilson, 'Normative and Interpretive Paradigms', loc. cit., p. 69.

46. ibid., p. 75.

47. ibid., p. 74.

6
Asking Questions and Using Words

Although the title of this chapter may appear rather wide-ranging, it focuses upon what is probably the most frequently used data source in contemporary sociology: the interview and questionnaire. As Benny and Hughes claim, 'Sociology has become the science of the interview. . . .'[1] Of course, a great many methods involve asking questions, including the methods discussed in Chapter 5 on participant observation, but the role of questions and their replies is given a rather special emphasis in interview and questionnaire methods.

Interviews and Questionnaires

An interview is a research setting in which the researcher asks the subject ('respondent') a series of questions relevant to the topic of research. The respondent's answers constitute the raw data analysed by the researcher. The questionnaire is similar in conception, except that the respondent answers written questions. Once again the answers, verbal or written, are the data for analysis. There are many variations of each of these methods, and an account of the major types will be presented. However, it is important first to realize that these methods are usually used in the context of a survey, the subject of the next chapter.

Interviews and questionnaires are distinguished mainly in terms of whether a researcher asks the questions of the respondent face-to-face, or whether they are written in a questionnaire completed by the respondent. Both depend upon the use of some verbal stimuli —a question—to elicit a verbal response from a subject. The presentation, arrangement and content of the verbal stimuli varies according to the purposes or whims of the investigator. To the extent that both depend on verbal stimuli, most of the following remarks are applicable to both the interview and the questionnaire. Special problems attaching uniquely to one or the other will be considered as the occasion warrants.

Interviews may initially be classified according to their degree of standardization. The most structured type is where the interviewer uses a schedule in which the wording and order of the questions must be rigidly adhered to for all respondents alike.[2] The assumption underlying this procedure is that if all respondents receive the same stimuli, then any variation in their replies must be a result of actual differences in their responses and not a product of variations in the stimuli. Thus, if one interviewer were to ask a question in one way and another interviewer to ask the same question in a different way, we could not be sure whether variations in the responses to these questions were a result of real differences between the respondents or of differences in the way the questions were asked.

At the other extreme is the non-standardized interview, in which the interviewer simply works from a list itemizing the information required from the respondent. The interviewer is free to ask questions how he likes and in the order he feels appropriate. The rationale underlying this form of interview is that it allows both researcher and respondent much greater latitude in answering questions and developing ideas in situations where a standardized interview might be too constraining. It allows the interviewer to adopt a flexible approach and enables him or her to develop points not perhaps originally envisaged in the research aims. Related to the non-standardized interview is the focused interview, which is unstandardized in the sense that the wording of questions is not specified but where there is, nonetheless, a definite focus on a topic germane to the research. The interviewer comes to the respondent with a list of topics derived from a preliminary consideration of the research problem and then directs his questioning in a way which establishes the credibility of the information being imparted.[3] Further beyond this lies the totally unstandardized interview, in which the interviewer tries to develop a permissive atmosphere so that the respondent feels free to develop ideas and opinions, hopefully uninfluenced by the questions or the interviewer, rather like an informal friendly conversation.

Finally, between the standardized and non-standardized interviews is the semi-standardized one in which the interviewer has to ask certain specific major questions but is free to probe beyond them as he sees fit. In this form of interviewing the relative weighting of standardized and unstandardized items depends very much on circumstances.

Part of the rationale behind these different types of interview is that each one is more or less suited to dealing with particular kinds of research problem. The unstructured, non-standardized interview, for example, is argued to be more appropriate for exploratory studies where little of a systematic nature is known either about the problem itself or the population from which the respondents are selected. Thus, if one knows little about the processes affecting people's responses to mass media messages, the researcher might well, as a step towards gaining more systematic knowledge, conduct a series of unstandardized interviews to see how people felt about the problem, probing all the time so as to refine his ideas. In some cases, this sort of procedure is used in a preliminary pilot investigation prior to the construction of more standardized interview schedules. The results of the non-standardized interviewing can then be used as a guide to framing appropriate questions about relevant issues in a language which can be understood by the population of interest. The standardized interview, it is claimed, offers advantages in cases where a large sample of people are to be interviewed. The systematic format allows relatively untrained interviewers to use the schedule, whereas the unstructured interview requires highly trained, flexibly minded personnel fully cognisant with the aims of the research. It is also often argued that the structured interview offers the advantages of quantification, allowing for a more rigorous testing of hypotheses. Certainly, the use of structured interviews implies that the researcher knows enough about a topic to be able to construct his items systematically, and with every confidence that they will be understood by both interviewer and respondent.

In some cases, the different types of interview are used conjointly. The standardized type used to collect 'face-sheet' information, such as age, sex and other demographic data, and a non-standardized one dealing with less 'hard' information, or information more varied and qualitative in character. There is evidence to suggest that closed questions are more likely to keep the respondent on course and provide, with reservations, responses comparable in validity and depth. Open questions, however, are useful for assessing the salience of a topic, and also when resources do not allow for sufficient pre-testing for the construction of closed items.[4] Though the decision to use either type is sometimes couched in terms of whether the research is exploratory or hypothesis-testing, it must also be born in mind that interviewing is costly in terms of staff, processing and analysis, and that these purely financial considerations are often relevant to the choice of interviewing form.

There is no doubt that the systematic use of interviews and questionnaires in conjunction with the survey, especially after 1945, greatly increased the amount of sociological data, though its quality and virtue is something else again.[5] The reasons for the pre-eminence of the interview are not hard to find. For one thing, it is quicker than most observational methods, and for another, it does not so obviously take place in the artificial environment of a laboratory. Further, it allows the researcher to cover a large area, both social and geographical, and the resultant data lends itself to quantitative analysis. But all these claims are dependent upon certain assumptions about the nature of the social reality which produces the data—assumptions which are becoming increasingly more questionable.

Presumptions of the Interview

The function, then, of the interview or questionnaire is to elicit particular information by means of some verbal stimuli, namely, a spoken or written question. It is assumed that the respondent has some information, ideas, attitudes or opinions on the subject of the research, and it is the purpose of the interview to obtain this information with a minimum of distortion. The advantage of using words as the data medium is that the interviewer immediately has access to a vast storehouse of knowledge: the respondent's verbal reporting on such personal matters as occupation, marital status, sex and past history as well as feelings, opinions or attitudes on whatever the researcher is inclined to inquire into. In short, the researcher is not limited to what he can immediately perceive, but is able to cover as many dimensions of as many people as is feasible within the limits of time and financial resources. 'Words are actions in miniature. Hence by the use of questions and answers we can obtain information about a vast number of actions in a short space of time, the actual observation and measurement of which would be impracticable.'[6]

Implicitly, the interview and questionnaire presume a model rather like Figure 11. This diagram tries to show how language— the data used by the researcher-interviewer—is a good indicator of thought and action. Attitudes and thoughts are assumed to be a prime influence on behaviour, and language a reflection of both. So, if a person gave the answer, 'I would vote X', in response to a question about his voting intention, this is assumed to be a good indicator of what he will do when the time comes to vote. If these assumptions are accepted, then, by using verbal reports, the investigator has, in principle, access to an almost infinite variety of meaningful information offering a short cut to collecting behavioural data by using individual reports of their own and other's behaviour.[7]

Obviously, one does not need to be a social scientist to have doubts about the model outlined. For one thing, people sometimes lie or elaborate on the 'true' situation to enhance their esteem, or

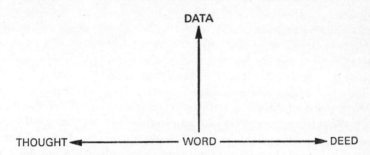

Figure 11. Implied model underlying verbal methods.

claim to do something one day but change their minds the next, and so on. Sociologists who use the interview method are also aware of these possibilities, and a great deal of effort has been devoted to improving the practical validity of the method by trying to devise means of detecting such departures from the 'truth'. These efforts are directed towards getting the respondent to reply to questions truthfully, unswayed or unbiased by such extraneous factors as the style of questioning or the characteristics of the interviewer. In general terms, the degree of correspondence between, say, a person's private thoughts and what he or she chooses to express is regarded as dependent upon individual, cultural and situational factors which will vary, and may or may not be controllable or even realized by the interviewer.

Most sources of invalidity are regarded as stemming from the fact that the interview situation, like most research or data-collection situations in sociology, is also a social situation subject to the same kind of dynamics which operate in 'normal' social life. The interview, in short, is not socially sterile, and hence the assumed correspondences between word, thought and deed may not hold. Illustrative of this is the way the 'social desirability' variable can effect responses to questions.[8] In one study of this factor, respondents were asked to rate personality trait items in terms of whether they considered them desirable or undesirable in others. A separate group of respondents were then asked to indicate whether the items were characteristic of themselves. A strong correlation was found between the judged desirability of an item and the probability of its appearance among the self-ratings. If these findings are applicable to the interview situation, then what the respondent says may be strongly influenced by the social desirability of saying it. In a similar way, a study by Dahrenwend, concerned mainly with the influence of social class and ethnicity on mental health status, suggested that many responses about the prevalence of mental health symptoms as likely as not reflect cultural differences in the social desirability of the modes of expressing distress and willingness to report it. He found that, with social class held constant, Puerto Ricans had a higher rate of mental illness (based on an inventory of symptoms) than did Jews, Irish or Negroes in a sample of the New York population. However, on subjecting the mental health inventory items to a social desirability rating, he found that Puerto Ricans regarded the items as less undesirable than did members of the other ethnic groups, and thus they may have been more willing to admit to such characteristics. Phillips and Clancy, developing the previous study, suggests that people's views concerning the desirability or otherwise of the psychiatric inventory items are determined partly by people looking around and making a judgement on how many of their peers show similar characteristics, and partly by a greater willingness of 'lower-class' individuals to admit to or report certain behaviours and experiences which 'upper-class' persons might rate as undesirable.[9]

If it is possible to generalize from such studies, and in many ways it would be safer to regard this as possible, then the implications are critical for the substantive theories developed from interview findings. To force home the example, the frequently found relationship between social class and mental health might be accounted for by the class differentials in the social desirability of the items constituting the mental-health inventory: a conclusion which could make nonsense out of any public policy designed to do something about this 'social problem' among the 'lower classes'. (Incidentally, this point stresses once again the necessity to examine alternative theories consistent with the data, some of which may be theories about how the data is a function of the instrument used.)

Other extraneous factors entering into the interviewer-respondent relationship are the fairly familiar ones noted earlier with respect to experimenters. Hyman, for example, found that white interviewers received more 'acceptable' responses from Negro respondents.[10] Similarly, Negro and Oriental interviewers obtained more socially acceptable answers concerning racial issues than did white interviewers.[11] Predictably, the sex of the interviewer is not exempt as a factor affecting responses.[12] The list could be expanded to include age, religion, social class and status, personality and so forth, all of which have been shown to affect responses.[13] The behaviour of the interviewer, too, has been shown to affect responses. One study has suggested that variations in respondent 'verbosity' often result from variations in interviewer willingness to probe: more aggressive interviewers tend to elicit more 'information'.[14] Also, the presence of others at the time of interview may effect responses. Taietz, in a study using the interview setting as a variable, found that when older Dutch adults were asked how they felt about their grown children living with them, their answers varied systematically with the presence of children.[15] College-age interviewers had a similar effect.

The other partner to the interview relationship, the respondent, is also a source of invalidity. Mention has already been made of the 'social desirability' variable. Other research has noted that the 'need for social approval' affects people's responses in various test situations. Persons characterized as having a high need for social approval tend to be more sensitive to situational demands and are more likely to respond affirmatively to social influences.[16] Also noted is the tendency of certain people to agree ('yea-saying') or disagree ('nay-saying') with items independent of their content.[17] Even on fairly standard 'empirical' information, the accuracy of respondent reporting is not as high as is often supposed. The few studies which have attempted to check respondent reports do not encourage much confidence. One study, for example, found that a significant number of respondents gave incorrect replies to questions about whether or not they voted. In some cases, these represented about 30 per cent inaccuracies, a startling figure given the crucial magnitudes on which the corroboration of theories often depends. Similar inaccuracies have been reported in the fields of birth-control use, health information, deviant behaviour and social welfare.[18]

The Process of Interviewing

Although the discussion so far would seem to be heading for a wholesale condemnation of the interview method, it would be wrong to jump to this conclusion too hastily. After all, it is not that interviewers have been unaware of these problems. Considerable attention has been paid to training interviewers and constructing appropriate questions in an effort to escape the biases to which the method is open. Let us first look at the interview situation itself. A great deal of discussion on interviewing technique centres on the need to create the sort of atmosphere that will minimize the respondent's need to distort, or give, 'not quite truthful', replies. To achieve this, most interview manuals stress the importance of the interviewer being exceedingly careful about expressing his own opinions and seeming to approve or disapprove of the respondent's answers. The interviewer needs to be encouraging and rewarding to the respondent while maintaining a permissive atmosphere but still avoiding evaluative gestures or comments that might communicate expectations.

The first contact between the interview and the respondent is crucial. At this stage, the task is to secure the co-operation of the respondent. The interviewer has to establish his legitimacy in the respondent's eyes and explain why he is standing on the doorstep. Unlike the participant observer, the interviewer does not 'enter' the interaction he is studying, but observes it second-hand, as it were, through the verbal reports of the respondent. To legitimate this process, auspices must be stated ('The Sociology Department at the University of ——— is understaking research into ———'). Sufficient information must be given about the research aims (but how much information will depend upon whether the researcher feels that too much knowledge about the aims might affect the respondent's replies unduly).[19] The respondent must also be encouraged to participate in the interview, and assurances given as to the confidentiality of replies. All this must be established in the first moments.

Once the respondent is satisfied about the legitimacy of the enterprise and its worth, the next task is to maintain interest and receive valid replies to the questions. The term generally used to refer to the most suitable kind of interviewer-respondent relationship is 'rapport'.[20] This notion turns upon the interviewer being able to communicate to the respondent trust, warmth, reassurance and likeableness: a formulation which might fit the shady salesman as much as the successful interviewer! The interviewer should never appear to threaten the respondent by destroying his or her confidence in the relationship. The respondent should be respected, and, as explained earlier, the interviewer should refrain from communicating approval or disapproval of replies.

What happens in detail depends very much on the type of interview being conducted. If a very structured interview schedule is to be used, the principle is that the questions, the verbal stimuli, should be administered in the same way to all respondents. They should be asked exactly those questions as stated on the schedule, and always in the order in which they are presented. If, on the other hand, it is one of the freer-ranging types, then the interviewer must be able to 'bring the respondent out', be able to handle lengthy conversations, to keep them moving and flowing well while making sure that all necessary topics are covered as fully as possible. In general, this latter type of interview is regarded as by far the most difficult to conduct successfully. Throughout both types it is of vital importance for each interview to be treated as a separate experience, otherwise the interviewer may begin to develop hypotheses, stereotypes and expectations that could influence his participation in the relationship and mislead him about what the respondent is and what he is saying.[21]

As important as these rather general considerations about the role of the interviewer and his aim of eliciting unbiased responses from the respondent are the questions themselves, whether used in an interview or a self-administered questionnaire. As we have seen, the entire enterprise of interviewing depends upon the questions, as verbal stimuli, eliciting verbal responses from the respondent, for it is these which provide the data for analysis. As such, the questions become the major unit around which the interview is constructed, and their design and selection should be such that they accurately elicit the data necessary to fulfil the aims of the research. Unfortunately, this is easier to exhort in theory than to achieve satisfactorily in practice.

Questionnaire Construction

There are many detailed accounts of questionnaire construction, but here are a few general points that, conventionally, must be born in mind. However, specific research needs and contexts may sometimes suggest variations from these general principles. After all, these are not rules but simple principles based on experience and commonsense.

The first step is to consider precisely what it is you want to find out and why. What data is relevant to the research problem? This is the most important question of all, for the answer will affect decisions about the data-collection method itself. If interviewing is chosen as the relevant research method, then the type of interview design needs to be decided upon. The next stage is to translate theoretical ideas into questions to be used in the interview or questionnaire. It is sometimes useful, when translating theoretical ideas into the operational format, if a prior pilot study is conducted where particular formulations can be tested out on a population as similar as possible to that intended for the main study. At this stage, decisions need to be made as to the type of question-and-answer to be used. The choice lies between 'open-ended' and 'closed' or 'fixed-alternative' questions.

The open-ended question is one which does not provide the respondent with a prearranged list of possible answers from which he or she must select an alternative. The fixed-alternative question, as indicated, provides a selection of possible answers, either 'yes', 'no', or multiple choice items (sometimes called a 'cafeteria question'). Examples of open-ended questions would be, 'Why did you come to work at this factory?'; 'How do you feel about the government?' In other words, they leave the respondent to provide his own answers. Fixed-alternative questions range from the fairly simple ones seeking a 'yes' or 'no' response to those giving a fairly elaborate and comprehensive list of alternatives. Usually the respondent's answer must be limited to the alternatives provided, though occasionally an open-ended category is included if the respondent positively feels that none of the offered alternatives fits his or her case. (If too many respondents fall into this category, it is almost certain that the alternatives provided are inadequate and that the question should be reformulated.)

Each type of question has advantages and disadvantages. To the extent that open-ended questions put less constraint on respondent's replies, there is less danger of the researcher forcing answers into categories which he feels to be important. Also, the extent to which the open-ended question is closer to natural conversation may aid spontaneity and encourage a freer expression of ideas. Unfortunately, coding open-ended questions is often difficult. Fixed-alternative questions are easier to code and provide more uniform information across relevant dimensions. It is not unusual for questionnaires to contain mixtures of the question types. Thus open-ended questions are often used for those topics where it is the respondent's own definitions, feelings or whatever which are required; and fixed-alternative questions used when information is needed on such fairly standard topics as age or years of schooling, where the possible alternatives are well known, or where attitude scales are involved.

As far as the wording of the question is concerned, it should ask precisely whatever it is that the researcher demands responses to, which is not always as easy as may seem. As far as possible, the language used should be suitable for, and hence understandable to, the interviewee. If the respondent is from the general public (whatever that means!), intuitively there would seem little point in asking a question phrased in esoteric language. In any case, if the interview or questionnaire is highly structured, then, in principle, the same stimuli should be applied equally to all and the words used should be understood by all respondents in the same way. Ambiguous and loaded words should normally be avoided, and these are not always self-evident, while the questions themselves should be as short as possible. The validity of responses can often be improved by tying questions down to specific events or items. For example, instead of asking, 'Do you often go to the cinema?' ask, 'How many times in the last month have you been to the cinema?' Care should also be taken not to predispose a particular answer, and the respondent's ego should be protected as far as possible. In other words, if not knowing something has a low social value, it is better not to ask questions such as, 'When was the last General Election?' Rather, it is better to ask, 'Do you happen to know the year of the last General Election?' suggesting that it is possible, without shame or disgrace, to admit honestly to not knowing. Above all, questions should be phrased to avoid putting the respondent in an unfavourable light by suggesting that other people might well feel the same way, and by not indicating that his or her responses are in any way exceptional, whatever the interviewer's personal feelings about a specific response.

In the case of alternative-answer questions, the alternatives should be exhaustive, covering all possible ranges of responses, including 'Don't know', be mutually exclusive and, of course, fit the frame of reference to the question. This point is especially relevant with self-administered questionnaires where no interviewer is present to remedy errors that might creep in. Visual presentation of the questionnaire can be important in that it needs to offer the respondent sufficient guidance and encouragement to complete it easily, simply and unambiguously. Instructions on how to answer particular questions, e.g. whether one and only one alternative is to be chosen or whether more may be selected, should be clearly provided.

The sequence of questions also needs careful consideration, since early questions may predispose answers to later ones. This, once again, is largely something which must be considered in terms of the aims of the research, though there are one or two general principles to bear in mind. One such is pure common sense. Don't ask, 'What did you vote in the last General Election?' and follow it by, 'Did you vote in the last General Election?' Funnelling is often useful: asking general questions on a theme and following them by more specific ones. This mode of question organization is sometimes used to filter the respondent through relevant sub-sets of questions. For example, if the respondent only has to answer certain sets of questions depending upon his earlier replies, the former question, along with appropriate instructions, directs him to the relevant sub-set. Thus, 'Did you vote in the last General Election? IF YES, please proceed to Question X', and so forth. Occasionally, closed items may be used as funnels for open-ended questions asking for elaboration of responses, and vice versa, depending on judgement.

The sequencing of questions also plays an important role in 'breaking in' the respondent smoothly and easily. Fairly conventional and less contentious questions should normally come early in the schedule, and more personal, sometimes intimate, ones later. It must always be remembered that the researcher's judgement of what is contentious is not always a good guide to what will be embarrassing to the respondent. There is also evidence to suggest that the designer of structured questionnaires should avoid monotony. Under-reporting can be interpreted as a consequence of the failure of the questionnaire to arouse the respondent's interest.

Processing Questionnaire Data

One great advantage of the interview or questionnaire is that they can be used to collect data from large samples of the population. At one extreme is the census with its near total coverage of the population of a country. The sheer size of the sample raises problems of processing the data contained in the questionnaires. Even a small sample, especially if covered by non-directive methods, can present tremendous processing problems. Fortunately there are methods of machine processing, such as the card sorter and computer, which are invaluable aids for data analysis. Before the stage of analysis, however, the questionnaire information must be coded into a form usable by the machine. Even if machine processing is not required, the information must be 'gutted' from the questionnaires or interview reports, whether for tabular presentation or for more qualitative accounts. It is a good idea, therefore, to have some idea of the codes to be used before the data has been collected and the questionnaire completed. These codes will be derived, of course, from the theoretical problem at which the study is aimed, and will also serve as a check that the empirical procedures—questions, codes, relationships among variables, sample characteristics, etc.—are adequate to the theoretical task.

If machine processing is to be used, then a coding frame has to be devised. Basically, a coding frame is a set of rules specifying correspondences between the responses on a schedule or from an interview, and positions on a punch card. This card (often referred to as an IBM card, a tribute to the best-known manufacturer of this kind of equipment) consists of eighty columns by ten rows, so that each response can be defined in terms of a coordinate position on the card. Thus, in the example shown in Figure 12, the respondent

Q. 12 How do you feel about X? (please tick the response closest to your feeling)		Card positions C_{12}
(a) Very favourable	____	1
(b) Favourable	____	2
(c) Indifferent	____	3
(d) Unfavourable	✓	4
(e) Very unfavourable	____	5
(f) No answer	____	9

Figure 12. Example of card coding.

has ticked alternative (d) to question No. 12, which is then coded as Column 12, position 4, and the card will be punched in this location. If the respondent had ticked alternative (a), the card would be punched in Column 12, position 1. Each question and possible responses have to be defined uniquely in terms of card positions. (Note: there are variations from the details given here, though the principle is the same. Local specialists will be in a position to advise.) Once all the responses have been processed in this manner, the data can be read electro-mechanically as appropriate by card sorters or computers. The data produced is numerical, the sophistication depending upon the computer programs available.

There are other ways of processing data from interviews or questionnaires, ranging from paper and pencil to cards with holes around their edges sorted with a knittng needle. The card sorter and computer are, however, the most widely used today.

A word about the resultant data. Naturally it varies depending upon the style of the interview and the mixture of question types. Non-standardized interview data will generally result in a research report illustrated by appropriate quotations from the interviews. The more standardized formats allow tabular presentation, often of a statistically high order.

The above guide-lines are a summary of what might be called the 'conventional wisdom' of interviewing and questionnaire design. If you like, they may be regarded as implicit theories about the ways to produce valid and reliable knowledge in interviewing contexts, and treating them as behavioural theories offers interesting possibilities for research and theoretical development.

Questions of Validity

It is important to remember that a question is simply a vehicle for eliciting data, or material which can be transformed into data. As such, the issues of validity and reliability appear once again, and in at least two ways. The first concerns the degree to which the question asked is a valid and reliable indicator of what the researcher wants to know. The second, strongly tied to the first, is whether the replies elicited are also valid and reliable.

Let it be said, right away, that there are no glib answers to either of these questions. Taking first the problem of the validity and reliability of the question itself, this will in many cases hardly seem a matter of issue. The variable 'age', for example, would seem to be reasonably validly indicated by the question, 'How old are you?' (The validity and reliability of the reply is another matter!) However, it is interesting to look at what the case for validity depends upon. Obviously, and paramountly, it depends upon a language, one understood by both interviewer and respondent. The effectiveness of the question depends upon its meaning being mutually understood. In cases of in-depth interviewing, where misunderstandings or non-understandings can be probed, it might be plausible to assume that some mutual sense of meaning can eventually be achieved. However, in standardized interviews and cross-cultural work there are rather less grounds for confidence. In the case of standardized interviews or questionnaires, the assumption is that the same stimulus, i.e. the same question, wording and all, has been applied to all respondents equally. The difficulty is in finding adequate grounds on which this assumption can be upheld. Unless such grounds can be found, the argument that such procedures provide more reliable information, because of less interviewer variability, cannot be supported.

Cross-Cultural Settings

What might such grounds be? One ground might be that the wording of the question is based upon extensive pre-testing on a population similar to that used in the main study, and that the results of this pre-testing give confidence that the intended meaning is adequately conveyed. Certainly, if the population is a familiar one, exhibiting little in the way of subcultural variation, this claim carries some force. If, on the other hand, the population is relatively culturally varied, then care must be taken to ensure that exact meaning is conveyed (often by the use of different wordings designed to measure the same variable) where appropriate question wordings would have to be devised for possible variations. More difficult are those items asking for less 'factual' types of response, for an opinion, the expression of an attitude or cultural orientation. This is especially problematic in the cross-cultural use of interviews and questionnaires. Here the problem is to obtain equivalence of meaning despite linguistic difference, since it is not always possible (or wise) to provide a literal translation of a question from one language to another. The Marathi speakers in India, for instance, have no concept that corresponds adequately to the notion of the generalized other, such as 'people', 'one', 'they', etc., and this would constitute an enormous difficulty for anyone carrying out cross-cultural questionnaire-type research involving Marathi speakers. It is necessary here to draw a distinction between formal and functional equivalence.[22] The former refers to the literal translation of verbal indicators from one language to another, the latter to obtaining equivalence in terms of meaning relevant to the members of the cultural group under consideration. The former is usually achieved by a foreign bilingual translating the questionnaire into his or her mother tongue and getting another bilingual to retranslate back into the original language.[23] The two translations can then be checked against each other. While this still does not solve the problem of meaning, it does achieve reasonably good linguistic equivalences.

A further complication is that a sequence of questions that provide a well-ordered set of stimuli in one language may produce a badly ordered set in another. The structure of the question itself and the alternatives it provides may appear odd in the eyes of some respondents, or, conversely, the replies odd in the eyes of the interviewer. Take, for example, the question, 'How do you feel about gambling from a moral point of view? Would you say that it is always wrong, usually wrong . . . hardly ever wrong?' What would the implications be if the response was, 'Isn't life a gamble?'[24] How is such a response to be coded in terms of the rationale behind the question: 'no answer', 'hardly ever wrong', 'don't know'? Concepts lying behind words are often delineated differently in different languages, and verbal equivalence is often little guide to these differences in meaning. The classic case is the term 'democracy' with its tremendously wide variations in meaning, not all of which are owing to political opportunism and cynicism, but also to real cultural differences of meaning. Similarly, in the Almond and Verba study, *The Civic Culture*, the following question was asked: 'Here are some important problems facing the people of this country. Which do you feel is most important to you?' One of the choices offered to the respondent was 'spiritual and moral betterment', and the combination of this with 'country's problems' in political interviews in Europe was rather an odd notion.[25]

Less dramatic, but as fundamental, are the different intercultural variations in such common-or-garden terms as 'friend'. The German lexical equivalent, 'freund', is reserved for a few intimates of long standing, but in English 'friend' can be applied to a wider circle of acquaintances.[26] Of course, problems such as these will vary in enormity between language groups and cultures. Nonetheless, it raises the issue of whether a question, as a stimulus to obtaining cognitively useful information, may itself be culturally specific. It assumes, in other words, a particular cultural role for language itself. Some researchers have reported that in technologically and economically underdeveloped societies it is much more difficult to find words high in cognitive meaning than is the case in Western, industrialized societies.[27] So, if questionnaires or interviews are used cross-culturally, great care must be taken to ensure that the wording of the question is appropriate to the job of eliciting valid responses. It must not be forgotten that 'a vocabulary is not merely a string of words; immanent within it are societal textures. . .'.[28]

There is yet a further and rather radical consideration relevant here which might suggest that semantic equivalence is a pure fiction.

Sapir and Whorf, in extensive studies of Hopi, Nootka, Shawnee and 'standard average European' language groups, claim that different linguistic communities perceive and conceive reality in different ways. A more extreme hypothesis advanced by them was that language, its structure and lexicon, determines thought. If these hypotheses are correct, any comparative analysis which relies on verbal stimuli and reporting becomes suspect since it is virtually impossible to obtain meaning equivalence.[29] Though the extreme version of the Sapir and Whorf hypothesis may be challenged—the Eskimo can, lexically, distinguish three different kinds of snow, but English speakers can also distinguish them even though they do not have one word for each 'snow-state'—it does raise rather awkward questions concerning the ability of verbal instruments to elicit meaningful and valid responses across linguistic and cultural boundaries, especially within the rather narrow confines of a questionnaire.[30]

The Behavioural Conventions of Interviewing

There are other features of the interview to be mentioned in connection with cross-cultural research, but which are also important in more localized contexts. Although the interview is a data-collection instrument it is also a social situation governed, deliberately or otherwise, by particular conventions. Some of these conventions derive from beliefs about the efficacy of certain styles of interviewing in eliciting less biased responses, such as those recommendations outlined above regarding the proper way in which interviewers should conduct themselves. Others, however, derive from the normal expectations of social intercourse prevailing in the culture, such as rules of etiquette, politeness, and so on. Further conventions are those attached to the interview as a behaviour setting in its own right.

Of these various conventions, Benney and Hughes argue for two which 'characterize most interviews and seem to give this particular mode of personal encounter its uniqueness', namely 'equality and comparability'.[31] The first of these, equality, involves the assumption that information is more valid if voluntarily given. Thus, the stress in many guides to interviewing is on the interview as a relationship freely entered into by both parties, but especially by the respondent. Hence it is a bargain entered such that 'for allowing the interviewer to direct [the] communication, the informant is assured that he will not meet with denial, contradiction, competition, or other harassment. As with all contractual relations, the fiction or convention of equality must govern the situation.'[32] Thus, by implication, the interviewer should try to minimize any inequalities, such as age, sex, intelligence, social status and expertness, which exist between the parties to the interview relationship. Certainly a great deal of interviewer training and exhortation in manuals is focused on precisely this point. But to what extent this convention actually operates is a moot point. The efficiency with which a 'middle-class' interviewer can minimize the sort of inequalities mentioned when interviewing, say, a 'working-class' respondent is bound to be problematic. It is even more of a potential problem when interviewing in other cultures: in ex-colonial societies, for example, where the superordinate-subordinate relationship between white and coloured may strongly violate the convention of equality.[33]

The second convention presumed by Benney and Hughes to prevail in the interview is comparability, which is 'designed to minimize the local, concrete, immediate circumstances of the particular encounter . . . and to emphasize only those aspects that can be kept general enough and demonstrable enough to be counted'.[34] In other words, no particular interview is an end in itself, but only has meaning in the context of other interviews being conducted at roughly the same time. Idiosyncratic qualities have to be eliminated in preference to those qualities which are generalizable across the range of interviews. This is, once again, the explicit rationale behind the standardized interview, but in this form it applies to other types equally. The particular encounter between interviewer X and respondent Y should yield information comparable to encounters between A and B, C and D, E and F, and so on.

All this suggests that the interview relationship is an encounter which can occur only within particular cultural and social climates which allow for relationships governed by such norms or conventions. Imagine conducting interviews in a climate where these conventions have little legitimacy or meaning, as in, say, societies with repressive internal controls; or where transitory contacts with strangers is viewed with suspicion; or where the norms supporting privacy are very strong.[35] It is considerations such as these which suggest that the interview, as a tool of social research, is heavily dependent upon the cultural conventions of everyday life, public and private. None of these remarks necessarily detract, by themselves, from the validity of the information produced by the interview or questionnaire in climates where it has some legitimacy or meaning. It does suggest, however, that the validity of the method needs to be warranted by thorough knowledge of the social context in which it is to be used.

Verbal Responses and Meaning

Although the problem of the validity of verbal instruments seems most salient in cross-cultural research, the same issues can be relevant within the same cultural group, and what is essentially at issue is whether a verbal stimulus can elicit a verbal response which is a good indicator of the respondent's meaning. Earlier in this chapter it was suggested that the verbal response to a question is the data from which certain things are implied or inferred about both the 'inner life' of the respondent and his outward behaviour. The model of man employed here is something like the following: people are moved by attitudes and beliefs they hold which are acted out, partially at least, in situations. Access to this 'inner life' can be obtained from an analysis of verbal behaviour, often directly, but also by more indirect methods.[36] Thus knowledge of the cluster of beliefs and attitudes which the person uses to structure and make sense of the world in which he lives is important in any explanation of social behaviour. However, identifying these clusters of belief is a complex matter, and various devices have been employed, the most common and least sophisticated of which are the 'opinion' or 'poll'-type questions: 'Which political party do you prefer?' 'Do you think the British should leave the Common Market?' In other words, they are questions which simply ask for a brief opinion on a topic of interest.

However, the claim is that opinions are closely related to an identifiable structure of attitudes which are more stable and more enduring features of the individual's 'inner world'.[37] Attitude scales have been devised to measure an almost endless variety of belief elements, including authoritarianism, neuroticism, dogmatism, conservatism, job satisfaction, social isolation, alienation, to mention but a few, and some have become fairly standard instruments used over and over again.[38] But no matter how fully such instruments are used, there remains the question of validating the theoretical assumptions upon which the interviewing method depends, namely, the correspondence between verbal and overt behaviour. Unfortunately, the first is difficult since we have no access to the 'inner' world except by inference from verbal to other behaviour. One strategy is to argue that this is relatively unimportant since 'the spoken word is a social act, the inner thought is not, and the sociologist has good reason to be most interested and concerned with the former, the psychologist perhaps with the latter.'[39] There is some plausibility in this view, except for the following reasons. It assumes that the interview is a social context comparable to other social situations where attitudes and other verbal assertions may be expressed. Is the interview representative as a situation of social intercourse? While it could be argued that the interview is not comparable or equivalent to other public situations, this is not to say that it cannot be made more so by appropriate arrangements and interviewer training. However, against this it can be argued rather forcefully that the interview does decontextualize the respondent by asking him questions about matters divorced from the actual circumstances to which they might refer. For example, to ask a series of questions designed to measure racial prejudice may be little guide to behaviour in a situation where the respondent is confronted by a black, has a black family move in next door, has to work alongside a black, and so on.

Verbal Responses and Behaviour

These considerations bring us towards a second issue in the methodology of interviewing and questionnaires: the relationship between verbal expression and behaviour. Earlier it was pointed out that the warrant for the method is that access to verbal behaviour can throw considerable light on whole worlds of social action largely inaccessible to researchers. Unfortunately, however, there is evidence to suggest that this warrant can no longer be accepted uncritically. As early as 1934, La Piere travelled with a Chinese couple in the United States, reporting the treatment they received in hotels, camping sites, motels and restaurants. Of the 251 establishments visited, only one refused to accommodate the couple. Six months later, La Piere sent a questionnaire to each. Half only were asked, 'Would you accept members of the Chinese race as guests in your establishment?' and the other half were asked additional questions about other ethnic groups. Only one 'yes' response was received. As early as this a discrepancy had been discovered between verbal attitudes and overt behaviour, and many others have been noted subsequently.[40]

There are two strategies for resolving this often noted discrepancy between thought and deed. One is to refine the methods still further to increase their predictive reliability and validity. Improvements in measurement theory and techniques, knowledge of interview behaviour and settings, and so on, are all designed to reduce this discrepancy. A more fundamental and more radical strategy regards the first of these steps as likely to lead to only marginal improvements, and argues for what amounts to an epistemological shift in the foundations of sociological research. Deutscher remarks: 'One of the more regretful consequences of our neglect of the relationship between words and deeds has been the development of a technology which is inappropriate to the understanding of human behaviour, and, conversely, the almost complete absence of a technology which can facilitate our learning about the conditions under which people in various categories do or do not "put their monies where their mouths are".'[41] What is being argued here is the inadequacy of the meaning system in which the interview is embedded, involving, as it does, an inadequate theory of social action which assumes a correspondence between word, thought and deed. There is, of course, no lack of alternative theories and implied methodologies, some of which have already been mentioned. The symbolic interactionists, for example, have argued that action, whether verbal or not, is a response to symbolic meanings embedded in particular situations.[42] Thus, the interview as a symbolic situation in its own right might, or is likely to, result in verbalization not compatible with other situations. A question put to a respondent about, for instance, Armenian women, leads to a response in terms of the words and what is perceived about the interviewer and the situation. Standing face to face with an Armenian woman involves the ex-respondent in acting towards a totally different set of symbols.[43]

If these considerations are correct, then they constitute a serious objection to the warrant underpinning much of the sociological knowledge acquired by the use of interviews and questionnaires. However, even if we refuse to go so far as to reject the method entirely, it is necessary to stress the need for a long look at the theory on which the method is based, the putative connection between words and deeds, and to look closely at the social use of language as it impinges both on research practice and human behaviour.[44] In this regard, close attention must be paid to the issues raised by, among others, Sapir and Whorf, not only from the point of view of improving instrumentation, but because it influences the very process of sociological thinking.

A step towards this end is the study of the interview itself. A great deal of effort has been devoted to removing bias in interviewer behaviour and performance, while deviations from the normative conventions of equality, comparability and courtesy are carefully monitored as potential sources of error. More positively, such discrepancies could be regarded as useful clues to the ways in which different people perceive, relate and communicate. This could be especially useful in cross-cultural research in helping to reveal the 'background expectancies' operant in research situations.[45] Indeed, this is true not only in cross-cultural research, for there is a dangerous insensitivity to the dimensions of language, especially when everyone appears to be speaking the same language. Cicourel sums up the danger neatly: 'the sociologist . . . cannot afford to treat his own language from the perspective of a native speaker, but must adopt the position of a cryptoanalyst approaching a strange language'.[46] For, within a single society, the sociologist seeks information from people and about people who live, speak and behave in different linguistic, cultural and social worlds, and there is a danger of the researcher, for the sake of his instrument, taking these as more similar than they might be.

Exercises

These particular exercises are intended to introduce you to using verbal stimuli and verbal responses as sociological data. Since the questionnaire and the interview are also frequently used in connection with the survey, you might, if possible, like to run the exercises here in conjunction with one or two of those presented in the next chapter.

Choose an area of sociological interest which you think can be illuminated by interviewing a group of people. In other words, try to pick a problem in which it makes sense to gather verbal reports from a group. Remember also when making your choice to limit yourself to areas within your capabilities of time and resources. Interviewing fellow students is often convenient, though not always commensurately interesting. In picking an area of interest, do not simply confine yourself to gathering opinions, e.g. opinions about the university or college, or the latest government measures. Go beyond public-opinion polling. You might like to examine, for instance, upbringing patterns and their influence upon political ideas, conceptions of authority and social class, occupational background and evaluations of education: problems that, in other words, challenge your ingenuity in relating verbal data to theoretical conceptions. Then, prepare an informal unstructured interview prospectus. Think about, then list, all the topics which can form the basis of a 'conversation' relevant to your theoretical problem. If you have chosen a problem in which upbringing—or, to be technical, socialization—is relevant, you might decide to talk about the respondent's relationship with his or her parents in terms of discipline, inducements, ease of relationships, values which seemed to have been stressed, parental encouragement and the like. In short, don't simply ask, 'What do you think is the relationship between your patterns of socialization and X?' (Though why not ask this is an interesting question in its own right, and one discussed in the final chapter.) You have to gather verbal data as indicators of some properties specified in your theoretical ideas. You are working between the theory language and a data language which puts a premium on verbal behaviour. In an interview of this sort, the aim is to gather verbal responses in a relatively free and easy manner relevant to the area of theoretical interest. It does not matter whether the topics are covered in a particular order, only that you cover them. Make sure that the prospectus for the interview is as full as possible. Don't omit fine detail if you think it important.

Choose three or four respondents who, in some way, represent the target group: students, housewives, husbands, Welsh separatists, pretentious intellectuals, criminals or whatever. Carry out these interview conversations with them, recording as fully as possible all the replies to your questions, the probes you used to elicit fuller responses, and the indicators of meaning like gesture, tone of voice and so on, which make the purely verbal formulations socially sensible. Do not forget to reassure your respondents about the anonymity of their replies. Always respect the confidentiality of your informants. Incidentally, tape recorders are often useful, although this moves the practical problem of recording back one stage further to the making of transcripts of the interviews.

Your resultant data will consist of your questions and probes, and their replies. Look through the material—it will look impossible —and see what it suggests in terms of your original theoretical ideas. Can you begin to generate concepts which might be illuminating? If so, do so. If the rest of the class has chosen the same area of theoretical interest—in any event, this is a good idea—compare ideas and data.

The next stage is to use the results of these informal, unstructured interviews to construct a more structured questionnaire. (This is the point at which you can connect this exercise with the survey.)

In other words, pick out ideas, themes, particular verbal formulations which respondents seem to feature as guides to formulating a more structured questionnaire. Don't forget the demographic and other face-sheet information. Remember, now, the other constraints upon you as a researcher, especially the fact that more subjects will be involved and so it will become difficult to interview many people in depth. Accordingly, questions will have to be 'efficient' in tapping dispositions. Try your hand at constructing verbal items of the 'agree' *versus* 'disagree' type, which may tap an attitude or value to some social object. Design the questionnaire and, if possible, administer it as the project for the next chapter.

Once this exercise is completed, you might like to think about the following sorts of questions:

What are the presumptions behind the use of verbal reports as data? Elucidate the theory or theories of instrumentation which underlie verbal methods and illustrate from the decisions you make during the exercise. Elaborate your theory or the assumptions as to why a particular verbal formulation is indicative of a theoretical concept.

Which method, the informal or the more structured questionnaire, is the more reliable? Why? At what cost?

Reflect upon the interviews you made as a social experience. What kind of relationship did you want to establish, and why? What bearing has this on the theories of instrumentation involved? Do you think you succeeded? If yes or no, how and why?

What is lost and/or gained by transforming the 'unstructured' data into a more formal questionnaire? Is this serious? What does it suggest about the nature of sociology and the material relevant to the enterprise?

One adaptation of this exercise is to select a sociological problem which requires to use as respondents the members of some sub-culture or sub-group, such as Gay Liberationists, Black Power supporters, anti-blood sports leagues, or some other cultural minority. The reason for choosing such a group is not because they are 'peculiar', except in a purely statistical sense, but simply that, in the absence of the opportunity to interview a different linguistic group, interviewing a set of people who have developed a language of their own to talk about and interpret the social world throws into relief the sorts of problems arising from the central role of language in the construction of questionnaires and in conducting interviews. Even though such people may speak the same tongue, as it were, their own sub-group language makes for problems of equivalence *versus* meaning when devising standardized verbal stimuli. It should lead one to reflect on the extent to which this is possible, or even desirable.

Notes and References

1. M. Benney and E. C. Hughes, 'Of Sociology and the Interview', *American Journal of Sociology*, 62, 1956, pp. 137–42.

2. See E. A. Richardson, B. S. Dahrenwend and D. Klein, *Interviewing: Its Forms and Functions*, Basic Books, New York, 1965; E. E. Maccoby and N. Maccoby, 'The Interview: A Tool of Social Science', in G. Lindzey (ed.), *Handbook of Social Psychology*, Vol. 1, Addison-Wesley, Reading, Mass., 1954.

3. R. K. Merton and P. L. Kendall, 'The Focussed Interview', *American Journal of Sociology*, 51, 1946, pp. 541–57; R. K. Merton, M. Friske and P. L. Kendall, *The Focussed Interview*, The Free Press, New York, 1956.

4. B. S. Dahrenwend, 'Some Effects of Open and Closed Questions on Respondents' Answers', *Human Organization*, 24, 1965, pp. 175–84; P. F. Lazarsfeld, 'The Controversy over Detailed Interviews: An Offer for Negotiation', *Public Opinion Quarterly*, 8, 1944, pp. 38–60. This is an early classic statement on the different functions of open and closed questions.

5. One study reported that 91·7 per cent of research articles in the *American Journal of Sociology* and the *American Sociological Review* based on primary data had made use of interviews and/or questionnaires. See J. Brown and B. G. Gilmartin, 'Sociology Today: Lacunae, Emphases, and Surfeits', *American Sociologist*, 4, 1969, pp. 283–91.

6. P. E. Vernon, *The Assessment of Psychological Qualities by Verbal Methods*, Medical Research Council, Industrial Health Board, Report No. 83, H.M.S.O., London.

7. See J. Galtung, *Theory and Methods of Social Research*, Allen & Unwin, London, 1967, pp. 111–28; and J. S. Coleman, 'The Methods of Sociology', in R. Bierstedt (ed.), *A Design for Sociology: Scope, Objectives and Methods*, American Academy of Political and Social Science, Philadelphia, 1969, pp. 86–114.

8. A. L. Edwards, 'The Relationship between the Judged Desirability of a Trait and the Probability that the Trait will be Endorsed', *Journal of Applied Psychology*, 37, 1953, pp. 90–3; *The Social Desirability Variable in Personality Assessment and Research*, Dryden Press, New York, 1957.

9. B. Dahrenwend, 'Social Status and Psychological Disorder: An

Issue of Substance and an Issue of Method', *American Sociological Review*, 31, 1966, pp. 14–34; D. L. Phillips and K. J. Clancy, 'Response Biases in Field Studies of Mental Illness', *American Sociological Review*, 35, 1970, pp. 503–15. Also reported in D. L. Phillips, *Knowledge from What?*, Rand McNally, Chicago, 1971, pp. 39–47. A. Sicinski, in 'Don't Know Answers on Cross-Cultural Surveys', *Public Opinion Quarterly*, 34, 1970, pp. 126–9, suggests that 'don't know' responses are affected by cultural predispositions to admit ignorance. Norwegians, for example, seem to prefer to hazard a guess rather than admit ignorance.

10. H. Hyman, *Interviewing in Social Research*, University of Chicago Press, Chicago, 1954. Note the date of this finding. Attitudes may be different today. For more recent evidence, see H. Schuman and J. M. Converse, 'The Effects of Black and White Interviewers on Black Responses in 1968', *Public Opinion Quarterly*, 35, 1971, pp. 44–68.

11. K. R. Athey, 'Two Experiments Showing the Effects of the Interviewer's Racial Background in Response to Questionnaires Concerning Racial Issues', *Journal of Applied Psychology*, 44, 1960, pp. 244–6; G. F. Summers and A. D. Hammonds, 'Effects of Racial Characteristics of Investigator on Self-Enumerated Responses to a Negro Prejudice Scale', *Social Forces*, 44, 1966, pp. 515–18.

12. M. Benney, D. Riesman and S. A. Star, 'Age and Sex in the Interview', *American Journal of Sociology*, 62, 1956, pp. 143–52.

13. See Phillips, *Knowledge from What?*, for a review of many of these findings; and his *Abandoning Method*, Jossey-Bass, San Francisco, 1973.

14. M. J. Shapiro, 'Discerning Interviewer Bias in Open-Ended Survey Responses', *Public Opinion Quarterly*, 34, 1970, pp. 412–15.

15. P. Taietz, 'Conflicting Group Norms and the "Third" Person in the Interview', *American Journal of Sociology*, 68, 1962, pp. 97–104.

16. D. Crowne and D. Marlow, *The Approval Motive*, John Wiley & Sons, New York, 1964.

17. A. Couch and K. Kenniston, 'Yeasayers and Naysayers: Agreeing Response Set as a Personality Variable', *Journal of Abnormal and Social Psychology*, 60, 1960, pp. 151–74; W. D. Wells found that 69 per cent of 'yeasayers' and only 18 per cent of 'naysayers' had made at least one unsubstantiated claim about possessing various popular magazines in their homes. 'How Chronic Over-Claimers Distort Survey Findings', *Journal of Advertising Research*, 3, 1963, pp. 8–18.

18. C. G. Bell and W. Buchanan, 'Reliable and Unreliable Respondents; Party Registration and Prestige Pressure', *Western Political Quarterly*,

29, 1966, pp. 37–43; D. Cahalan, 'Correlates of Respondent Accuracy in the Denver Validity Study', *Public Opinion Quarterly*, 32, 1968, pp. 607–21; L. W. Green, 'East Pakistan: Knowledge and Use of Contraceptives', *Studies in Family Planning*, 39, 1969, pp. 9–14; J. P. Clark and L. Tifft, 'Polygraph and Interview Validation of Self-Reported Deviant Behaviour', *American Sociological Review*, 31, 1966, pp. 516–23.

19. As in most sociological research, there is an ethical dimension to this. Most professional sociological associations have a code of conduct to govern field research.

20. Converse and Schuman indicate that current advice to interviewers at the Institute of Social Research, Michigan, lays less stress on 'rapport' and more on an impersonal, professional approach. See J. M. Converse and H. Schuman, *Conversations at Random*, John Wiley & Sons, New York, 1974, p. 94 n. 25.

21. Of course, each interview is a unique experience, and no matter how good a training the interviewer has received, particular problems will always crop up which need to be faced and solved in the interview situation. Converse and Schuman in *Conversations at Random* relate a story I particularly like about one such problem faced by a student interviewer who wrote in response to his experience, 'You sit in a lady's living room, look through cracked, broken-out windows at blocks and blocks of gutted "has-been" homes. You walk across a sagging, creaking floor and look into narrow eyes peering at you beneath a dresser . . . a child. Now you, ask the big question in the neighbourhood problem section, "Have you had any trouble because of neighbours not keeping up their property?"'

22. See, e.g., R. Rommelweit and J. Israel, 'Notes on the Standardization of Experimental Manipulations and Measurements in Cross-National Research', *Journal of Social Issues*, 10, 1954, pp. 61–8; S. Ervin and R. T. Bower, 'Translation Problems in International Surveys', *Public Opinion Quarterly*, 16, 1952, pp. 595–604.

23. R. E. Mitchell, 'Survey Materials Collected in the Developing Countries: Sampling, Measurement, and Interviewing Obstacles in Intra- and International Comparisons', *International Social Science Journal*, 17, 1965.

24. Converse and Schuman, *Conversations at Random*, p. 17.

25. E. Scheuch, 'The Cross-Cultural Use of Sample Surveys: Problems of Comparability', in S. Rokkan (ed.), *Comparative Research Across Cultures and Nations*, Mouton, Paris, 1968. The original Almond and Verba study is *The Civic Culture*, Little, Brown, New York, 1965.

26. I. Deutscher, 'Asking Questions Cross-Culturally: Some Problems of Linguistic Comparability', in H. Becker *et al.* (eds.), *Institutions and the Person*, Aldine, Chicago, 1968, pp. 318–41.

27. ibid.

28. C. Wright Mills, 'Language, Logic and Culture', in I. Horowitz (ed.), *Power, Politics and People*, Oxford University Press, New York, 1963, p. 433.

29. See R. M. Marsh, *Comparative Sociology*, Harcourt, Brace & World, New York, 1967; E. Sapir, 'Conceptual Categories in Primitive Languages', *Science*, 74, 1931; B. Whorf, *Collected Papers in Metalinguistics*, Department of State, Foreign Service Institute, Washington, 1952.

30. See H. P. Phillips, 'Problems of Translation and Meaning in Field Work', *Human Organization*, 17, 1960, pp. 184–92.

31. Benney and Hughes, 'Of Sociology and the Interview', loc. cit.

32. ibid.; see also T. Caplow, 'The Dynamics of Information Interviewing', *American Journal of Sociology*, 62, 1956, pp. 167–71.

33. Galtung, *Theory and Methods of Social Research*, p. 123.

34. Benney and Hughes, 'Of Sociology and the Interview', loc. cit.

35. Deutscher, 'Asking Questions Cross-Culturally', loc cit.: 'There are . . . cultural differences in both those things people are able to talk about and those things they are willing to talk about.'

36. Such indirect methods include projective techniques such as 'ink-blot tests' and sentence or story completion methods.

37. The theory of attitudes has a long and formidable research history. A good text book account is P. F. Secord and C. W. Backman, *Social Psychology*, McGraw-Hill, New York, 1964. On attitude measurement, see B. F. Green, 'Attitude Measurement', in Lindzey (ed.), *Handbook of Social Psychology*, pp. 335–469; H. S. Upshaw, 'Attitude Measurement', in H. M. Blalock and A. Blalock (eds.), *Methodology in Social Research*, McGraw-Hill, New York, 1968; and A. L. Edwards, *Techniques of Attitude Scale Construction*, Appleton-Century-Crofts, New York, 1957.

38. See, e.g., C. M. Bonjean *et al.*, *Sociological Measurement: An Inventory of Scales and Indices*, Chandler, San Francisco, 1969.

39. Galtung, *Theory and Methods of Social Research*, p. 124.

40. R. T. La Piere, 'Attitudes versus Actions', *Social Forces*, 13, 1934, pp. 230–37. Various devices were employed to control for previous visits by sending similar questions to establishments not visited by the researchers. The distribution of replies was the same in each case. Other relevant material in L. S. Linn, 'Verbal Attitudes and Overt Behaviour: A Study of Racial Discrimination', *Social Forces*,

43, 1965, pp. 353–64; C. R. Tittle and R. J. Hill, 'Attitude Measurement and the Prediction of Behaviour: An Evaluation of Conditions and Measurement Techniques', *Sociometry*, 30, 1967, pp. 199–213; and R. Brannon *et al.*, 'Attitudes and Action: A Field Experiment Joined to a General Population Survey', *American Sociological Review*, 38, 1973.

41.   Deutscher, 'Asking Questions Cross-Culturally', loc. cit.

42.   Earlier, of course, psychoanalytic theories had suggested in the strongest terms that people repress some feelings, emotions and experiences into the subconscious with the result that they are unable to verbalize them in 'normal' ways.

43.   Example from Deutscher, 'Asking Questions Cross-Culturally', loc. cit.

44.   See the important developments represented in D. Sudnow (ed.), *Studies in Social Interaction*, The Free Press, New York, 1972.

45.   R. Anderson, 'On the Comparability of Meaningful Stimuli in Cross-Cultural Research', *Sociometry*, 30, 1967, pp. 124–36.

46.   A. Cicourel, *Method and Measurement in Sociology*, The Free Press, New York, 1964, p. 175; and his *Theory and Method in a Study of Argentine Fertility*, John Wiley & Sons, New York, 1974, is an extended study of the interview.

7
The Survey and Multivariate Analysis

In conjunction with verbal methods, the survey is possibly the most widely used research design in sociology. Though it is used in a number of other social sciences, few have embraced it so enthusiastically. The history of the survey goes back to the early censuses of the nineteenth century. Booth's surveys of the London poor and Le Play's study of income and expenditure in France were among the most important precursors of the modern survey method.[1] More recent developments have been influenced by the invention of high-speed data-processing machines, public-opinion polling and other market-research techniques, and important innovations in probability-sampling theory. This chapter is mainly concerned with the survey as a research process together with some typical procedures of analysis and their implications for sociological theory. Since most surveys also make use of questionnaires and/or interviews, many of the points already discussed in Chapter 6 should be born in mind throughout what follows.

Types of Survey

A survey is a systematic collection of standardized information from a sample chosen to represent a predefined universe or population for the purpose of analysing relationships between variables.[2] More simply, a survey is a research process which tries to provide knowledge about a defined group or aggregate—for example, voters, the homeless, the middle class, manual workers, women, married women—usually by selecting a sample to represent the whole. The universe or population is itself defined by the research interest and is not necessarily to be equated with the population of a town, city or other geographical region. Thus, 'all women of marriageable age', 'all people of voting age', 'all delinquents in Lancaster', could all be populations in this sense. The primary data produced by the survey is generally of the form talked about in Chapter 6, namely, respondents' answers to various questions about themselves or others, about their attitudes, and about their relationships. Surveys are also conducted to gather information about the physical environment—about, say, housing conditions, and so on.

Surveys fall into two major types: the descriptive and the analytical.[3] The former, as the name implies, is used in cases where description of the distribution of a phenomenon is required; the latter where explanation rather than sheer description is the aim. The focus of the descriptive survey is 'essentially precise measurement of one or more dependent variables in some defined population or sample of that population'.[4] One of the most familiar of descriptive surveys is the census, in which information is sought on the distribution of such items as births, deaths, housing conditions or incomes. The major purpose of such a survey is to obtain an accurate statement of the frequency of a phenomenon: how many members of a population have a particular characteristic, or how often certain events occur, and such like. Since accurate enumeration of the population is the aim, good representative sampling is critical.

The analytic or explanatory survey follows, in many respects, the logic of experimental design by trying to sort out relationships between variables, except that the manipulation of these variables is achieved through the design of the survey itself, or by tabular and statistical manipulation of the survey data. This type of survey is less orientated to traditional representativeness, and more towards the selection of a sample which will be appropriate for the testing of specific hypotheses. The mode of analysis used in the analytic survey is a set of techniques known as 'multivariate analysis', which involves measuring a relationship between an independent and a dependent variable, and then introducing an additional variable as a test factor to see if this makes any difference to the original relationship.

Indicators

One of the major initial requirements before undertaking any survey, descriptive or explanatory, is a clear conceptualization of the phenomena to be surveyed. If the survey is descriptive, it is important to know what is being counted; and if the survey is analytical, then a precise determination of any relationship depends upon a clear and unambiguous delineation of the variables. This process usually begins by the researcher fully explicating the phenomena he wishes to survey. This is often not as easy as might be supposed. Kinsey, for example, in his study of sexual behaviour, required the rather surprising total of about 300 items to cover the domain of this activity adequately.[5] Empirical indicators must cover as many aspects or dimensions of a concept as possible. In many cases, especially in sociology, difficulties will arise because of loose usage, ambiguity and genuinely varying reference and meaning.

Translating concepts into empirical indicators often requires considerable ingenuity. The general issues here can be illustrated as follows. Suppose a researcher is interested in political activism and wants to discover social factors associated with this category of behaviour. Any indicator of this dependent variable needs to be precisely and unambiguously enough defined for the researcher to decide whether or not any act is classifiable as political activism.[7] What are the options open as empirical indicators for this concept? What does political activism involve? Is it a matter of being wholeheartedly committed to a party programme, or is it something slightly different—say, a heightened degree of interest and knowledge about politics in general? All these kinds of question are relevant to the choice of measures. In many cases, especially with concepts like political activism, the researcher will probably quickly reach the conclusion that it is a complex notion better measured by a number of indicators. But notice what this process involves. Explicating a concept and selecting appropriate indicators is rather like sketching out a theory about the nature of the subject in question. With political activism, the researcher might regard purely behavioural indices as adequate measures—such things as contributing to party funds, helping with campaigns, addressing envelopes, regularly reading party literature and so on—on the supposition that people would not expend this amount of energy and resources unless they had a positive psychological commitment to and interest in politics. So, the validity of the behavioural indices of political activism depends upon the truth of the underlying theory which links psychological commitment to particular courses of action.

Alternative theories might, of course, lead to the selection of different indicators. A good parallel example occurs in some researches on religious commitment in which certain ambiguous, even contradictory, findings pointed to a weakness in the measures of religious commitment and the validity of the theories underpinning them. One piece of research found that high-status people were more religious, on the whole, than low-status persons; but other research found the reverse to be true. Part of this apparent contradiction was caused by the fact that different indicators of religiosity had been used in the different studies: the former result relied on behavioural indices, the latter on attitudinal or belief measures. In other words, the latter indices had been based on the argument that religious commitment need not necessarily be associated with conventional religious behaviour such as attendance at church.[8] These problems of definition can, however, be theoretically fruitful: in this particular case, it led to a refinement of the notion of religiosity and the theories involved. Religiosity came to be regarded as a multi-dimensional phenomenon which had to be measured accordingly. Where political activism is concerned, it might be argued that purely behavioural indices, as with religiosity, are not enough, but that attitudinal, cognitive and affective indices are also required. On the other hand, it could be maintained that politics is of a different order from religion and that behavioural indices are, for all intents and purposes, adequate. There is no simple way of making a choice, except within the context of the theoretical ideas which justify the link between concept and indicator. In any event, as we saw in the case of religiosity, making such links clear may result in the development of theory and a step forward in sociological analysis.

Nonetheless, given the frequent necessity for multiple indicators of a phenomenon, the practical problems arising from their use are often dealt with by a range of formal and quasi-formal procedures. These methods—and they are not limited to survey research situations— normally involve evaluating raw data in terms of some measurement model which thereby places a structure on to the data, enabling the researcher to choose indices according to the assumptions contained in the model. None of these methods can be used independently of the first phase of index construction just outlined, namely of conceptualizing a phenomenon and developing precise theoretical imagery. However, once a researcher has chosen his operational measures, the methods offer ways of evaluating the indices which have been chosen according the particular criteria. Most are predicated on the idea that, at the present state of the research game, it is unlikely that any one index will prove to be a satisfactory measure of a complex concept. Therefore some method of combining several operational measures into a meaningful pattern is needed: a pattern which is a product of the phenomena being measured, and accordingly an indicator of it. For example, suppose that in a survey of political behaviour a researcher was concerned to delineate political activists. One way of detecting this group is by classifying as activists all those who respond affirmatively to the question, 'Are you a member of a political party?' Although this might be suitable for some purposes, it could be criticized on the grounds that the notion of activism involves more than membership alone. Holding a membership card may indicate a wide range of behaviours, from simply being a formal member to being highly involved in all party organizational activities. So, on the questionnaire, the investigator might ask more questions directly related to the kind of political activity in which the respondent might be involved, such as attending meetings regularly or being committed to certain beliefs. Unfortunately, while several indicators would intuitively seem better than one, this is not much help unless we can show how the separate indicators are related to reflect the property being measured. To do this, certain assumptions must be made about the property's nature. Thus, we might begin by regarding political activism as an ordinal property so that people can be classified according to whether they were more or less politically active. This means examining the data to see if the operational measures we have chosen display ordinality. More formally, we have to see whether the items referring to political activism, I_1, I_2, I_3, I_4, . . . I_n, satisfy the requirements of an ordinal scale, so that if a person endorsed I_3 he would also endorse I_1 and I_2, but not necessarily those items 'higher' in the scale where the subscripts indicate the order of items from the 'lowest' to the 'highest'. So, assuming these conditions to apply with our items about political activism, if a respondent said he was an official in a party, we would know also that he attended meetings regularly, gave contributions to funds, and all the other activities which could be regarded as 'less' active than holding an official position. If we went further than this, and mapped the items on to an ordinal number system so that the most active, according to our conception, received the highest score, we would have a scale of political activism. This would mean that, assuming the data satisfied the model, we could predict from the score, which items had been endorsed; all of which gives some credence to our belief that we are measuring, with our items, an ordinal property.[9]

The model just outlined can be used to determine whether a set of items—not necessarily questionnaire items—satisfy a particular structure, in this case a partial ordering. It can also be used to decide which indices are 'good' or 'bad', which seem to be measuring the same underlying property and which do not. There are other and more sophisticated models that, in principle, do much the same job as the one discussed, though some may be more applicable to certain kinds of problems than others.[10]

However, while methods such as these are useful for assessing the validity of indices after the data has been collected, the initial problem at the beginning of a survey is to have a clear conceptualization of the phenomenon to be surveyed. This is especially important if the survey is to be a *sample* survey—as by far the majority of surveys are.

Sampling

The purpose of sampling theory is to offer a basis upon which generalizations can be made from a sample to some population or universe. Sampling, as we have seen, consists of obtaining information from a portion of a larger group about the whole. Since the study of an entire universe of cases is seldom practicable, the researcher is often driven to studying only a selection. For him to generalize validly to the universe, the cases must be selected in accordance with certain principles that justify the generalization, namely, the principles of sampling. Fundamental to the idea of generalizing from a sample of cases to a population is the concept of random selection. By random selection, we mean that each element of the total population, however this is defined, has a known probability of being selected for the sample. If random sampling procedures are followed, the sample, it is argued, may be used to support inferences about the population with some precision.

Suppose that a researcher wanted to predict the outcome of a particular election. Assume that the electorate consisted of 250,000 persons, and that of these 47 per cent planned to vote for the Labour candidate, 38 per cent for the Conservative, the remainder being either 'don't knows' or 'abstainers'. The problem for the investigator, given that he cannot survey everyone, is to select a sample that does not over-represent voters from one party rather than another, but which reflects the distribution of voting choices within the population. If, for example, his sample happened to contain all Labour voters, this would not enable him to predict the election with accuracy—to say the least! Therefore he needs to select the sample in such a way that the sample values will be a good estimate (with a known degree of likelihood) of the population values. For this he needs to select his cases randomly. According to probability theory, if successive samples of the same size are taken from a known universe, the sample values will differ between samples. However, if the sample size is increased, the sample values will approximate more and more closely to those of the population. We know, for example, that if a coin is tossed 10 times on successive occasions, sometimes we would get 5 heads and 5 tails, sometimes 9 heads and 1 tail, sometimes 4 heads and 6 tails, and so on. But, if the coin is tossed 100 times instead of 10, the relative frequency of heads and tails would be closer to 50/50, or what we would expect by chance alone using a perfect coin. Similarly, then, in our hypothetical population of 47 per cent Labour voters, 38 per cent Conservative voters, and the rest 'don't know' or non-voters, a sample of 10 will, in all probability, result in the over-representation of one or the other of these groups. Fortunately, the larger the sample, assuming it has been selected randomly, the more likely it is to give sample proportions closer to those existing in the total population. There is nothing certain about this; it is simply that the larger the sample, the higher the probability is that it will yield more accurate estimates of the total population values. This *ceteris paribus* clause is important, because random sampling cannot remove all sources of bias. Bias can still enter, both at the initial-design stage and at the data-collection stage. Nevertheless, for present purposes we can assume that, as sample size increases, so chance variation from the selection of an unrepresentative sample will be reduced. However, it is important to note that, after a certain sample size, efficiency declines in relative terms; that is, after a certain point, increasing the size of the sample gives only a marginal gain in accuracy. So the researchers' problem is to select a sample size which maximizes efficiency with regard to available resources and the degree of accuracy he requires.

Sampling Methods

These are the main points about the purpose and use of random sampling. In practice, there are three major sampling methods: (a) simple random sampling, (b) stratified sampling and (c) cluster sampling.[11] *Simple random sampling* is, as the name suggests, a random sample of cases from a listing. Normally the researcher lists the universe of cases (individuals, firms, communities or whatever), and using a table of random numbers, selects sufficient units to constitute the sample required.

Unfortunately, simple random sampling will occasionally give lopsided samples, and while the risk is small, *stratified sampling* is designed to preclude this risk. In this method, the universe is first of all divided into strata, each of which is homogeneous with respect to some characteristic. Each of these strata are then randomly sampled according to their proportion in the population. Thus, if a researcher felt that 'sex' was crucial to his hypothesis, he might first determine the proportion of males and females in the universe, then sample within these strata according to this proportion. So, if there is a ratio of males to females of 2 : 1, he will randomly sample from the two strata, preserving this ratio in the sample. This method can increase the representativeness of samples of a given size by ensuring that enough cases are drawn from all elements in the population. Stratification, if done with reasonable care to obtain homogeneous strata, will nearly always result in a more precise estimate of the total population values than will a simple random sample.

Cluster sampling is a method in which groupings, or clusters, of units to be sampled are first selected by a probability sample. In the case of a researcher trying to predict the outcome of an election, instead of drawing up a list of all the electorate (which could be expensive), he might divide the constituency into areas and sample the areas (first-stage cluster sampling); and then, within each cluster selected, sample the individuals (second-stage cluster sample). Cluster sampling is useful in its saving of time and money, but carries a danger of misrepresentation unless the initial clustering is based upon a sound knowledge of the total population in terms of the geographical distribution of such major variables as age, sex or occupational status. Thus, if cluster sampling a city, it would be sensible to make sure that the areas are representative of the usual variables considered important to political and social behaviour.[12] While cluster sampling is less precise than random sampling, its use is generally dictated by cost and administrative convenience. In resource terms, it tends to be more efficient than random sampling. Cluster sampling tends to reduce the resource cost per respondent so that an increase in sample size can often achieve greater precision than a simple random sample of the same overall resource cost.

An incidental sampling procedure that ought to be mentioned is *quota sampling*, a non-random method in which the interviewer is given a list of certain types of individuals, of whom he must interview a certain number. This procedure is, in fact, mostly used in public-opinion polling, but because the selection of cases is not based on any random sampling procedure, no significance tests can be applied to determine the accuracy of the sample results.

G

These, then, are the basic sampling methods, and the choice of any of them for any particular research project will need to be considered carefully. One of the more important issues which a researcher must resolve is whether he is primarily interested in representativeness, the analysis of variables, or both, since samples selected for descriptive surveys are not always satisfactory from the point of view of analytic surveys, and vice versa. As already mentioned, to secure a representative sample the investigator needs a clear definition of the conceptual universe, a firm statement of the empirical frame of the universe, and a random sampling procedure. This implies a fairly definite and definable universe of concern, such as 'all TV owners', 'all the voters in Bradford', 'the population of delinquents from the University of Lancaster in the last six years'. What are difficult to sample are universes of very general concern, or which are too vague to define with any firm boundary. Suppose a researcher wanted to sample all societies, how could he do this? If he sampled all known societies, the criticism could be levelled that this is not representative of all societies since the distinction itself between 'known' and 'unknown' is a biasing factor; a product of processes of temporal recording which are not random processes. Indeed, the testing of general hypotheses—'All X's are Y's'—is better achieved by procedures which select cases in such a way as to obtain the appropriate combination of variable values.[13] This sort of sampling is often referred to as 'focused sampling', in which the researcher selects cases so as to concentrate on variables in which he is interested, and it is often married to principles of experimental design. As was discussed in Chapter 4 on experiments (pages 87–8), random sampling procedures often enter at some stage. However, one possible difficulty is that such samples may conflict with the ideals of representativeness, so making it statistically difficult to justify generalization of the findings to some universe, even if this is known.

Apart from the issue of representativeness *versus* analysis, another vitally important issue relevant to the kind of sociological theories generated from survey data is the choice of units. Most surveys sample individuals and then proceed to collect verbal responses from the sample. Thus, not only may individualism be implied in the use of questionnaires or interviews (only individuals can respond to questionnaires), it may also be implied in the sampling procedure itself, which, more often than not, samples individuals. This means that the surveyor may well have failed to sample the groups and processes of which the separate individuals are a part.[14] Accordingly, though it may be easy to make statements, on the basis of survey findings, such as, 'X per cent of the sample held opinion (or attitude, or property) Y', the relevance of this in terms of some notion of social structure or social system could be hard to determine. To give a simple example, suppose we wanted to assess the effect of public attitudes towards divorce in influencing changes in the law relating to the dissolution of marriage. Taking a poll of the general public over the years, and correlating any changes in public opinion with changes in the law, would hardly be satisfactory, for the relationship between public opinion and changes in the law is part of a complex social process involving interactions between the general public, Members of Parliament, government advisers, members of the legal profession, moral pressure groups, churches and so on. The problem is that the logic of the survey implies that every unit is equal to every other unit. Thus, when counting and then asserting that X per cent of a sample have property Y, we are treating each unit as equal to each other unit: one of the basic principles of measurement. But, in most images of society, there is the presumption that individuals are differentially located in a social domain with hierarchical and structural dimensions. So, in the above example, it matters who holds a particular opinion and where that person is (or those persons are) located in the social and political decision-making process. (This problem is roughly equivalent to that noted in Chapter 6 on the interview, in that the person answering a questionnaire is also located in every-day social processes and situations which might well affect his responses. In other words, the interview too often regards itself as a sterile context, independent of the social process.)

Moreover, the very structure of society may well have a bearing on those available for sampling purposes. According to Galtung, surveys tend to be carried out among the 'social centre' at the expense of the 'periphery': 'The illiterates, the aged, the non-participants, the destitute, the vagabonds, the geographically isolated periphery, etc.'[15] Those who constitute the 'social centre' are more likely to be listable for sampling purposes, more likely to be able and available to answer questionnaires, more likely to be used to the relatively easy and commonplace relationship of the interviewer and respondent, and so on. Less easy as sample targets are those who lack the social skills or resources, even willingness (and this includes the élite members of a society) to answer survey questionnaires.

In the light of all this it might be argued that sociologists have perhaps concentrated too much on random sampling methods, with their attendant constraints. To sample randomly implies that a list can be made (at least in principle) of all the members of a population, for, unless the researcher can say how any one member of a population can be found, it cannot be assumed that every member of that population has an equal chance of being included in the sample.[16] This requirement is essential to random sampling, and yet unlistable populations are more common than is realized. Convenient lists such as street directories, electoral registers, telephone directories or whatever, though they are listings of *some* population, are not always adequate listings of populations of *sociological* concern. In the case of many research questions, the population at issue is often impossible to list with any completeness. How, for example, would we list the populations of deviants, of paranoids, of conformists, of the alienated, and so on? The choices facing the researcher (apart from abandoning empirical research) are difficult. One common tactic is to redefine judiciously the research population to one that is listable, so running the risk of making the sample injudicious from the point of sociological theory. In many cases, arbitrary samples, with their attendant risks of non-randomness, are the only alternatives. Nonetheless, such samples can be immensely fruitful in examining interesting theoretical relationships among particular variables.

The lesson to be learnt from this is the necessity for a careful consideration of the social unit to be sampled, given the nature of the research problem, and whether description or analysis is the aim of the survey. The use of the survey method and the random selection of individuals may well involve 'democratic' and 'individualistic' assumptions inappropriate to the theoretical model in which the researcher is interested. A simple counting of how many individuals intend to vote for which party could be useful for predicting the outcome of an election, since, broadly speaking, 1 man = 1 vote: a presumption of both the electoral process and the counting procedures normally employed in surveys of this type. However, it will tell us little about the operation of political power through the social process. For these sorts of question, it is necessary to select samples more in accord with the image of the social processes that we have in mind. This would require more purposive sampling by, for example, sampling individuals according to social position, membership of influential groups, degrees of political power, or sample situations of a certain sort, or whatever the theoretical model would require.

Multivariate Analysis

Despite its limitations, there is little doubt that one of the very real achievements of the survey method has been the large amount of quantifiable data which it has provided over an exceedingly wide range of subject matter, and often with reference to very large aggregates of people.[17] As said earlier, it is not merely simple counting statements of the form, 'X per cent of sample S have property P', that may be made on the evidence of survey results, important as these are; but also that the data can often be used to quantitative expression to relationships between two or more variables. Figure 13 is a representation of the basic idea used in the analysis of

Variable Y

	Y	Not Y	Marginal
X	a	b	a + b
Not X	c	d	c + d
Marginal	a + c	b + d·	N = a + b + c + d

Variable X

Figure 13. Basic unit of analysis of survey data : the contingency table.

relationships. Any individual unit (a person, an event, a group or whatever) is locatable in terms of the coordinates defining values of the variables X and Y. These could be any variable property, such as scores on an attitude scale, membership of a particular group or possessing some social property. Such a device is termed a 'property space'.[18] The dimensions used to locate any unit in such a property space can be of many kinds. The simplest kind—shown here—is the dichotomous attribute, such as voter/non-voter, male/female, white/non-white, Labour/Conservative. On other occasions, the attributes may be rank-ordered according to whether, for example, political interest is 'high', 'medium' or 'low'. More rarely, as far as sociology is concerned, the attribute may be continuous, having a zero point and equal intervals, as is the case with age, income or size of community. In all cases, rank-ordered and continuous variables can be reduced to simple dichotomies. Thus, an age distribution can be dichotomized on the basis of some appropriate point, such as 'over 21/under 21', or 'below average age/above average age'. Whether or not this is necessary with any particular research data depends upon the quality of the data and what the researcher wants to ask of it. In any event, the logic of the analysis is much the same.

The simplest way to use data presented in this way is inspection of the marginal totals. These show how many of the units counted do or do not possess a particular attribute. If the sample were randomly drawn, it would also, within certain limits, tell the researcher about the distribution of the attribute within the total population from which the sample was drawn. Analysis begins when the values in the other cells are used. In questionnaire terms, this would be when the answers to one question were related to answers to another; an analysis represented in its simplest form in Figure 13. Setting out data in this way means that the joint distribution of attributes, whether these be answers to items on a questionnaire or other properties in which the investigator is interested, can be examined. Figure 14 is a two-way table setting out a hypothetical relationship between race and propensity to vote. Inspection of the cells of the cross-tabulation gives the frequencies with which certain categories derived from the variables concerned

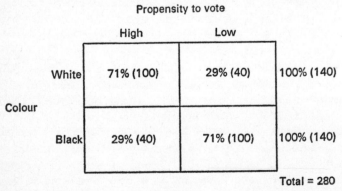

Figure 14. Hypothetical relationship between colour and propensity to vote.

occur: white and high propensity to vote; white and low propensity to vote; black and high propensity to vote; and, finally, black and low propensity to vote. This adds to the information contained in the marginals, not only by reporting how many white or how many blacks there are, or merely how many people have a high or a low propensity to vote, but also how many there are of each combination of the two variables. In terms of theory building and testing, this is a considerable advance, for the structure of data arranged in this way can be used to reflect the structure of some of a theory's propositions which state empirical relationships between attributes. The researcher can go on to measure the strength of the relationship, using appropriate measures of association.[19]

The basic structure just outlined is used, with the inevitable complications, for one of the major analytic procedures used in examining survey data, 'the study and interpretation of complex interrelations among a multiplicity of characteristics', or *multivariate analysis*.[20] The idea is to introduce into the basic two variable crosstabulation a third variable to elaborate and elucidate the original one. The association between race and propensity to vote is shown, using hypothetical data, in Figure 14. However, it is more than likely that the researcher will be aware of other variables connected to the two just been considered, perhaps between colour and level of education, between education and propensity to vote. He may know that whites have usually received more education than blacks and that more educated people have a higher propensity to vote. Therefore may not the original relationship found between colour and propensity to vote be a result of the greater level of education among whites and have little to do with racial or ethnic characteristics? In other words, the researcher begins to interpret the original relationship that he discovered in his effort to discover the causes of the variations he has found in the dependent variable.

The effects of introducing a third variable are illustrated in Figure 15. What this shows is that within groups consisting of individuals with the same level of education, colour is still a factor associated with the dependent variable, the propensity to vote, but not in a simple way. By exploiting this procedure with other possible variables, some idea of their causal priority and the interactions among them can be made. In an important way, it is a process discussed before, namely, testing out alternative theories and seeking those which explain most of the variance in the dependent variable. It is also important to note that one of these theories will be that the relationship is spurious, that it is due to the opera-

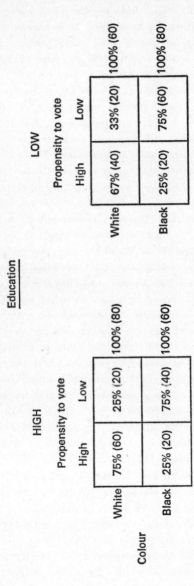

Figure 15. Hypothetical relationship between colour, propensity to vote, controlling level of education.

tion of some other factor, or factors, which determines both of the variables used in the original relationship.[21]

The above is a relatively simple statement of the idea of multivariate analysis. However, there are one or two points of interpretation which need to be considered.

The importance of multivariate analysis lies in its usefulness for explicating theoretically relevant relationships within data. A theory might predict, for example, a relationship between two variables, and yet, in a survey situation unlike in an experiment, it will be difficult to isolate these variables from the effects of others in the situation. Accordingly, to rule out alternative theories and confounding factors, other methods, such as multivariate analysis, must be employed.[22] Since the survey researcher is not working in an experimental situation, he may not be able to control for possible other factors, and there is a limit to which statistical controls can take account of every potential confounding factor, even assuming that relevant data is available. Though the advent of high-speed data-processing machines, such as computers, enables the researcher to search many, many possible relationships in his data, he normally proceeds on hunches derived from the theoretical models which inform the research. We must bear in mind also that the choice of which variable is dependent and which is independent is suggested by the theoretical model and not by the data itself.

The specification of relationships has been at the centre of survey analysts' attention for a long time, not only as a descriptive tool, but also as a device of considerable analytic and theoretical potential. For one thing, it is a procedure enabling the researcher to examine the conditions under which a relationship applies, or does not apply, or, if so, in what degree, so increasing the fineness of the study and enriching the theory based upon it.[23] Further developments of the techniques include attempts to link multivariate analysis with some formal and systematic notions of causation by setting up a series of multivariate regression equations as a formal model to be tested against available data. (These are discussed in Chapter 4.)

Powerful as multivariate techniques might be, their theoretical relevance cannot be decided by technique alone. Although the survey and its associated methods do offer opportunities to gather masses of quantitative information about large aggregates of people, the theoretical import of such data is not always obvious or universally acclaimed. Mention has already been made of the democratic and individualistic bias of many survey designs in that they fail to give due weight to theoretical models involving notions of structure. Other more fundamental objections are to be found in the criticism, simply stated, that survey design and analysis 'seeks to reduce human group life to variables and their relations'.[24]

Critiques of Variable Analysis

In detail, this objection involves an attack by the more humanistic tradition of sociology on the positivistic presuppositions of the survey method. It is rather more than a metaphysical sally, however, since it does involve detailed and serious methodological issues. Although the survey offers an opportunity to the researcher to analyse a large number of variables, there is little in the way of rules or guides to govern which variables are important. Instead, 'variables may be selected on the basis of a specious impression of what is important, on the basis of conventional usage, on the basis of what can be secured through a given instrument or technique, on the basis of the demands of some doctrine, or on the basis of an imaginative ingenuity in devising a new term'.[25] Undoubtedly such practices are to be found among survey researchers (since they are human and hence not perfect), but the crux of the objection is that 'variable analysis' does not take seriously enough the interpretative features of social life, and that it is too often used without careful or thorough knowledge of the sociological phenomena to be examined.

To illustrate this point, let us suppose that the relationship between colour and propensity to vote had been explicated as fully as possible and still left us with colour as an independent variable exerting an effect on the dependent variable, the propensity to vote. How is this to be explained? What is it about the variable 'colour' that accounts for the lower propensity to vote? Is it biologically rooted, or has it to do with the role expectations attaching to different coloured people within our culture? Is it a matter of socialization, blacks being socialized to take less interest in public affairs and regarding them as a white preserve? What, sociologically, does 'colour' stand for which can account for the variation in the propensity to vote? If the analyst has any sense, he will already have some ideas about these questions prior to the design and execution of the survey, and assuming that data is available, will have checked out as many alternative explanations as possible through the elaboration procedures. But, while variables such as 'colour' may appear simple and unitary in sociological contexts, they are also extremely complex. 'Black' and 'white' stand for an almost incredible variety of phenomena, sets of role expectations, personal resources, world outlooks, different cultural goals, and so on, and to understand how these work to establish the relationships discovered by variable analysis, we need to understand the 'process of definition intervening between the events of experience presupposed by the independent variable and the formed behaviour represented by the dependent variable'.[26]

There are really two related criticisms. The first is that variable analysis, largely because of its quantitative nature, requires variables to be defined precisely and unambiguously. Unfortunately, the argument runs, such precision is often spurious in that it is rarely reflected in the social reality being examined. The very coding procedures and question formats used in surveys serve to reduce the variety in individual responses to fairly clear-cut, firmly bounded categories necessary for variable analysis. Cicourel's study of interviewing shows how interviewers and coders reduced respondents' replies so as to produce consistency across respondents in ways which were normal but hardly warranted in the transcripts of the interviews. Instead, a consistency was established through the coders' own commonsense knowledge.[27] And this consistent picture owed more to the coders' practices than it did to the reality reputedly being studied. The second criticism is that variable analysis presupposes, but fails to take adequate account of, some sort of intervening medium, namely, the creative interpretative process in which human beings engage as an inescapable feature of their social lives. In short, 'the very features which give variable analysis its high merit—the qualitative constancy of the variables, their clean-cut simplicity, their ease of manipulation . . . their ability to be brought into decisive relation—are the features that lead variable analysis to gloss over the character of the real operating factors in group life. . .'.[28]

These criticisms begin to take on the appearance of a fundamental disagreement about the ontological and epistemological bases of sociology, a confrontation between opposed views about the nature of social reality and the means of obtaining knowledge of that reality. The survey and variable analysis are criticized for their inability to gather relevant knowledge about interpretative processes. This must be acquired by methods which allow the researcher to understand the definitions which people use as they use them in interactive situations: methods such as participant observation. To make sociological sense out of variable relationships within survey data, meanings have to be imputed to actors on the basis of very little knowledge of the meanings and interpretations used. This particular problem is compounded by the fact that the survey rarely deals with behaviour that is a response to a behaviour setting, but rather with behaviour elicited in response to stimuli within settings—the interview, for example, whose effects are intended to be neutralized or regarded as irrelevant to the responses to the stimuli.[29] This is an assumption already seriously questioned (pages 161–3).

Survey findings are nearly always 'after-the-fact' correlations or relationships to which the analyst must give some meaning. This meaning, naturally enough, is provided by some theory which structures the interpretation of the variable relationships. Unfortunately, most theories of relevance to survey data concepts—such as 'class', 'political beliefs', 'religion', 'associational activities'—which, when rendered into operational forms, owe their structure more to the exigencies of measurement than to the social realm in which social actors live and which the concepts are supposed to portray.[30] For example, the variable 'class', though measured in a variety of ways, is known to be correlated with many other variables used in sociological analysis. What is missing, however, is knowledge of how such a variable enters into actors' everyday worlds to produce the behaviour the concept is claimed to explain. Such links are largely imputed on the basis of the analyst's own commonsense knowledge, which he may or may not share with those under study.[31] So, quite apart from the survey's reliance on verbal methods, there are serious objections to the status of the knowledge produced by survey methods and variable analysis: objections which stem from different conceptions of the nature of sociology and its subject-matter. Although it is not necessary to regard such criticisms as constituting a wholesale condemnation of the survey method, they do point towards a weakness of the method, namely, that it fails, by and large, to provide knowledge of those processes which are needed to make sense out of the associations between variables, namely, actors' meanings.

Exercises

The major point to bear in mind as far as this exercise is concerned is not to be too ambitious in the scope of your survey. It is better to finish a small survey well within your resources of time, effort and personnel than to leave a large one frustratingly incomplete. A major survey requires a large supporting organization of interviewers, coders and data-processing facilities. If the institution in which you are studying has these, well and good; if not, cut your survey cloth to suit your resources coat. In any event, it is an obvious advantage if the class as a whole takes part in the survey.

It will, again, be an advantage to use the formal structured questionnaire you devised in connection with the exercise here. If, however, you decide to choose another topic of investigation, you will still have to construct a further questionnaire. The first major research decision you will have to make concerns the nature of your target population: who is to be surveyed, and, most importantly, why? Get your theoretical ideas as straight and clear as possible, and think about how your target group is relevant to testing out these ideas. Is your survey to be descriptive or analytic? This brings us to the next question for decision, namely, sampling procedure. Here the question of resources comes to the fore, especially with regard to sample size. Think about each of the methods of sampling discussed in the chapter and whether or not representativeness is important (as it is if your survey is descriptive), or whether you intend to aim for a sample which can illuminate relationships of theoretical interest. What are the consequences of this decision? Are convenient lists of your target population available? If not, are there other convenient ones—street and telephone directories, registers of voters, lists of organizational members, and so on— which might constitute a sampling frame? If no satisfactory list is available, what can you do? What are the implications of your decision?

When selecting a sample, fix on a sample size which you can handle. If there are only ten of you in the class to administer a three-page questionnaire spending an average of two hours a week on a methods course, a sample size of 750 is going to take a long, long time. In my experience, about ten respondents per interviewer per four-hour week is an approximate average, but clearly this will depend upon other factors to do with the availability of sample members, total sample size and type of questionnaire, and the travelling time between interviews. A self-administered questionnaire is often quicker, meaning that the same number of interviewers can handle more respondents in the same time, though this is often offset by the usually low response rate characteristic of such questionnaires. However, it may be that the possible bias by low response can be assessed in some way. So, although your sample may be smaller than desired, it is better to accept this than stretch your resources too far. One additional point to do with sample size: if you intend a descriptive survey about, say, housing conditions within one town, then representativeness is important. If, on the other hand, you intend an analytic survey, studying, say, the relationship between social class and student subject choice, then it is important for your sample to include enough cases which reflect the major variables you intend to use in your analysis. The reason for this is that the extent to which you can introduce interpreting factors in your multivariate cross-tabulations will depend upon the size of your sample, otherwise certain statistical measures and tests become inappropriate. Moreover, the smaller marginal frequencies are, the correspondingly greater will be the effect of any errors. A rough conventional guide is that you should aim at an *expected* frequency per cell of about twenty, although sometimes ten is just about allowable. Note, this does not mean the actual frequency you find in the cells, only the expected frequency once you have categorized the sample in terms of the major variables. So, in this case, it is a good idea to draw up a list of the major analyses you intend to see what kind and how many cases you will need.

Having decided all these and other questions of practical import, carry out your interviewing or deliver your questionnaires. Think about what you are going to do about any non-respondents.

When this stage is completed—and, take my word for it, the organizational problems of a survey, even a small one, are often horrendous; interviewers fail to fulfil their quota, some respondents are never in, questionnaires are lost, etc.—the next job is to code the responses. No doubt, when originally constructing the questionnaire or interview schedule, you will have devised codes for the responses. If you are going to process by machine, either card sorter or computer, see the relevant specialists for guidance. In fact, it is a better idea to see such people before finalizing your questionnaire. During the coding stage, it is more than likely that you will come across responses which are 'ambiguous' in terms of your coding scheme. You will have to decide whether or not to devise new codes, classify such responses as 'don't know' or 'no answer', or whether some agreement can be reached among the coders as to what such a response might mean. Devising new codes is often impracticable once most of the coding has already been done. In any case, whatever you do, reflect upon what it is you are doing and what knowledge about the subjects you are using as a resource to make sense out of the ambiguous response.

The final step is to analyse your data, using the logic of multivariate analysis to make it relevant to your theoretical problem. Make sure, before doing this, that you have mastered some simple mathematical and statistical tools, especially percentaging. Write up your report.

Now the problems begin when you start to think about the following kinds of question:

Contrast the kind of data produced by this method with that gathered by observational methods. What are the major differences? Do they involve different assumptions about the nature of sociology? Are the two different kinds of method complementary to one another, and, if so, when would you use each one?

Are the relationships discovered in your cross-tabular variable analysis complete, or is other knowledge not provided in the data necessary to make sense of them? If so, what is this knowledge and what are the consequences for sociological theory and analysis?

Are the principles of experimental design as embodied in the logic of multivariate analysis really applicable in this context?

What are the ultimate warrants or theories of instrumentation upon which the survey depends? Are they plausible?

Notes and References

1. For a history of survey research, see N. Glazer, 'The Rise of Social Research in Europe', in D. Lerner (ed.), *The Human Meaning of the Social Sciences*, Meridian Books, New York, 1959.

2. See C. Y. Glock (ed.), *Survey Research in the Social Sciences*, Russell Sage, New York, 1967, pp. 4–5.

3. This distinction is given in what is still perhaps the fullest treatment of survey methods, H. Hyman, *Survey Design and Analysis*, The Free Press, Glencoe, 1955, p. 66. See also A. N. Oppenheim, *Questionnaire Design and Attitude Measurement*, Heinemann, London, 1966, p. 7.

4. Hyman, *Survey Design and Analysis*, p. 68.

5. A. C. Kinsey and C. E. Martin, *Sexual Behaviour in the Human Male*, Sanders, Philadelphia, 1948. See also J. Madge, *The Origins of Scientific Sociology*, Tavistock Publications, London, 1963 for an excellent discussion of Kinsey's work.

6. See R. G. Dumont and W. J. Wilson, 'Aspects of Concept Formation, Explication, and Theory Construction in Sociology', *American Sociological Review*, 32, 1967, pp. 985–95.

7. An excellent practical guide to these and other problems of survey

research is J. A. Davis, *Elementary Survey Analysis*, Prentice-Hall, Englewood Cliffs, 1971.

8. N. J. Demerath, *Social Class and American Protestantism*, Rand McNally, Chicago, 1965.

9. The model outline is a truncated version of Guttman scaling. L. Guttman, 'The Basis of Scalogram Analysis', in S. Stouffer *et al.*, *Measurement and Prediction*, Princeton University Press, Princeton, 1950, pp. 172–212. A clear exposition is to be found in A. L. Edwards, *Techniques of Attitude Scaling*, Appleton-Century-Crofts, New York, 1957. P. J. Runkel and J. E. McGrath, *Research in Human Behaviour*, Holt, Rinehart & Winston, New York, 1972, contains discussion of more elaborate models.

10. Many of the models are too complex to summarize here. Two texts of use are D. Child, *The Essentials of Factor Analysis*, Holt, Rinehart & Winston, London, 1970; and B. Everitt, *Cluster Analysis*, Heinemann, London, 1974.

11. One of the best texts on sampling is L. Kish, *Survey Sampling*, John Wiley & Sons, New York, 1965. Also useful is F. Conway, *Sampling*, Allen & Unwin, London, 1967.

12. See E. Shevky and W. Bell, *Social Area Analysis*, Stanford University Press, Stanford, 1955, for a theory and technique to characterize the social areas within cities. This kind of analysis could be useful for selecting appropriate areas for clustering.

13. S. F. Camilleri, 'Theory, Probability and Induction in Social Research', *American Sociological Review*, 27, 1962, pp. 170–78.

14. J. Galtung, *Theory and Methods of Social Research*, Allen & Unwin, London, 1967, p. 150.

15. ibid., p. 154.

16. Runkel and McGrath, *Research in Human Behaviour*, pp. 133–8.

17. See Glock (ed.), *Survey Research in the Social Sciences*, for a review of many of these achievements.

18. A. H. Barton, 'The Concept of Property-Space in Social Research', in P. F. Lazarsfeld and M. Rosenberg (eds.), *The Language of Social Research*, The Free Press, New York, 1955, pp. 50–57.

19. For a much fuller and entertainingly written discussion, see Davis, *Elementary Survey Analysis*.

20. Lazarsfeld and Rosenberg (eds.), *The Language of Social Research*, p. 111. Other expositions include Davis, *Elementary Survey Analysis*; Hyman, *Survey Design and Analysis*. R. Boudon, *The Logic of Sociological Explanation*, Penguin Books, Harmondsworth, 1974, gives a much more sophisticated analysis of the logic of multivariate methods and their place in sociological explanation.

21. H. Simon, 'Spurious Correlation: A Causal Interpretation', *Journal of the American Statistical Association*, 49, 1954, pp. 467–79.

22. See H. Blalock, *Causal Inferences in Non-Experimental Research*, University of North Carolina Press, Chapel Hill, 1964.

23. M. Rosenberg, *The Logic of Survey Analysis*, Basic Books, New York, 1968, esp. Chapters 5 and 6.

24. H. Blumer, 'Sociological Analysis and the Variable', *American Sociological Review*, 21, 1956, pp. 683–90.

25. ibid.

26. ibid.

27. A. V. Cicourel, *Theory and Method in a Study of Argentine Fertility*, John Wiley & Sons, New York, 1974.

28. Blumer, 'Sociological Analysis and the Variable', loc. cit.

29. Runkel and McGrath, *Research in Human Behaviour*, p. 109.

30. A. V. Cicourel, *Method and Measurement in Sociology*, The Free Press, New York, 1964, p. 118.

31. Some of the implications of this kind of argument are to be found in Berger's recommendation that 'age' be defined as a cultural rather than a structural variable. This would alter the purely quantitative determination of age and make the structure of its properties more problematic. See B. Berger, 'How Long is a Generation?', *British Journal of Sociology*, 11, 1960, pp. 10–23.

8
Cross-Societal Inquiry, Typologies and Levels of Analysis

During the past decade or so, sociologists and researchers in related disciplines, such as political science, have increasingly undertaken cross-societial investigations, so re-emphasizing an original element in the sociological tradition. Indeed, the awareness of other ways of living, of other cultures, was a tremendous stimulus to the rise of sociology as a discipline. The recent renewed emphasis on cross-societal research has been encouraged for two major reasons. First, as a possible palliative to the insularity of a discipline developed mainly in two regions of the world, North America and Europe; and secondly, as an extension of the comparative method by bringing systematic evidence to bear on sociological theories. This latter theme was one developed early in this century by social anthropologists who urged the need for a comparative methodology, 'the aim being to explore the varieties of forms of social life as a basis for the theoretical study of human social phenomena'.[1] In other words, they argued for the use of data from other societies in a controlled and comparative manner to build theories which would encompass the whole variety of human experience. This early lead has been built upon by contemporary researchers using a more sophisticated comparative methodology to replace the rather *ad hoc* comparisons with apt illustrations used in the early days, by using a more sensitive selection of cases coupled with modern developments in research technology, such as the survey and forms of quantitative analysis. Thus social science researchers have revived in a more systematic form their obligation to compare.

They realized that effective comparison is not achieved simply by placing a 'fact' from one society against a 'fact' from another, but that this needs to be done within a methodological and theoretical framework which makes the compared data relevant. The *ad hoc* comparisons which typified early comparative work were rarely warranted by a logic in which the data gathered was part of an overall design. However, it should go without saying that such comparisons should not be underrated, since they may, and did, point to weaknesses in generalizations derived from the study of one cultural area. For example, the Western view of the family and its role within society was seriously qualified as a result of examinations of the family within other societies. The major difficulty with such comparisons, useful though they may be in discouraging overhasty generalization, is the lack of control over possible explanatory factors.

As already suggested, the idea of comparison as a tool of analysis is by no means new—the logic of experimental design, for example, merely formalizes this age-old principle. Yet, in the context of the development of sociology, it did assume a rather special emphasis. This emphasis derived from the central role played by the concept of 'society' in conceptual repertoire of sociology, which, in turn, derived from the recognition that society, however it may be defined, 'exerts' some effect on the behaviour and values of its members, and that, further, given the variations between societies, membership in a different society should make differences to the ways in which human beings behave. Although this observation may seem trivial to modern ears, it is nonetheless one of the fundamental 'domain assumptions' of sociology, and especially that branch of sociology variously known as 'comparative sociology', 'cross-cultural analysis' or 'cross-societal research'. There are a number of implications which may be derived from this assumption, but before looking at them in detail, it is as well to note that it is possible to hold a contrary view, namely, that membership in different societies or cultures makes no sociological difference. If, for example, we were to hold the view that man has a basic unalterable human nature—an idea which has a long history in human thought, though one held with greater or lesser conviction at various times—then whether an individual is from Lagos or Hartlepool is irrelevant to understanding behaviour resulting from this basic human nature.[2] In other words, it is possible to argue that there are certain constants which affect social life and which are apparent in all societies, past and present.

Cross-Societal Designs

If it is argued that membership in different societies produces variabilities in human behaviour, the problem is to make this methodologically and theoretically relevant. To obtain some leverage on the issues, let us take an example. Suppose that, in Britain, a study had shown that unionization was most pronounced among the lower-paid, less skilled workers, while a similar study in Holland had shown the better paid, more skilled workers to exhibit a greater degree of unionization than did the lower paid and less skilled. What could be made of this? One source of the apparent contradiction is that the studies may have used different indicators, instruments and samples. But, if it is assumed that the studies were similar in both design and execution, then the contrary findings will make it difficult to form any global generalization about the relationship between occupational reward, skill and unionization. However, we do know that the studies were carried out in two different societies, Britain and Holland, and it is a fairly safe guess that the responsibility for the discrepant findings lies in factors differentiating the social patterns of the two countries. Another way of stating the point is that the proper names, 'Britain' and 'Holland', stand for 'variables that influence the phenomena being explained but have not yet been considered'.[3] Thus, the divergent findings can be seen as the result of a particular constellation of factors occurring within the set of spatio-temporal parameters denoted by the names 'Britain' and 'Holland'. And, although no self-respecting researcher would stop at this juncture, but would go on to look at other factors which might explain the discrepant findings, it is necessary to look in more detail at what this might involve methodologically.

Sociologists, even more than natural scientists, work and gather data in situations where they have only minimal control over when and how phenomena appear. Thus, to study the relationship between unionization and occupational factors in Hartlepool in 1974 is to study relationships among phenomena produced by processes which 'happen' to coalesce at that time and that place; and although sociologists often write as if the relationships they found were generalizable to all relevant times and places, the justification for this is not always self-evident. Herein lies the importance of comparative research—comparative both spatially and temporally—and the need to devise suitable warrants for generalizing beyond single instances. Suppose, then, that in addition to Hartlepool the study was carried out in Boston, Lyon, Zaragoza and Berlin. Would this enable us to make a safer generalization? As usual, it will depend. If the various studies showed the same results, we might feel reassured, on intuitive grounds alone, that the relationship was generalizable to other times and places. This 'feeling' might then be reinforced by appropriate methods of statistical inference. But if, as is more than likely, there was a discrepancy in the results, the problem is to explain why this should be so. Unfortunately, this will be no easy matter, for all the studies have been carried out in different societies and so we are left with the problem of sorting out from the host of factors subsumed under the proper names of these societies those factors responsible for the variations in the recorded data.

Similar Systems Designs

How can the number of possible factors be reduced to manageable proportions to enable the sociologist to determine both the scope and the limits of any desired generalization? One strategy is to systematize the comparison in ways familiar to the experimenter, by 'controlling out' as many factors as possible and so reducing the number of possible explanatory variables. The traditional way of achieving this in cross-societal work is to select for comparative study societies which are as similar as possible, so that, if important differences are found among otherwise similar societies, there will only be a small number of factors to which these differences could be attributed.[4] Alford's study of class voting in Britain, Australia, New Zealand, the United States and Canada was based on this logic. He claimed that the countries chosen shared important features such as a pluralistic political process, two-party systems, little basis for the rise of coalition governments and a common cultural heritage.[5] Other 'blocs' of countries used in this way include Scandinavia, Latin America, the Mediterranean societies of southern Europe and so on. As these examples suggest, the simplest principle of control is often geographical contiguity, the assumption being that geographically close societies will be similar in many ways: economically, historically, linguistically and culturally. While there is a plausible argument to be made in certain cases, geographical contiguity does not always imply social similarity. Moreover, even if two or more contiguous societies are similar, this may not only be a result of mere geographical closeness, but also of other factors—all having subsistence economies, for example. In such cases, it is often difficult to sort out those features arising from cultural transmission from those arising from the operation of factors connected with the sociological characteristics of the societies involved. This dilemma is known as Galton's problem. Galton raised the issue in 1889 at a meeting of the Royal Anthropological Society when he pointed out that cross-societal correlations could be explained by diffusion, borrowing or migration. In other words, features are often highly correlated simply because they are found within neighbouring tribes and not because they are systemically related.[6] Clearly depending upon the nature of the problem, the possibility of diffusion and so on will have to be controlled.

A related cat among the methodological pigeons is contained in the idea of functional equivalents.[7] This notion—a respectable one, though heavily criticized—suggests that formally similar institutions may perform different functions in different societies. Similarly, it also suggests that formally different institutions may perform the same functions in different societies. For example, a society with little in the way of a formally structured, highly integrated religious system may have those functions performed by such functional equivalents as nationalism or political ideologies. Accordingly, in this case any attempt at matching would have to be done on the basis of functional equivalents rather than formal equivalence. These problems are by no means unusual. Categorizing certain ritual patterns like magic, religion or proto-science is a familiar example of the problem from the history of anthropological thought: the interpretation clearly affects the basis on which an attempted matching is to be achieved.

In general, then, the foci of these 'most similar systems' designs are known inter-societal differences and similarities, the similarities being regarded as 'controlled variables', the differences as sources of explanatory factors. By maximizing the similarities and minimizing the differences, the number of potentially explanatory factors is reduced. Factors common to the societies chosen are regarded as irrelevant to differences in the phenomena to be explained.

Problems of Assessing Similarity

Although this design has a putative rigour, in practice, matters are often a little different. The degree of similarity claimed for a group of societies often seems more a function of the level of abstraction than of any systematic attempt to measure and match societal profiles. For example, in most of the social sciences frequent comparisons are made between all or some of the industrial societies of the United States, Britain, Japan, France, Germany, the Soviet Union and so on. The rationale normally offered is that these countries are indicative of some type of social order or system, that is, industrial society. Selecting these societies for comparison should, the argument runs, hold constant certain common features; in this case, those features which have to do with their being 'industrial'.

In other words, these features are 'abstracted out' of the complex of variables which may characterize any historical society and then used to claim that the societies are similar in 'relevant respects'. Since sociology abounds in such devices, such as *'gemeinschaft'* and *'gesellscahft'*, 'folk' and 'urban', 'capitalist' and 'socialist', 'democratic' and totalitarian', 'traditional' and 'modern', it is necessary to discuss their methodological basis more thoroughly.

Typologies

The typology, like many of the techniques and ideas discussed throughout this text, is not limited to any one area of research in its application. It is probably true to say, however, that its development as a conceptual and empirical tool has, historically speaking, been stimulated by problems of comparative cross-societal research, as notably illustrated in the work of Max Weber.[8]

A typology is a special kind of concept which involves abstraction and the selection of particular features reorganized into a theoretically interesting configuration. To explain this more fully, let us examine matters in the context of the question of what is meant by the assertion that Britain and the United States are similar? Clearly, each of the proper names, 'Britain' and the 'United States', stand for a unique constellation of variables (an almost infinite number, if we include all the possible ways of conceptually 'carving up' these two societies), and so the assertion of similarity cannot mean that they are *literally* identical, but only identical in relevant respects. Relevance is determined by some inclusion rule, which, in turn, is derived from some analytical construct. So, if the researcher is interested in similarities of industrial societies, he would explicate the concept, 'industrial society', which would also provide the inclusion rule needed. Thus, he might formulate the following definition: 'An industrial society has a high ratio of capital to labour, a factory system of production, and an elaborate division of labour.' The inclusion principle, or rule, is the definition, and it states that all societies which display the features specified are 'industrial', and that those which do not are 'non-industrial', whatever else they might be. What such a rule does is to introduce order into variety and uniqueness by using a more general concept at a higher level of abstraction. This is a familiar aspect of all conceptualization, for, as McKinney puts it, 'to conceptualize means to generalize to some degree'.[9]

But, while generalization necessarily involves a loss of uniqueness, empirical research normally means dealing with and creating data out of particular phenomena. This means that there will always be cases difficult to encompass within the inclusion rules which delineate a category or type. There will always be borderline and ambiguous cases, and so no one type can lead to a completely precise delineation of a set of phenomena. This is more likely the higher the generality of the concepts in question.[10] However, the arguments for the use of typologies is not based on any claimed ability they may have to achieve accurate description. Rather, their purpose is to organize experience in a theoretically interesting manner. They abstract out what are regarded as 'essential' elements in particular phenomena and organize them into a 'unified conceptual pattern' and offer a 'means by which concrete occurrences can be compared, potentially measured, and comprehended within a system of general categories that may be developed to comprise the type'.[11] As pragmatic and heuristic devices, no claim is made that a type presents a valid empirical description of things in the world. Indeed, as was suggested, if the type is applied in empirical analysis, deviations from the construct will arise, as is both necessary and desirable. For, in this sense, the type acts as a baseline for measurement, however crude that measurement might be; and holding the relationships within the type invariant is a conceptual equivalent to the experimental strategy of controlling out confounding variables. This is the role performed by such notions as a 'perfect vaccuum' or 'perfect fluidity' in the natural sciences. It is here that the type departs from normal classification in that its elements are organized into some structure, logical whole or 'configurational significance'.[12]

The construction of typologies, then, is a theoretical enterprise essential to organizing data and ideas into some meaningful structure. In other words, the type is distinguished from the simple category or classification by the fact that the selection of elements to be included is dependent upon some evaluation of their theoretical importance. That is, there is a presumption that the elements 'hang together' in some way. Precisely how they 'hang together' is a matter for debate, but what is certain is that there are no hard-and-fast rules specifying how 'configurational significance' is achieved. Weber emphasized the 'ideal type' as a 'one-sided accentuation' of reality, an exaggeration of the essential features of a phenomenon designed to set off the phenomenon from those with which it stands in contrast. For Weber, its purpose was to serve as a comparative device. Thus the ideal type of bureaucratic organization, with its stress on hierarchy, impersonal and universalistic norms, the separation of office from office-holder and so on, served to isolate those basic and essential elements distinguishing this form of organization from others. Used as a first analytical step, the ideal type gives a preliminary ordering of the phenomenon being studied. Moreover, the organization of elements within the type offer implicit hypotheses to the affect that certain features will be related to other features. To use the example of bureaucracy once again, the inclusion of hierarchy, impersonal and universalistic norms and the rest, represents a theory to the effect that these elements will occur together in a society which attaches a high value to efficiency.[13] Also, departures from the ideal type can be used as cases for exploring the conditions under which variations are likely to occur.

However, the 'ideal type', though probably never intended by Weber to be anything more than a first-order approximation, was criticized for its 'one-sided accentuation', and Becker's notion of a 'constructed type' tried to bring typology development closer to empirical reality.[14] Although this type is also constructed out of elements regarded as theoretically important, the resultant configuration is designed to be 'objectively probable'. Exaggeration is not involved to anything like the same degree as in the ideal type, though the process of construction is, again, a simplifying and abstracting one, selecting out those features regarded as essential to the phenomenon in question, but leaving in sufficient detail to make the type, as said before, 'objectively probable'. For example, the ideal type of 'folk society' might be described as a small, isolated society with no division of labour which possesses a sacred value system. Of course, no such society is likely to be found anywhere in the world, past, present or future, nor, formulated as an ideal type, is this to be expected. In the case of the constructed type, suitable qualification, such as no division of labour *except* for age and sex, are included to make the type objectively possible, even though empirical cases are likely to show some deviation.[15]

The differences between these two versions of typologies are often subtle and need not yet concern us too much. Both represent attempts to put together a conceptual apparatus for comparing social forms and processes. Neither is intended as an end-product of analysis, only as its beginning. In terms of the problem with which we set out, comparison is not achieved by unequivocal matching but rather by a conceptual ordering which serves as a framework for further analysis and the generation of theoretical ideas.

However, to the positivistically inclined tradition of social inquiry, these modes of typology construction seem too divorced from empirical considerations and to play too fast-and-loose with the way the world is. Moreover, their relative lack of precisely formulated inclusion rules, and unsophisticated means for measuring deviations from the type, make them rather too crude for complex analyses. This is an important point when choosing cases for cross-societal work. 'Folk' and 'urban' types of society, to take one example, might be useful as nascent theories in a capsulated form, but leave much to be desired as a means of selecting empirical cases for analysis. To meet this kind of need, Lazarsfeld and his colleagues formulated a number of typological procedures.

They argued that each typology can be regarded as a selection of attributes, and that measuring individual cases in terms of these attributes enables the analyst to place them in a 'property-space' bounded by the attributes concerned.[16] For example, the components of the definition of 'industrial society' offered above can be taken as attributes which each have two values—'high' and 'low'—so giving the property space in Figure 16. (Note that, depending upon the nature of the attributes and the sophistication of indices available to measure them, they can be treated as orders higher than dichotomies.) The two extreme types—or, if you like, the empirical versions of the 'ideal' or polar types—are labelled in the appropriate cells. The other cells represent different combinations of the three attributes, and some of them, depending partly on how the attributes are defined, may be illogical or empirically impossible. Although the logic of the property space is a way of generating types in what is perhaps a more formal and systematic manner, by itself it does not automatically provide any theoretical rationale for the types generated. This must still, as always, be provided by the researcher.[17]

However, if we take the example represented in Figure 16 by way of illustration, we can see how the types represented by each of the cells can be made theoretically relevant. Such a property space may have been generated to examine theories of industrial development. It could be argued, for example, that the attributes are related in systemic ways, and that, through time, types which are not consistent—having a factory system of production but a low capital to labour ratio, or a relatively low division of labour, for instance—will be unstable. This can be tested, using the property space as a data matrix, by locating empirical instances within the cells. Like the cross-tabulation discussed in Chapter 7, the frequencies in the cells would confirm or deny the prediction made in the theory. Also other factors, such as stage of political development, types of stratification system and so on, can be correlated with each type.

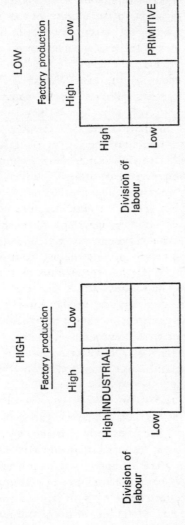

Figure 16. Property-space typology for economic dimensions of societies.

Although each method of typology construction has received its fair share of criticism, one thing which does seem to emerge is that each serves a rather different purpose in the process of inquiry. The 'ideal type' construction serves to throw into relief the elemental characteristics of a phenomenon or event, a process which necessarily results in a loss of descriptive verisimilitude. But description is not the intention; formulating concepts and relationships as an aid to further, more detailed analysis, is. The more empirically based typologies are by no means alternatives to the more 'impressionistic' ones, though many of the functions served by ideal types in the past may have been superseded by developments in empirical method. In this regard, the more empirically based typologies are perhaps more suited to cross-societal work where the overall design employed is the 'most similar systems' design, for, if certain variables are to be held constant, the researcher needs to know precisely what is and what is not being held constant. However, the discussion of typologies serves to illustrate, among other things, one of the major difficulties of the 'most similar systems' design in cross-societal work, namely, the problems posed by developing generalized concepts in an effort to reduce the variability in concrete social systems and thereby provide a measure of explanatory control. While it goes without saying that general concepts are necessary to any discipline with scientific pretensions, the point is that their use within cross-societal work raises questions of fundamental importance to the inter-relationship between sociological theory and sociological data. To bring out some of these issues, let us contrast the 'most similar systems' design with an alternative design which does not initially depend on matching social systems in terms of their similarities.

Most Different Systems Design[18]

This design takes, as its starting-point, variation in observed behaviour at the level of the individual, group or aggregate, but unlike the 'most similar systems' design, it does not give any *a priori* special place to the *social system* factors in the explanation of the variations being studied. For instance, if, when studying the relationship between occupational reward, skill and unionization, the same result were to be found for Hartlepool, Zaragoza and Boston, then the social system differences between Britain, Spain and the United States would be irrelevant to explaining the discovered relationship. For, if the relationship between the three factors were the same in the three cities, then the samples used could all, as it were, have been drawn from the same population. In other words, the cross-societal character of the study is simply an extension of the process of replicating studies on other samples and has less to do with the characteristics of nations or societies *per se*. This kind of design, unlike the former, aims at eliminating irrelevant systemic factors. Of course, if the relationship was not the same in the three cities, then reference would need to be made to factors at the social-system level differentiating the societies involved.

Though the differences between the two strategies should not be overemphasized, they differ mainly in terms of initial assumptions. In the case of the 'most similar systems' design, there is an *a priori* assumption about the level at which important explanatory factors operate, namely, the social system. Moreover, once the design has been formulated, alternative levels are difficult to consider. The 'most different systems' design, on the other hand, leaves open the question at which level the explanatory variables operate. If a population of individuals is sampled from several communities within several countries, then differences between individuals will be tested both within and across communities and within and across countries. If communities differ, factors operating at community level will be considered, and if nations are found to differ, then factors at the national level will be considered. If neither communities nor countries differ, the entire analysis will remain at the individual level and no social system factors need be taken into account.[19]

Both these designs in their different ways make some reference to phenomena at different analytical levels. The 'most similar systems' design uses societies and their attributes as the major unit of analysis; and the 'most different systems' design, while beginning with units 'below' the level of the social system, is prepared, if analysis requires it, to move to the social system level. In other words, each design recognizes that sociological analysis has to deal with multi-levelled phenomena, and it is to a consideration of some of the problems involved in this to which we now turn.

Levels of Analysis

'Every sociologist is keenly sensitive to the distinction between the individual and the group', but, as Lazarsfeld and his co-authors go on to point out, the distinction is not without its problems.[20] The idea of members and collective is relatively easy to grasp at the conceptual level, but in the context of empirical work is downright frustrating. Sociologists often talk about individuals being members of various kinds of groups or collectives—families, political parties, juvenile gangs, social classes, mutual-admiration societies, nations, societies, and so on—the obvious presumption being that membership in such collectives makes a difference to the socially relevant ways in which actors act, feel and behave. In other words, there is a strong sense in sociology of a hierarchical ordering of phenomena which must be taken into account. Figure 17 suggests one simple way to illustrate this notion of levels.

Figure 17. Simple classification of levels of social phenomena.

Level	Examples
Individual	Me, you, your friend, the girl next door, personal income, personal sadness.
Small group	Friendship clique, me and the girl next door, neighbourhood, work group.
Aggregate	All people with personal incomes above average, married women in Lancaster, buyers of Elton John's records.
Larger collective or group	Community, city, nation state, society.

Though almost all sociological perspectives contain some notion of different levels of phenomena, variously conceptualized, the implications for empirical analysis are not as clear as the fainthearted might hope.[21] The idea of individual properties is fairly obvious. 'The intention to vote', 'personal income', 'sexual satisfaction', 'degree of alienation', are all, whatever else they may be, properties that could be attributed to individuals. Moreover, a great deal of the raw data produced by many of the techniques used in empirical research is obtained from individual persons. Only individuals can answer questionnaires, only the actions of individuals can be observed, and only individuals can be manipulated in the laboratory. However, the data derived from individuals is not always used solely at the individual level of analysis. For example, a researcher might wish to conduct a survey into the attitudes of aircraft workers to disarmament with the intention of determining their attitude as a group. Alternatively, he or she might be interested in the stability of political systems, and part of his primary data might include analysis of rates of internal violence, country by country, the rates of violence being, of course, derived from acts by individuals. Or, a study might be concerned with the relationship between social class cleavage and political stability. In all these examples, there is a recognition of the need to take the idea of multi-levelled phenomena seriously, if only in the sense that most of the data used will ultimately have derived from individual persons.

The sociological tradition has always made various approaches to the relationship between different levels of phenomena. Some regard the individual as the primary sociological unit, higher-order collectives being simply epiphenomena—theoretical constructions or abstractions. These may serve some heuristic purpose, but the 'real' causal processes are always to be found at the level of the individual. Indeed, a fairly prevalent tradition in sociology and social psychology is to explain higher-order phenomena by relative frequencies observed at a lower level of the social system. Thus, data on individual behaviour, such as mobility aspirations, is used to account for higher-order social-system characteristics, such as the rigidity of a status system.[22] Other theoretical perspectives begin their conceptualization at the level of the social system, regarding individual behaviour as a product of higher-order processes.[23]

Occasionally, one or other of these perspectives explicitly or implicitly posits a consistency across levels which Wagner terms the 'homology thesis'. Parsons, for example, argues for a theoretical continuity from the primary group to the social system, allowing generalizations from one level to another.[24] Other points of view, however, reject this model of simple continuity; and this is the 'discontinuity thesis', sometimes adopted by both micro- and macro-theorists, who see as a necessary part of sociological analysis the task of understanding how phenomena at different levels interact to produce the patterns in which the researcher is interested. This rather simplified account of the metatheoretical positions on the issue of levels is important since it is paralleled by methodological problems similarly concerned with the translatability of data across levels. Moreover, different positions are not always consistently held when it comes to data. Some of those who reject the homology thesis sometimes make simplifying assumptions when, for example, gathering data by random sampling so as to obtain 'structural' information, or when formulating mathematical models assumed to hold for more than one level.[25]

Collective Phenomena

The methodological problems begin with concepts that refer to, or at least hint at, phenomena above the level of individual or interpersonal interaction. Sociology has traditionally recognized different kinds of collective, most simply expressed in the distinction between 'aggregate' and 'group'. The former kind of collective is simply a class or set of individuals—'manual workers', 'men', 'women', 'people with cross-eyes'—delineated according to some property or properties held in common. A group, on the other hand, is in its sociological sense regarded as something more than aggregate (though properties held in common by a set of persons could form the basis of group interaction), as something more than a simple enumeration of members according to some common property. A group is held to involve such things as consciousness of kind among its members, a definable pattern of interaction, and so on. Thus, assuming that in each particular case the following examples conformed to whatever definition of 'groupness' was offered, groups could include political parties, families, trade unions, factories, corporations, societies and nation states. Although this distinction could be elaborated further to talk about different kinds of groups and collectives, the problem addressed here arises from the attempt to translate such notions into empirical research operations and is concerned with the nature of the data used as indicators of collective properties.

As was indicated earlier, most sociological data is derived, at some point, from individuals. Such data may consist of verbal reports, observations of actions or characteristics which are then transformed, by appropriate techniques, into indicators of various sorts. Some of these operations include transforming such data into indicators of collective properties. For instance, enumerating the personal wages (property of an individual) of the members of an occupational group (a collective), and dividing the sum by the number of members to obtain an average wage of the members of the collective. This collective indicator can be compared with similar indices for other occupational groups in the same or other countries, and so on. This kind of collective property is formally defined by Lazarsfeld and Menzel as an 'analytic' property: one obtained by performing some mathematical operation upon some property of each individual member, and it could include such things as the average rent paid in a town, the proportion of cities in a country that have a cathedral, the correlation between age and social status in a community as a measure of the norms regarding old age, etc.[26] A 'structural' property, on the other hand, is arrived at by performing some mathematical operation on data about the relations of each member to some or all other members of the collective. This could include such relational properties as degree of cliquishness of a school class as measured by non-overlapping sociometric choices, or the concentration of power in a state by the relative influence which key groups have over certain decisions. Finally, properties of collectives not based on information derived from the properties of individual members are termed 'global'; these include such things as characterizing people according to the frequency with which themes of 'achievement motive' appear in folk tales, the density of settlement of a region, and the 'warlikeness' of nations by the ratio of the national budget allocated to arms as opposed to education and welfare. While this classification of collective properties is not always unambiguous in practice, it will serve to demonstrate some of the issues involved.

Indicants of Collective Phenomena

It was shown earlier that many of the statements occurring in sociological theories are not confined to any one level. Empirical analysts often reflect this in how they operate with properties regarded as individually based, and with other properties which they regard as collective. The problem is working between levels, or deciding upon the relationships considered to govern the inferences sought between one level and another as well as the consistency of these rules with those involved in the theory language. Clearly, the kind of inferences considered warrantable depend very heavily upon the theoretical interpretation of the relationship between different orders of phenomena. In the data language, for example, if individual data is available, the inferences from one level to another—in this case, from the individual to the collective—are warranted by the very procedures which have been used to construct collective properties out of the properties of the individual members—in this case, there being no direct measurement of the collective properties. However, such interpretations are not always compatible with assumptions in the theory language. Taking the number of 'democratic personalities' within states as an index of the degree to which a political system is democratic would hardly be justifiable if the theory language defines 'democracy' as a referent of political systems.

This issue has affinities with some of the problems raised in connection with the survey. Though we may construct an 'analytic' or 'structural' collective property by means of some relatively straightforward mathematical operation, such as averaging the individual properties of the members of the collective, there remains the question

H

of the compatibility of the mathematical rules with the assumptions we wish to make about the nature of the collective. Suppose, for example, that a researcher wished to construct a profile of social class, or of a nation state for that matter, characterizing the collective by average scores on a number of properties such as income, degree of political participation, family size, and the like. Whatever else has been done, the researcher has succeeded in reducing individual variations into summary measures. In addition, the mathematical procedure of simple averaging gives each member of the set an equal weight in the derivation of the collective property, and (more food for thought) any grouping operation of this kind tends to inflate the size of correlations over what would have been found had the data remained ungrouped at the micro-level.[27] Whether or not any of the problems are serious depends upon the purposes of the research, and also upon the theoretical assumptions one wishes to make about the nature of the collective. One danger is that by using collective indices like those discussed, a serious illusion of simplicity may be created, distorting the social reality we have set out to investigate. In short, the decision whether or not to use a particular operation for aggregating individual observations into some collective measure needs to be warranted by a suitable theory to specify how individual interactions produce the collective phenomena. Such theories are not always readily available.[28]

Aggregate Data and Ecological Analysis

This problem if inter-level relationships is made even more acute when data from all levels is unavailable, as is often the case in cross-societal work. While cross-national surveys have become more common, they are normally limited to a few societies at a time because of cost and other difficulties of administration. Accordingly, for these and other reasons, a number of researchers have tried to make more use of the 'aggregate' or 'ecological' data often obtained at public expense as a by-product of such social accounting as elections or administrative and economic statistics. Though one of the terms used here, 'ecological', first referred to the study of the influence of the physical and biological environment on the behaviour and development of organisms, in the social sciences it has come to refer to the study of units at some level above that of the individual actor, using data normally referring to the distribution of some property within certain areas or regional units.[29]

There are various reasons for choosing unit levels above that of the individual, ranging from the wish to study these levels as phenomena in their own right to there being little choice since data at the individual level is unavailable. This latter reason is especially pertinent to official statistics, where the primary individual data may either be kept secret, as with electoral votes, or cannot be made available for administrative, judicial or economic reasons.[30] In such cases, aggregate distributions for various kinds of territorial units, such as constituencies or census tracts, even for whole countries, are available, but not the primary individual data from which the distributions are derived. Nonetheless, studies using such data have amassed an impressive catalogue of findings which can be used for intra- and inter-societal comparisons.[31] However, it should be no surprise to discover a certain unease about the use of such data: an unease based not only on the problem we have been discussing.

One source of this unease derives from doubts about the accuracy of the numbers reported for large aggregates. The accuracy of accounting procedures varies from country to country, and even in the most developed societies sample surveys have revealed weakness in census data. Enumerating large numbers of people may often mean that the researcher has less control over individual observations. These problems may become serious when comparing aggregate data between nations, since at least some of the differences may be a result of variations in the accuracy of accounting rather than of 'real' social differences. An additional problem is in defining the units being counted. Even in developed countries, for example, there are ambiguities in the definition of 'household', whether it is a consumption unit, a unit around one provider, a unit involving the shared use of incomes, or whatever. Similar difficulties arise over the comparability of figures relating to such matters as crime rates, owing to cultural variations in the definitions of specific crimes. Even relatively unequivocal notions like 'income' must be treated with caution when using such data to signify differences in standards of living and comparing societies with different economic and social systems.[32] Though definitions of some categories may be reasonably simple and standard, their meanings can differ between societies. A good example is provided by educational statistics: secondary education in European societies has a different meaning, both in terms of curricula and social significance, from that in the United States. Other factors affecting the value of official statistics can have to do with the significance of such figures for domestic and international politics. Economic and defence statistics are manipulated for political reasons in almost every state, and so need to be treated with caution. Finally, it should be remembered that the categories, employed for official accounting purposes may or may not be consonant with those required by the researcher's problem.[33]

Inferences from Aggregate Data

The most interesting methodological difficulty with the use of aggregate data occurs, however, when it is wished to make inferences from the aggregate to the individual level. This difficulty was first pointed out in an early paper by W. S. Robinson where he demonstrated that an ecological correlation is not equal to its corresponding individual correlation, and that the former cannot be used, without strict qualification, for the latter.[34] The argument was illustrated by showing that the correlation between colour and literacy for nine geographical regions used by the United States Census Bureau's 1930 census was far higher (0·9) than the correlation for individuals (0·2), where colour and illiteracy were treated as properties of individuals rather than of geographical regions. Where states were treated as ecological areas, yet another set of correlations was derived. The lesson Robinson was trying to underline was that individually referring hypotheses must be tested or examined using individual level data. The criticism is not against using ecological or aggregate data, but against its use to infer relationships at the individual level.[35]

Attempts have been made to control or estimate the size of the errors involved when making inferences from the macro- to the micro-level and vice versa.[36] However, the problem is not just one of technique, but also one of theory, and it has to do with the sociological interpretations given to the idea of multi-levelled phenomena. If you like, it has to do with establishing suitable correspondences between the theory language and the data language. The status of aggregate measures depends not only upon the technical processes required to construct them, but also upon their compatibility with the theoretical and epistomological presuppositions we entertain about social life. To illustrate the point, take an example from small-group research not untypical of the kind of statements which may occur in other contexts: 'A group remembers its previous activities; it is the basis often for its unity, and the interdependence feelings that may exist now. A group employs this background of experience in its approach to group goals.'[37]

At its face value, such a statement can mean a number of things. It may be taken as a heuristic image or model, an analytical construct; groups, like persons, can have a memory, can have goals, and so on. More literally, the term 'group', and other statements attached to it, can be taken as a shorthand expression for its individual members, who are, as a result of their common experiences, sufficiently similar for it to be possible to refer to them in a manner of speaking as a single entity by means of the concept 'group'. In this case, we might regard the statement as infelicitous, but there would be no implication that the group is, in any sense, a conscious entity. Alternatively, we might argue that the statement does not imply either of these, that it is not elaborating a conceptual model, nor is intended as a convenient manner of speaking, but rather that it indicates that we should treat groups as independent phenomena in their own right. Which of these interpretations is plausible depends upon the meta-theoretical position the researcher wishes to accept. Whichever it is will affect his choice of operations and the measures used to indicate the collective concepts. If the interpretation or theoretical meaning is that the statements about the group's activities are intended as shorthand expressions for individual properties, then aggregative operations may be suitable. In other words, groups could be compared by using such 'analytic' properties as the proportion of members who have been in the group for a particular period correlated with similar measures for the degree of unity and feelings of interdependence among the membership.

If, on the other hand, the interpretation is that the notion of group refers to phenomena in some sense independent of the properties of individual members, would an aggregative operation be plausible? Could analytic or 'structural' properties be used as meaningful indicators? These questions are the methodological equivalents of theoretical questions which are to do with the individual and the collective and the relationship between the whole and its parts.[38] They are questions which are bound up with philosophical and theoretical considerations.

Inter-Level Designs

Attempts have been made to construct research designs to allow for the expression of phenomena at different levels. One such strategy is known as 'contextual analysis': relating individual measures to the social context or milieu in which the individual lives. In this way, Stouffer observed that soldiers' attitudes towards promotion could best be explained by relating them to relative opportunities for actual promotion within military units.[39] The strategy consists of looking for conditional relationships, using a collective variable as a test factor. That is, of looking at the relationship between an individual property, say, sex and scholastic achievement, within the context of a collective property, such as type of school. Such strategies, it is claimed, can go a long way to overcoming the atomistic tendencies of cross-sectional surveys, and they are clearly important in cross-societal work where multi-levelled analysis is necessary. Also, they give due weight to the idea that individuals live in 'domains' or organized social entities, taking seriously the idea of social structure. Similar analyses using aggregate data have been used in cross-societal studies. Alker, for example, has shown that some variables which are uncorrelated in a large sample of nations nonetheless have regionally significant associations, but that other universal relationships had no validity within particular geographical contexts. Thus an almost nonexistent correlation between McClelland's 'achievement motivation' scores and *per capita* income hides a strong positive correlation between these variables in Latin America and a moderately negative correlation in European countries. There are other examples.[40]

Lazarsfeld and Menzel describe four properties which can be used to characterize individuals within groups.[41] 'Absolute properties' of members are derived without recourse to any information about the collective, or about the relationship of the member to others in the collective. For example, income, age and level of education are absolute properties in this sense. 'Relational properties', on the other hand, are derived from information about the relationship a member may have with other members. The number of sociometric choices a member receives would be one such property. 'Comparative properties' describe a member by comparing his value on some absolute or relational property and the distribution of that property over the whole collective; an example would be a ranking in terms of sibling birth order from first born to last born. Finally, a 'contextual property' characterizes a member by a property of the collective. Workers in large factories are more likely to become unionized than are workers in small factories. Being a worker in a large (or small) factory is a contextual property.

Though not without its problems, this classification, like that discussed earlier (pages 212–13), does point towards serious theoretical and methodological problems when dealing with data across levels. It is perhaps in the study of the values and normative orientations of groups and other collectives that the issues come to the fore most markedly.[42] The problem here is to distinguish the effects of individual values from those supposed to characterize the collective or group. This is not always easy, given the lack of suitable theory linking individual with collective phenomena.

Conclusions

Unfortunately, space prevents a fuller discussion of all the matters involved in these issues, but, as pointed out earlier, they have relevance beyond cross-societal work. Indeed, they are relevant to survey analysis and to any attempt to build an empirically based macro-sociology. Nonetheless, attempts to develop systematic, often quantitative, studies of many societies simultaneously have perhaps brought such issues to the fore. Cross-societal research, almost by definition, raises the problem of working between levels. The very notion of society—itself posing operational problems of stomach-aching proportions—presupposes levels above that of the individual. Describing collectives and trying to establish macro-relations, as many cross-societal researchers have tried to do, raises problems about the nature and structure of the data and its relationship to the theoretical formulations it tries to support. Also, as mentioned before, there are many differing perspectives on these matters which tie in with some of the themes discussed throughout the text. What is certain, however—and this is a problem for theory as well as methodology—is the need to construct theories which will better legitimize the relationships across levels of analysis. In other words, the task is to narrow the gap between individuals and the macro-relations posited in a variety of studies.

Exercises

It is unlikely that you will be lucky enough to go to another country as part of your sociological studies. So we shall have to do what we can *in situ*, so to speak.

1. Take the distinction often made between 'industrial' and 'pre-industrial' societies. Look at relevant literature and draw up the major dimensions upon which the distinction rests, e.g. structural differentiation basis of solidarity, types of value system, political structure and so on. You will find many such suggested dimensions in the literature not always in agreement with one another. Use these dimensions as elements with which to draw a profile of the two types of society. Decide what evidence or indicators you are going to use for each dimension, and using suitable library sources, pick

examples of each type If you are feeling ambitious, you might like to develop more sophisticated dimensions, and assuming that each dimension can in principle vary independently, collect examples to see if there is any clustering empirically. For example, see whether a greater degree of social differentiation is associated with secular value systems. How would you explain such a finding?

2. In many sociological theories, reference is made to such phenomena as societal values or societal norms or to a culture, and are regarded as global properties of collectives, not simply as individual properties. Try to find such formulations and evaluate their importance. Why, for example, is it felt necessary to establish the 'externality' of social values and norms? In what sense can we speak of collective properties? Try to devise a study which could plausibly demonstrate the independent causal efficacy of societal or group over individual values.

Notes and References

1. A. R. Radcliffe-Brown, 'The Comparative Method in Social Anthropology', in E. Etzioni and F. R. Dubos (eds.), *Comparative Perspectives: Theories and Methods*, Little, Brown, Boston, 1970, pp. 17–24. Those anthropologists interested in formulating general laws of social life were faced with the ever-present problem of the number of exceptions or deviant cases to any formulated law. This later led a number of them to argue that anthropology and sociology could only achieve the discovery of regularities rather than of laws. On the insularity of sociology, see R. Bendix, 'Concepts in Comparative Historical Analysis', in S. Rokkan (ed.), *Comparative Research across Cultures and Nations*, Mouton, Paris, 1968, pp. 67–81.

2. See A. R. Wolf, 'New Perspectives in Comparative Anthropology', in Etzioni and Dubos (eds.), *Comparative Perspectives*, pp. 69–71, where it is suggested that recent anthropological thinking is tending to stress the limits to human variability.

3. A. Przeworski and H. Teune, *The Logic of Comparative Social Inquiry*, John Wiley & Sons, New York, 1970, pp. 26–30.

4. See R. Narroll, 'Some Thoughts on Comparative Method in Cultural Anthropology', in H. M. and A. Blalock (eds.), *Methodology of Research*, McGraw-Hill, New York, 1968, pp. 236–77; and Przeworski and Teune, *The Logic of Comparative Social Inquiry*, Chapter 2.

5. R. Alford, *Party and Society*, Rand McNally, New York, 1963.

6. R. Narroll, 'Galton's Problem: The Logic of Cross-cultural Research', *Social Research*, 32, 1965, pp. 428–5; R. Narroll and R. G.

D'Andrade, 'Two Further Solutions to Galton's Problem', *American Anthropologist*, 65, 1963, pp. 1053–67.

7. See R. K. Merton, *Social Theory and Social Structure*, The Free Press, Glencoe, 1956, pp. 33–5.

8. Most of Weber's work is interesting in its use of typologies, but see esp. *The Theory of Social and Economic Organisation*, translated by A. M. Henderson and T. Parsons, The Free Press, Glencoe, 1947; and *The Methodology of the Social Sciences*, translated and edited by E. A. Shils and H. A. Finch, The Free Press, Glencoe, 1949.

9. J. C. McKinney, *Constructive Typology and Social Theory*, Appleton-Century-Crofts, New York, 1966, p. 9. This book presents a full discussion of the methodology of typologies.

10. For these and other reasons, Bendix argues that scholars, especially those in comparative studies, should use concepts more limited in their applicability, rather than universals which 'are so emptied of content they require specification in order to be applied to some body of evidence . . .'—R. Bendix, 'The Comparative Analysis of Historical Change', in T. Burns and S. B. Paul (eds.), *Social Theory and Economic Change*, Tavistock Publications London, 1967, pp. 67–86; see also his 'Concepts and Generalisations in Comparative Sociological Studies', *American Sociological Review*, 28, 1963, pp. 532–9.

11. McKinney, *Constructive Typology and Social Theory*, p. 12.

12. ibid., p. 15.

13. Weber argued that the grounds for inclusion should be 'logical consistency'.

14. H. Becker, *Through Values to Social Interpretation*, Duke University Press, Durham, N.C., 1950, esp. Chapter 2. Also, R. F. Winch, 'Heuristic and Empirical Typologies', *American Sociological Review*, 12, 1947, pp. 68–75.

15. Example taken from G. Sjoberg and R. Nett, *A Methodology for Social Research*, Harper & Row, New York, 1968, p. 252.

16. See A. H. Barton, 'The Concept of Property-Space in Social Research', in P. F. Lazarsfeld and M. Rosenberg (eds.), *The Language of Social Research*, The Free Press, Glencoe, 1955, pp. 40–53.

17. Try to think of concepts to describe the cases in the other cells of Figure 16. Use the property-space structure on other typologies, say, Weber's ideal-type bureaucracy, making each element vary independently of the others to see how the method works as a theory-generating technique.

18. Przeworski and Teune, *The Logic of Comparative Social Inquiry*, pp. 34–9.

19. ibid.

20. P. F. Lazarsfeld, A. K. Pasanella and M. Rosenberg (eds.), *Continuities in the Language of Social Research*, The Free Press, New York, 1972, p. 219.

21. See H. R. Wagner, 'The Displacement of Scope: A Problem of the Relationship Between Small-scale and Large-scale Sociological Theories', *American Journal of Sociology*, 69, 1964, pp. 571–84, for a pertinent discussion on the attempts by various sociological theories to cope with this problem of levels.

22. See, for example, G. C. Homans, *Social Behaviour in Its Elementary Forms*, Routledge & Kegan Paul, London, 1961; and E. K. Scheuch, 'Social Context and Individual Behaviour', in M. Dogan and S. Rokkan (eds.), *Quantitative Ecological Analysis in the Social Sciences*, MIT Press, Cambridge, Mass., 1969, pp. 133–4.

23. This, for example, is implicit in the Marxist tradition.

24. The general systems approach also finds this idea a useful one. See F. K. Berrien, *General and Social Systems*, Rutgers University Press, New Brunswick, 1968. See also T. Parsons, 'The Relation between Small Groups and the Larger System', in R. Grinkler (ed.), *Toward a Unified Theory of Behaviour*, Basic Books, New York, 1956, pp. 190–200.

25. See M. T. Hannan, 'Problems of Aggregation', in H. M. Blalock (ed.), *Causal Models in the Social Sciences*, Macmillan, London, 1971, pp. 473–508; and J. Galtung, *Theory and Methods of Social Research*, Allen & Unwin, London, 1967, pp. 37–48, esp. section on 'Fallacy of the Wrong Level'.

26. P. F. Lazarsfeld and H. Menzel, 'On the Relation between Individual and Collective Properties', in A. Etzioni (ed.), *Complex Organizations: A Sociological Reader*, 2nd edition, Holt, Rinehart & Winston, New York, 1969, pp. 499–516.

27. G. Yule and M. G. Kendall, *An Introduction to the Theory of Statistics*, Charles Griffin, London, 1950, pp. 311–12.

28. A similar problem arises in the use of random sampling where it is assumed that individuals are only randomly related; a curious supposition, if one believes, as sociology does, that individuals interact in patterned ways.

29. Dogan and Rokkan (eds.), *Quantitative Ecological Analysis*, p. 4.

30. See S. Rokkan, 'Mass Suffrage, Secret Voting and Political Participation', *European Journal of Sociology*, 2, 1961.

31. This kind of analysis is perhaps most fully developed in cross-national voting, participation and political cleavage studies. See selection of articles in Dogan and Rokkan (eds.), *Quantitative Ecological Analysis*.

32. On these and allied problems, see E. K. Scheuch, 'Cross-National Comparisons Using Aggregate Data', in R. L. Merrit and S. Rokkan (eds.), *Comparing Nations*, Yale University Press, New Haven, 1966, pp. 135–64.

33. Similar kinds of problem attach to the efforts of Murdock and his associates to construct a databank known as the Human Relations Area File: an attempt to codify most of what is known about societies throughout the world, past and present. See P. Diesing, *Patterns of Discovery in the Social Sciences*, Routledge & Kegan Paul, London, 1972, pp. 192–5; also A. J. F. Köbben, 'The Logic of Cross-Cultural Analysis: Why Exceptions?', in S. Rokkan (ed.), *Comparative Research across Cultures and Nations*, pp. 17–53, includes an exhaustive list of the methodological problems involved in making cross-cultural generalizations.

34. W. S. Robinson, 'Ecological Correlations and the Behaviour of Individuals', *American Sociological Review*, 15, 1950, pp. 351–7. See also H. Alker, 'A Typology of Ecological Fallacies', in Dogan and Rokkan (eds.), *Quantitative Ecological Analysis*, pp. 69–86.

35. See H. Menzel, 'Comment on Robinson's Ecological Correlation and the Behaviour of Individuals', *American Sociological Review*, 15, 1950, p. 674; and M. T. Hannan, *Aggregation and Disaggregation in Sociology*, D. C. Heath, Lexington, 1971, for an excellent review of the technical issues involved.

36. Briefly, as far as aggregation is concerned, it is problematic when data-sets are aggregated non-randomly, i.e. when the aggregation criterion is systematically related to one or more of the variables in the model. What appears to happen is that the relative variation in the variables is affected. Moreover, aggregate data is often based on summary statistics which reduce the variety at the macro-level so that correlations at this level tend to be higher than those at the micro-level. See Hannan, *Aggregation and Disaggregation in Sociology*, for details.

37. M. H. Horowitz and H. V. Perlmutter, quoted in J. S. Coleman *et al.*, *Macrosociology; Research and Theory*, Allyn & Bacon, Boston, 1970, p. 15.

38. See, for example, E. Nagel, 'On the Statement "the Whole is More than the Sum of Its Parts"', in Lazarsfeld and Rosenberg (eds.), *The Language of Social Research*, pp. 519–27.

39. S. Stouffer *et al.*, *The American Soldier*, 1, Princeton University Press, Princeton, 1949.

40. H. Alker, 'Regionalism versus Universalism in Comparing Nations', in B. Russett *et al.*, *World Handbook of Political and Social Indicators*, Yale University Press, New Haven, 1964; and Math-

ematics and Politics, Macmillan, New York, 1965, Chapter 5, for a co-variance model relevant to this kind of problem.

41. Lazarsfeld and Menzel, 'On the Relation between Individual and Collective Properties', loc. cit.

42. Relevant literature on this includes P. M. Blau, 'Structural Effects', *American Sociological Review*, 25, 1960, pp. 178–93; A. S. Tannenbaum and J. G. Backman, 'Structural *versus* Individual Effects', *American Journal of Sociology*, 69, 1964, pp. 585–95; J. A. Davies *et al.*, 'A Technique for Analysing the Effects of Group Composition', *American Sociological Review*, 26, 1961, pp. 215–25.

9
Time Is of the Essence

Almost every statement made in sociological analysis contains, often implicitly rather than explicitly, some reference to time. The ideas of social change, of social development and social process indicate, if only cursorily, how time is rooted in most of the basic ideas within the discipline. However, time as a problem for methodology and substantive theory tends to be relegated to the 'Sunday School League of Sociological Issues', despite its centrality in principle.

The Methodological Importance of Time

A fairly full consideration of time and its relevance for methodology is important. For one thing, time is one of the basic parameters of social life. It enters into the very idea of social organization and is a feature recognized and socially defined, though in different ways, in all societies. Age, rites of passage, the factory whistle, timetables, the seasons' round and the like are all events which give temporal order to social life.[1] Similarly, in their various ways, the members of any society are orientated not only towards the present, but also to the future and the past. A people's sense of their own history may help to form their beliefs about the status and nature of their country. In short, social life is inextricably embedded in a sense of time.[2] A further reason why sociologists need to be attuned to the notion of time is that it forms one of the major parameters, along with space, which affect the generalizability of any particular sociological theory. Moreover, most sociological theories, whether about social change or not, contain some reference to 'action-over-time'. Even structural functionalism, a theory often criticized for its apparent lack of concern with change, implies the movement of system parts, and where there is movement there is time.[3] This temporal component within sociological theory is important for its implications for empirical work in that it matters at what point in the temporal process the data is gathered. Suppose that over a long period of time, within a social system, various elements, A, B, C and D, have the values described by the curves shown in Figure 18. The elements could be any sociologically relevant attributes, such as the degree of political stability, the level of economic activity, the distribution of achievement motive, the amount of political violence, the predominance of particular cultural themes, population size, and so on. Notice that the processes shown have different shapes, some wave-like, others declining, others increasing over time. Accordingly, it will matter at which point in time an investigator enters the stream to gather his data. If an investigator chose point x, this will produce a very different picture from points y and z, and if these are isolated, 'one-off' observations, then the resultant theory could be based on a highly misleading description of the processes concerned. This is relevant to the point made elsewhere that the non-experimental character of much sociological work means that the events the researcher is studying are time-dependent in that they have occurred at that time and in that place owing to the effects of many, many factors. In our rather simplified example, the relationship between elements A, B, C and D found by an investigator at time z may be temporally 'untypical', and without knowledge of the processes over time, any resultant generalization would be inadequate.[4]

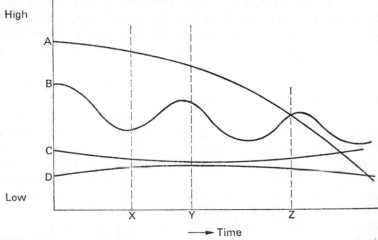

Figure 18. Temporal processes.

A third reason for taking time seriously is the need to determine cause-and-effect. Assuming that the investigator wishes to talk in the language of cause-and-effect, then he must pay strict attention to the axiom which states that causes occur before effects. Any analysis claiming to establish causal laws must inevitably make some determination of the temporal order of the factors entering into the analysis. It would, for example, necessitate making some justifiable claim that the independent variable occurred prior to the dependent one.

These then are three different reasons why time is an important consideration for sociology, both theoretically and methodologically. Now to discuss some study designs which incorporate time as an element, and some problems which arise when time is taken as an ingredient of theory.

Time-Based Research Designs: The Panel Study

To highlight the importance of research designs which 'build in' time, as it were, as an element of the design itself, it is useful to remember some of the problems which can arise with the cross-sectional survey. The 'one-shot' cross-sectional survey selects data by intersecting the stream of social process, using verbal reports taken at a particular point to reconstruct past, present and future acts or intentions. The difficulty with such studies is, however, that it is not always easy to establish a temporal order for the variables. More often than not, this has to be inferred and is not given in the structure of the data itself. In the United States, early mass-communications studies had noted that people who listened to a particular programme were more likely to buy the product it advertised. Although such a finding might be eagerly seized upon by advertisers as evidence for the efficacy of their calling, other explanations are more than possible. It might be, for example, that people bought the product for quite instrumental reasons and then listened to the advertisement by way of reassurance for their choice and expenditure. Similarly, in assessing the efficacy of political broadcasts, it is essential to know whether or not prior opinions and attitudes determine the selection of party programmes which are watched or listened to. Also, asking respondents to report on past experiences may result in data which owes more to selective memory, or to a reconstruction of the past in terms of the present, than it does to actual events in the past. Nor is the methodological case for the cross-sectional survey much improved by studies which have shown that responses to the same items on the questionnaire —even items supposed to tap deep-seated attitudes—often vary, almost randomly, over time.[5] In all these cases, it is crucial to determine the time order of variables as a step towards ruling out some of the other possible explanations. One research strategy designed to do this is the panel study.

This research design consists of repeating observations over time on the *same* set of people in order to register any changes that occur in attitudes, affiliations, relationships or whatever.[6] To see the advantages of this design over the 'one-shot' cross-sectional survey for particular kinds of problem, let us examine Figure 19. This

January (t + 1)

		Big-enders	Little-enders	Totals (t
	Big-enders	30	40	70
December (t)				
	Little-enders	20	10	30
	Totals (t + 1)	50	50	100

Figure 19. Voting intentions (hypothetical).

tabulates the numbers of people who intended to vote for one of two parties at one period of time against the number who intended to vote for the same parties at a later time. The same people are involved through both time periods. Suppose, however, that the individuals used in this fictitious survey had been asked their voting intention at one time only, December (Time 1). This would have indicated a strong leaning toward the Big-enders' party, 70 to 30. However, the researcher knows full well that voting intentions some time before a poll tend to be less sure guides for predicting the outcome of an election than those taken nearer polling day. So, let us assume that the researcher interviews a *different* set of people in January (t + 1) and finds (total t + 1) that the Big-enders have been losing support to the Little-enders; indeed, during the month there has been a net shift of 20 per cent, indicating a late swing to the Little-enders party. However, if instead of interviewing different people the researcher had interviewed the *same* individuals on the two occasions, as is, in fact, shown in Figure 19, a rather more complicated picture would have been revealed. Although the Big-enders have lost support during the month, they have also gained during the same period from the Little-enders, who have lost, at $t+1$, some two thirds of the supporters they had at time t. The net result, and the only one relevant to the outcome of the election, is that the Big-enders have lost rather more than they have gained. Nonetheless, from the point of view of research into the process of voting decision and similar processes, the results of the panel study are of considerable theoretical importance. What they show is not a simple movement from one party to another, but extensive switching in both directions. This could not have been predicted using only the marginal (or total) figures for each time period alone. It is essential, if these submerged trends are to be isolated, for the analysis to be based upon the same individuals over successive time periods.[7] 'Turnover' analysis, as this is sometimes called, enables the researcher to get underneath the net shift to the changing patterns of, in this case, opinions and voting. This form of analysis, coupled with additional data felt to be relevant to the problem, will enable the researcher to explore the causal impact of a host of variables on the processes in which he is interested.[8]

Familiar problems which again should be noted in connection with panel studies are 'control effects' and 'sample mortality'. The former, as we have seen, arises when results occur owing to the effects of the investigation itself. Such effects are potentially confounding in panel studies because of the necessity to reinterview the same individuals through successive time periods. The respondents may become sensitized to the issues, or bored, or change their responses so as to appear 'socially desirable' to the interviewers, and so on. Ways of assessing control effects include the selection of matched control samples interviewed, unlike the panel, only once, so giving some guide on the likelihood of artifacts arising from the research process itself.

'Sample mortality' refers to the tendency of some members to leave the sample through reasons which include boredom, feelings about the invasion of privacy, moving away from the area, and so on: all more than likely with research over an extended period. The loss of respondents through these self-selection processes introduces a possible bias. Unlike cross-sectional samples, substitutes cannot be used in panel studies, for the obvious reason that the logic of the method requires that the same people be interviewed at successive periods. The usual way out is to analyse the character-

istics of the missing persons to check them against those who stay
the course and see if there is any noticeable feature about them
which may introduce a bias in the results.

Uncertainty of Response

Another issue which makes matters less than simple in panel studies
is to distinguish between two kinds of change: changes in opinions
and changes owing to uncertainties of response. In the turnover
analysis just illustrated, it was shown that respondents had been
switching, like demented yo-yo's, from one party to another. So,
it is necessary to determine, as far as possible, whether the variation
in responses from time to time is owing to change—in this case,
change in voting intention owing to changes in opinions and
attitudes—or to uncertainties that arise from the instruments used
to measure intentions. That is, it is necessary to distinguish two
types of variability: change and uncertainty of response. This is
important for the following reasons. In examining, say, the process
of voting decision, we might be rather more interested in those
factors which result in 'real' changes of opinion and support and
less concerned with those which result in what might be termed
random responses or uncertainties. This is not to say that uncertainties of response are always dull or of no interest. Indeed,
they are very relevant to the attitude theories and their associated
theories of instrumentation; between the notion of 'having an attitude' and the instruments used to measure it. If responses show
uncertainties, this may say a great deal about the measuring instruments and the theories of verbal behaviour upon which they depend.
One strategy to separate out these two sorts of variability is to
compare, over time, responses with some model derived from
assumptions made about the nature of the change.

To illustrate this, let us use the example provided in Figure 19.
The data represents the hypothetical vote intentions of a hypothetical set of people interviewed at two separate points in time, t
and t+1. Note that these are observations at two points in time
only; and no doubt members of the sample will have opinions at
times other than those publicly elicited by the researcher. Some will
have the same opinion and some will have different opinions at
any given time. If, however, it is assumed that no sudden and
influential event had occurred to cause people to change their
opinions at other than a 'normal' rate, then, it could be argued,
that the rate of change from t+1 to another time point, t+2, could
be reasonably estimated from the rate of change from t to t+1. In

other words, by assuming a stable rate of change, we can generate predictions and see if they square with subsequent data. Using the data in Figure 19 to provide estimates of rates of change, of the 70 Big-enders at t, 40 have changed to the Little-enders at t+1 (call this B to L), so the transition is 40 from 70, or 40/70 (·6), This means that, from t to t+1, 30 Big-enders stayed (call this B to B), giving a rate of 30/70 (·4). The rate of those staying Little-enders (L to L), is 10/30 (·3), and the rate at which Little-enders have shifted to Big-enders (L to B) is 20/30 (·7). The transition rates for all possible changes and non-changes from t to t+1 is given in Table 1.

Transition states t to t+1	Transition rates
Big-ender to Big-ender (BB)	·4
Big-ender to Little-ender (BL)	·6
Little-ender to Big-ender (LB)	·7
Little-ender to Little-ender (LL)	·3

Table 1. Transition rates.

To construct a prediction matrix for changes t+1 to t+2, the transition rates are applied to the relevant frequencies in Figure 19, giving the changes from t to t+1. Notice that we are now dealing with three time points, and so members of the sample will have had the opportunity to change twice, so the frequencies predicted for t+2 will be composed of those who stay the same from t through t+1 to t+2, those who, at t+1, changed but now change back at t+2, and those who stayed with their original preference at t to t+1, but who, at t+2, change their preference. Figure 20 gives the predicted figures for t+2. The figures in each cell are arrived at by multiplying the appropriate cells in Figure 19 by the transition rates given in Table 1. Thus, cell (a) in Figure 20 consists of those who were Big-enders at t and who stayed so right through (B to B to B), plus those who changed back at t+2 (B to L to B). So, multiplying BB in Figure 19 by the transition rate appropriate (·4), we get BBB, or 12 who stayed loyal to the Big-enders throughout. Multiplying those who changed from Little-enders at t to Big-enders at t+t by the transition rate L to B governing the probability of their changing back to Big-enders at t+2, we get 40×·7, or 28. Adding these to the total of Big-enders who stayed loyal gives a total for the Big-enders, at t+2, of 40. The same procedure

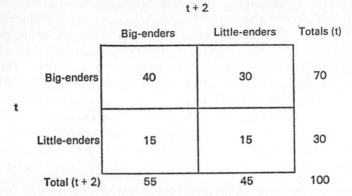

Figure 20. Voting intention: turnover table, t to t+2.

is used to complete the other cells. (The types of changes and their frequencies can, of course, be presented separately, depending upon the purpose of the analysis.)

Given this prediction for t+2, the erstwhile researcher could have conducted a further survey to check his results against those predicted on the assumption of a stable rate of change. If the results were a close approximation to those predicted, then this could be taken as grounds for the responses being not random but representing changes in preferences owing to relevant social processes. The random model would have to assume that the uncertainties were short term, leading to small perturbations in the marginal frequencies from time to time, but leaving the proportions going to each party roughly the same. That is, it would argue that the changes noted from t to t+1 were simply fluctuations around a stable trend. Of course, this simplified illustration fails to give such strong evidence as might be hoped for separating out uncertainties of response from changes, and measurement at other periods would be better.[9] However, it does hopefully give some idea of the kind of analyses possible when time is part of the research design. Moreover, it makes more possible the development of theories which take social processes into account than is the case with cross-sectional research.

The Trend Study and Time Series

Panel studies, though they do not offer an opportunity to monitor processes continuously, involve a research design which tries to use time not only as a way of obtaining a better description of social processes, but also to assist in the sorting out of causal order; in this, it is like the experiment. Of course, the sociologist's interest in time-ordered data is not always susceptible to this kind of design, especially since it means collecting data as the social processes unfold. The trend study, on the other hand, differs from the panel study in that selected properties are monitored over a continuous stretch of time rather than at discrete time points. Obviously the possibility of such a study will depend upon the availability of sufficient continuous data : a likelihood considerably enhanced by the trend over the past century—in industrial societies at least—of improved and more extensive methods of public accounting, as reflected in the census, poll records and the collation of various kinds of economic information.

Year	USA	England	France	Germany	Other	Unknown	Total
1800–09	2	8	9	5	2	1	27
1810–19	3	14	19	6	2	3	47
1820–29	1	12	26	12	5	1	57
1830–39	4	20	18	25	3	1	71
1840–49	6	14	13	28	7	–	68
1850–59	7	12	11	32	4	3	69
1860–69	5	5	10	33	7	2	62
1870–79	5	7	7	37	6	1	63
1880–89	18	12	19	74	19	5	147
1890–99	26	13	18	44	24	11	136
1900–09	28	18	13	61	20	8	148
1910–19	40	13	8	20	11	7	99
1920–29	27	3	3	7	2	2	44

Table 2. Numbers of discoveries in the medical sciences by nations, 1800–1926.

Table 2 presents the trends in medical discoveries for the United States, England, France and Germany for the period 1800 to 1926.[10] Two different trends are revealed. Between 1810 and 1819, there is a rise in the number of discoveries made by France and Britain, followed, in the next decade, by Germany. By 1840, France and Britain have passed their peaks and begin to decline until the 1870s. The second trend begins in about 1880, when France, Germany and Britain begin an upsurge, followed closely by the United States. Both waves show the simultaneous exploitation of discoveries in a number of fields applied to medical science. The problem is to explain the changes in the relative shares of the countries during the period. Early French supremacy in the beginning of the century was followed closely by Britain, giving way to Germany through the second half of the century while the United States's share rapidly increased from the 1880s until, by the end of the period covered, it became the largest contributor.

As usual, the tactic is to rule out as many of the alternative explanations as possible. Some of these have to do with the accuracy of recording 'discoveries'; a particular case of the general problem attaching to data of this kind. Assuming, however, that there are suitable grounds for treating the data as reasonably plausible, what else could account for the patterns observed? One fairly obvious possibility is that medical discoveries, being complex matters, are dependent upon processes not presented in the table. It may be, for example, that each country varied in the scientific ideas available to its members. Ben-David suggests that this is implausible, in this case, there being ample evidence of international communication within the scientific community as a whole. Other factors which come to mind are population growth and increases in national income. That is, the number of medical discoveries made within a country could be a simple function of the number of scientists, which, in turn, is a function of the size of the population. If so, the trends are to be explained by a simple demographic argument: the greater the population, the greater the number of scientists and, by extension, the greater the number of discoveries made. In both these explanations—population size and growth of national income—Ben-David's analysis suggests that neither have much to do with the frequencies of discoveries in each country. His own explanation is that the trends are a result of the extent to which the countries concerned 'exploited, through enterprise and organizational measures, the possibilities inherent in the state of science'. Both Germany and the United States 'were quicker than France and Britain in the recognition of new disciplines, the creation of specialized scientific jobs and facilities for research, and the introduction of large-scale systematic training for research'.[11]

This process of sorting out alternative explanations should, by now, be fairly familiar. However, with regard to trend data one or two interesting problems arise. A glance at the data in Table 2 and reference back to Figure 19 should suggest something fairly familiar to statisticians, namely, that the pattern revealed by any trend curve is partly dependent upon the time periods or intervals selected to present the data, as well as on the host of factors which explain the trends. The data on scientific discoveries, for example, is presented for every ten years, each figure being an average for each decade. The reason for presenting the data in this way is, presumably, that yearly data would have produced a more confusing picture. Year-by-year figures would probably have shown considerable variation, producing a less than smooth and definite trend. Presenting the data decade by decade averages out yearly variations to reveal a more consistent curve. Naturally, this is achieved at the cost of variety; removing, in other words, variations which we should have had to consider if we had been dealing with scientific discoveries in a shorter time period, say over twenty years rather than a century. Alternatively, if the time period had been extended over four centuries, we might have been forced to use longer intervals than a decade. The point is not that there is anything necessarily wrong with manipulating the time intervals in this way; merely, at this stage, to note one consequence.

A second interesting feature of time-series analysis, and one partly related to the issue of time intervals, is that the longer the time interval, the more general one's explanation of the trend is likely to be. Hence we are less interested in why the number of discoveries made in the United States between 1850 and 1969 dropped from 7 to 5, and more concerned with the longer-term shifts in the frequencies of discoveries. The shorter-term changes are likely to be attributed to 'historical' or 'unique factors', and the longer-term processes to more general social processes. Whether or not this is always justifiable remains to be seen. What, for example, are we to make of the decline in discoveries in all countries in the penultimate decade? Are these a result of the temporary effects of the First World War, or to more general social changes, or to both? This is a problem for theory as well as technique.

Components of Time Series

To meet these kind of issues, time-series analysts regard any time-series data as a product of four components: (a) the secular trend, (b) seasonal fluctuations, (c) cyclical movement and (d) irregular variation.[12] Using time as the independent variable, the 'secular trend' is the long-range movement of a dependent variable over an extended period. In the example used, the secular trend in medical discoveries would, over a long period, have shown a general upward direction. Other examples would be the rise in the world's population since man first set foot on the planet, airline passenger miles, pollution, the consumption of fossil fuels, the destructive power of military weapons, and so on. Other phenomena, of course, may show a decline, no change, or both rises and falls. 'Seasonal fluctuations' are that component of the dependent variable which shows a regular variation, usually annually, such as the peaks in shop sales just before Christmas, or the demand for heating fuel for household use being higher in winter than in summer. Seasonal factors may account for some of the departures from the general secular trend. 'Cyclical movement' is characterized by wide swings, usually of a year or more in duration, of a temporary nature brought about by non-recurring events. Since cycles are caused by a host of factors and vary in both length and intensity, they are often the most difficult to isolate. An example from economics would be distortions in economic growth caused by wars or external military threat.[13] These three components of a time series are known as systematic influences. 'Irregular variations', on the other hand, are swings which are unpredictable, and hence are often referred to as random factors. Owing to the difficulties of separating longer-term cyclical movements from random factors, short-term perturbations are the ones normally included in the irregular variations category.

Thus any time series consists, in varying degrees, of the above components, and the analysis of any set of time series data will endeavour to unravel them. In this way, long- and short-term influences can be examined or used as controls, depending upon the nature of the problem. For example, if we are measuring the effects of economic conditions, such as recession or growth on, say, crime rates, and if there is a case for believing that for both economic growth and crime rates there is a general secular trend upward, then this can be controlled so that shorter-term economic effects can be examined. In other words, the long-term secular trend in increasing national wealth, plus long-term trends in increasing crime rates, can be controlled so that shorter-term economic effects can be examined.

Trend studies, assuming suitable data to be available, enable the investigator to examine processes which operate through different temporal amplitudes. Points at which processes interact can be examined to see whether they mutually reinforce each other or cause disturbances. They also offer a potential, more exploited by economists and planners than by sociologists, of using knowledge of past trends to make future forecasts. Unfortunately, trend analysis is generally restricted to quantitative data of the kind especially prolific in demography and economics. It is not hard to see the reason, since plotting processes over time and comparing the relative amounts of a property between different time periods requires some determinate procedure which can normally only be provided by quantitative measurement. This means that such studies are subject to the weaknesses inherent in operationalizing concepts and devising appropriate measurement systems. Little attention has therefore been given to the 'softer' variables, such as cultural trends, values and the like, so beloved of sociologists.[14] In many ways this is a pity, for the logic of trend studies, especially that element concerned with identifying the different components making up any set of time-series data, would seem to make it a useful technique for analysing many sorts of social process, from small-scale fluctuations to large-scale cultural movements. As Sorokin's work suggests, there may be general cultural themes with amplitudes of centuries which influence, in their turn, other processes of shorter duration. All of which suggests a further possibility of generating models of social change and social process which operate, over time, in rhythmic ways: a revival of an idea held in the nineteenth century, yet exploited much more in other social sciences than in sociology. In economics, for example, the analysis of economic cycles has long been of central concern. Conventionally, economists distinguish between the short-term cycles of approximately three years, an intermediate cycle of nine to ten years, and the long-term, or Krondratieff, cycle of approximately fifty years. Moreover, to hark back to an issue mentioned right at the beginning of this chapter, there is a lesson for sociologists in that some economic literature makes the suggestion that certain economic theories, such as that of Keynes, though having applicability in the short term, are unsuitable for analysing processes of the Krondratieff type which reflected 'not only major economic trends . . . but all facets of national life—from prosperity to social unrest to involvement in foreign affairs', including in the downturn 'a strong shift to political conservatism' ![15]

Time and Sociological Theory

These remarks, however, bring us to a rather subtle point about temporal analysis. It has already been suggested that both panel and trend studies offer designs and research strategies by which an investigator can exert some control over the temporal priority of the factors that enter into an analysis. But, while these are important methodological devices, there still remains the problem of building time into the formulations of sociological theory. In trend analysis, for example, it has been pointed out that the variability shown by a time-series curve can fluctuate depending upon the time intervals used in presenting the data. Thus the analyst can present an 'illusion' of smooth change or erratic change depending upon the choice of perspective. This is similar to the historiographic practice of 'blocking off' time periods into epochs—the Middle Ages, the Age of Reason, the Domesday Book and beyond, the Tudors—which, though not unjustified according to certain perspectives, may possibly break into the stream of process too artificially.[16] The problem is to relate these practical procedures to theories of social change.

The idea of social change and its correlative notions has for a long time been a contentious issue in sociological theory. Theoreticians regularly engaged in mutual polemics over whether this or that theory copes with social change or presents an adequate conception of it. Thus, Marxist-orientated sociologists criticize structural-functional theories for their lack of concern with change and are criticized in turn by those who argue that the Marxist notion of change is too predeterminate. Whatever the answer to these theoretical debates, the problem is, methodologically speaking, to fit such ideas to the nature of the data as it presents itself over time. Part of the difficulty is that temporal perspective partly affects the choice of elements within any theory of social change, and we have already seen how the shape of temporal data is partly dependent on the intervals used and the time-series component chosen. To make matters worse, there is a suggestion that it may not be to its best advantage to arrange data according to calendric time. In other words, it has been suggested that sociologists, and maybe social scientists in general, hold too strongly to a conception of chronological or calendric time.

Conceptions of Time

The conception of time predominant in most of the social sciences is that of chronological time, 'composed of successive events which are actually or potentially interrelated, so that their succession in time can be said to be of consequence'.[17] The implications of this conception are three-fold. First, it assumes that knowledge of the moment when an event occurred will help account for its occurrence. Secondly, because of the homogeneity and irreversible direction of chronological time, conventional historiography tends to focus on what are regarded as more or less continuous large-scale sequences of events to be traced through the years; the creation of an illusion of continuity. Thirdly, the conception of flowing time often leads to a desire to translate 'the formal property of an irreversible flow into content—to conceive . . . of the historical process as a whole and to assign to that whole certain qualities', such as progress, evolution, steps towards a more hopeful future, democratization, development and so on.[18] In other words, there is a strong suggestion that our conception of time—in this case, as a chronological process—influences both the presentation and the interpretation of data, and hence it may be that other conceptions of time are more profitable. It is possible, for instance, to posit a multiplicity of times, regarding the historical universe as having a non-homogeneous temporal structure. This idea is not, of course, new. In many areas of historical scholarship, some phenomena are often regarded as following certain phases according to an immanent logic, chronological time being irrelevant to their intelligible sequence.[19] That is, the formal simultaneity of events in chronological or calendric time may well be irrelevant, and the understanding of these events dependent much more on the place an event occupies in the structure of the time it, as it were, carries within itself. This is similar to a distinction made by Nisbet between 'historical' and 'developmental' perspectives in social thought. The former tradition, maintained by the great historians from Herodotus and Thucydides through the medieval chroniclers and down to Gibbon and beyond, sees the past 'as a kind of genealogy of events, acts, happenings, and persons, each a point in recorded time that is theoretically specifiable, even datable'.[20] For developmentalists, however, the past is conceived as 'more or less timeless sequences of emergent *changes*'.[21] The historical view depends upon a conception of time in terms of moments, days, years emphasizing the exactness of the time-and-place relationship. While time obviously matters for the developmentalist, far more attention is given to arriving at correct before-and-after relationships than to what is regarded as a futile effort at fixing changes impossible to date with any precision. After all, how can change conceived as growth possibly be dated. More important is determining the phases which distinguish patterns of growth.

The methodological importance of this distinction has already been noted in other connections when it was pointed out that any investigator dealing with empirical phenomena is looking at them at a particular place and a particular time; in effect, in selecting cases for study, space and time are being sampled, but often in unknown ways. However, one consequence of this is that if the time frame for data presentation is calendric, time regarded as a 'matrix of meaningful process', then the analysis may force together simultaneous events which are 'intrinsically asynchronous', it being possible to regard any point in calendric time as a 'meeting place for chance encounters'.[22] This would be the temporal equivalent of the statistician's dictum that correlation does not imply cause: simultaneity does not imply causal connection either. As far as studies involving time are concerned, if they operate on a conception of calendric time, this raises difficulties of interpretation since empirical instances can always be regarded as samples of unknown universes which 'happen' to occur at a particular temporal point, tempting the investigator to treat simultaneous events as related without satisfactory warrants. One implication of this, for example, is that there may be no adequate licence to generalize from one set of data at one point in time to other points in time.[23] A large part of the difficulty is the commitment to the idea of calendric time, itself a product of a particular cultural milieu and maintained by social organizational requirements. In short, there is little conception within sociological theory of a sense of time which may get around the sort of problems just noted. Even developmentally inclined sociologists tend to examine and test their ideas on data, which is often ordered in calendric time.

It was mentioned earlier that instead of dealing with calendric time, sociologists should attempt, as a prior field of inquiry, to examine the time structure or shape immanent in phenomena. What precisely this would involve is rather hard to say. Other disciplines accept the idea of different time systems rather more readily than do sociologists, rejecting the conventional notion of chronological time. Sorokin, for example, summarizes some of the biologist's objection to chronological time in that it is 'external to the vital processes; it makes equal that which is biologically unequal . . .'. For example, all persons of the same calendric age are not necessarily at the same stage of physiological development. 'Hence, the advisability of measuring biological time by its own clock—the clock of the organism itself—but not primarily by the clock based upon the revolution of the earth.'[24]

While these remarks may well be relatively uncontentious, it is rather harder to see what could stand as social clocks equivalent to biological clocks, or social time equivalent to biological time. Certainly, it is obvious that socially relevant temporal frameworks are varied and dependent upon social contexts and meanings. Calendric time itself grew out of particular socio-cultural settings and is maintained by particular forms of social organization. The development of mechanical clocks and using the earth's rotation as a temporal yardstick was encouraged as social organization began to require more systematically ordered temporal units. The units used today—seconds, minutes, hours, days, weeks, months, years and so on—are simply an ordered model appropriate to a particular culture, whereas the time units relevant to other cultures are more suited to the patterns of social organization which underpin them. Pre-industrial peoples, for example, tend to have only fragmentary, discontinuous indications of time, but they are, nonetheless, entirely suitable to their purpose. They are unconcerned whether there are exactly four seasons in the year, in the sense in which we would understand this, or whether they occur at the same calendric point in each year. More important is the sequence of seasons for the peoples' economic and social activities. Time is for them a mirror of their daily, seasonal and annual activities, and these activities themselves are the time units, the points of reference for other purposes and events, social and non-social. By contrast, in industrial societies time largely takes its sense from the nature of work. Time is 'spent', 'saved', 'added', 'used' and 'lost': it does not simply 'pass'. Involved is a notion of time which is manipulable and rooted in the organizational routines of work, rest and play: a conception very different from those more typical in pre-industrial societies.[25] Other situations in social life display different conceptions of time appropriate to the contexts concerned. Some time statements within our own society indicate flexible time frames for structuring the routines necessary for daily life. Thus, 'See you tomorrow', 'We'll meet at lunchtime today', 'The end of this term', 'When I was young', 'It's about time you stopped drinking so much', and so on, which, though commonplace, give temporal reference by marking features of the social process in ways meaningful to members. Nor should they be understood as loose expressions which, if stated precisely, could be mapped on to a frame of chronological time. Instead, they have their own purpose to perform in social interaction, and represent systems of time, rooted in the features of the social processes themselves and chronological time, as a standardized frame, largely irrelevant to their meaning and use within members' discourse.

Conclusions

What does all this brief discussion suggest? While it is conceivable to regard social time as a multiplicity of time frames, it is more difficult to decide whether it is useful to do so. Although the conventional use of time as a frame for the study of social process has the disadvantages noted earlier, it is, at least, convenient in the absence of better suggestions. The idea of time frames bonded to social processes themselves, as suggested by analogy with biology and other natural sciences, is not always easy to appreciate in reference to social phenomena. As for macro-sociological phenomena, there are models available which have time shapes built into them. Exponential curves used to describe population growth are examples which can be applied to many processes of interest to the social scientist, such as industrial growth. But, apart from Sorokin, few sociologists have tried to tackle the temporal rhythms involved in 'softer', less quantifiable phenomena, such as cultural themes. Moreover, before much progress can be made, it is necessary for social theorists to take seriously the time shapes involved in phenomena, for only by doing so can measurement problems be sorted out. As far as micro-relations are concerned, theorists have to begin to examine how time is rooted in social organization itself.

Exercises

In this chapter, time was considered as a factor essential to establishing the causal priority of variables and as a feature of the social process.

1. In this first exercise, what you are asked to do is collect some time-series data and analyse it. (This latter part may well require you to consult some relevant statistics textbook.) You could collect data on various crimes over a period of years, trying perhaps to relate these to similarly ordered economic factors. Alternatively, educational statistics are also fairly easily obtainable. Be imaginative, but be careful. Many time-series figures are often standardized from a base-year. Watch for this. Also, this project will force you to the library to find statistical source books, which is no bad experience.

Once the figures are collected, try to discern some patterns and account for them. Try to sort out the various components of the time series. Can you explain them? Think back to the idea of quasi-experiments and see if this approach is applicable to your attempts to explain patterns in the data.

2. This second exercise will require careful planning since you will be using a panel design to study opinion change. Pick some subject-matter about which people might have opinions, e.g. proposed

government legislation, relations with a foreign government, immigration, proposed road route, and so on. Or, if you like, get hold of a well-corroborated attitude scale and use this. Construct or borrow some verbal items to elicit the opinion or attitude from respondents. You might also like to include some more 'factual' items to see whether the responses to these are over time more stable than the attitudinal items. But keep your questionnaire short.

Now, here's where the prior planning comes in. Plan to interview your target group—once again, pick a sample size which the class can handle—at least three times over intervals of, say, a month between interviews. Do not forget that you have to interview the *same* people each time, so think about what you are going to do about those respondents who do not complete the course. Students are a convenient target group, since they are perhaps more easily accessible. Also, do not forget to think of some suitable statement to warrant your return to interview the respondents: a statement which does not give the game away.

Once the sets of interviews are complete, do the panel analysis. Look for the following kinds of things. Are the responses stable over time? In other words, do the responses at t_1 correlate with those at t_2, and these in turn with those at t_3? Is there any sign of a general movement of opinion change, or does the 'turnover' indicate switching in a number of directions? If the responses show some fluctuation, to what do you attribute this: to opinion or attitude change, or to weaknesses in the instruments used? Is it possible that respondents became sensitized? What implications does panel analysis have for the cross-sectional survey and the sociology built upon it?

3. This exercise is less concerned with time as a future of research design and has more to do with time as a parameter of interpersonal social organization.

Many observers have noted that the social meaning of time varies between societies and cultures. (See E. T. Hall, *The Silent Language*, Doubleday, New York, 1959 for an illuminating discussion.) So, for a day or so keep your eyes and ears open and collect as many instances of the way in which time enters into everyday life. For example, you might collect expressions like the following. 'We waited twenty minutes, and when he didn't turn up to give the lecture, we all left'; 'See you sometime'; 'Oh, I'll do it soon'; 'What time is it by your watch?'; 'When shall we break the news to them?' All of these stand for richnesses of meaning which, though we use them as a resource in our everyday lives, are rarely studied by sociology. However, time meanings are not necessarily indicated verbally. Gestures, the pacing of events, waiting times and so on are all relevant. Collect some of these instances and think about what they indicate about the meanings people use to order their lives temporally. Can the meanings or acts be understood apart from the situations in which they occur? How is time a parameter of social organization? Do your analyses have any methodological implications?

4. Finally, take some developmental model. There are a number available in sociology and political sociology from those to do with the process of industrialization, the rise of the nation state, evolutionary models and so on. One rather large question: how would you verify the model?

Notes and References

1. W. E. Moore, 'The Temporal Structure of Organizations', in E. A. Tiryakian (ed.), *Sociological Theory, Values and Sociocultural Change*, The Free Press, Glencoe, 1963, pp. 161–9.

2. For an interesting attempt to build a model of the actor's past, present and future orientations as they are relevant to social action, see W. Bell and J. A. Mau (eds.), *The Sociology of the Future*, Russell Sage Foundation, New York, 1971; and F. L. Polak, *The Image of the Future*, Vols. I and II, Oceana, New York, 1961.

3. See H. Martins, 'Time and Theory in Sociology', in J. Rex (ed.), *Approaches to Sociology*, Routledge & Kegan Paul, London, 1974, pp. 246–95; and E. Gellner, 'Time and Theory in Social Anthropology', in Gellner, *Cause and Meaning in the Social Sciences*, Routledge & Kegan Paul, London, 1973, pp 88–106. Erikson, however, argues that the 'everyday vocabularies of sociology are very largely geared to lateral connections in social life' and do not 'translate easily into narrative figures'—K. T. Erikson, 'Sociology and the Historical Perspective', in Bell and Mau (eds.), *The Sociology of the Future*, pp. 68–9.

4. One illuminating attempt to build a systems model with interactions over time is D. Meadows *et al.*, *The Limits to Growth*, Earth Island, London, 1972, which is based upon the work of J. Forrester, *The World Dynamics*, Wright-Allen, Cambridge, Mass., 1971.

5. P. E. Converse, 'Attitudes and Non-attitudes: Continuation of a Dialogue', in E. R. Tufte (ed.), *The Quantitative Analysis of Social Problems*, Addison-Wesley, Reading, Mass., 1970, pp. 168–89.

6. See P. F. Lazarsfeld, 'The Use of Panels in Social Research', in P.

F. Lazarsfeld *et al.*, *Continuities in the Language of Social Research*, The Free Press, New York, 1972, pp. 330–7; and W. D. Wall and H. L. Williams, *Longtitudinal Studies and their Contribution to the Social Sciences*, Heinemann, London, 1965.

7. P. F. Lazarsfeld *et al.*, *The People's Choice*, Columbia University Press, New York, 1948, is a study of voting decisions using panel data based on seven months of re-interviewing the same individuals each month. It should be pointed out that the largest collection of panel data is provided by and for governments for national accounting and welfare purposes.

8. See, for example, L. Goodman, 'Statistical Methods for Analysing Processes of Change', *American Journal of Sociology*, 68, 1962, pp. 57–87; T. W. Anderson, 'Probability Models for Analysing Time Changes and Attitudes', in P. F. Lazarsfeld (ed.), *Mathematical Thinking in the Social Sciences*, The Free Press, Glencoe, 1954; L. M. Wiggins, *Panel Analysis*, Elsevier, Amsterdam, 1973; and J. S. Coleman, *Models of Change and Response Uncertainty*, Prentice-Hall, Englewood Cliffs, 1964.

9. See ibid., for a more extensive discussion. Also, O. J. Bartos, *Simple Models of Group Behaviour*, Columbia University Press, New York, 1967, Chapter 3; J. G. Kemeny and J. L. Snell, *Mathematical Models in the Social Sciences*, Ginn & Co., Boston, 1962, Chapter 5; and P. Doreian, *Mathematics and the Study of Social Relations*, Weidenfeld & Nicolson, London, 1970, Chapter 8.

10. The table is taken from J. Ben-David, 'Scientific Productivity and Academic Organization in Nineteenth-Century Medicine', *American Sociological Review*, 25, 1960, pp. 828–43. Reprinted in W. J. Cahnman and A. Boskoff (eds.), *Sociology and History*, The Free Press, Glencoe, 1964, pp. 516–35.

11. ibid.

12. L. L. Lapin, *Statistics for Modern Business Decisions*, Harcourt, Brace & Jovanovich, New York, 1973, Chapter 15, gives a good comprehensive account of some of the methods used in time-series analysis.

13. It is possible, of course, to regard events such as these as 'natural' outcomes of long-term social developments: the Marxian idea of societies carrying in them the germs of their own destruction, for example.

14. P. Sorokin, *Social and Cultural Dynamics*, 4 vols., American Book Co., New York, 1937–41, is perhaps the most outstanding example to the contrary.

15. See G. Barraclough, 'The End of an Era', *New York Review of Books*, 21, 27 June 1974, for a review of some of the literature.

I

16. See, for example, G. Gurvitch, 'The Social Structure and Multiplicity of Times', in Tiryakian (ed.), *Sociological Values*. Gurvitch terms the historian's use of time as 'reconstructed time'.

17. S. Kracauer, *History: The Last Things Before the Last*, Oxford University Press, New York, 1969, p. 140.

18. ibid., p. 141.

19. ibid., p. 142. Also, J. McHale, *The Future of the Future*, Brazillier, New York, 1969, esp. Chapter 2.

20. R. A. Nisbet, *Social Change and History*, Oxford University Press, London, 1969, p. 30. Also G. Gurvitch, *The Spectrum of Social Time*, Dordrecht, 1964.

21. Nisbet, *Social Change and History*, p. 21.

22. The quotes are from Kracauer, *History*.

23. This point can be overdrawn to a crippling degree.

24. P. Sorokin, *Sociocultural Causality, Space, Time*, Russell & Russell, New York, 1964, p. 163. The whole of this section is well worth reading.

25. ibid., p. 175; and J. E. T. Eldridge, *Sociology and Industrial Life*, Nelson, London, 1973, pp. 47-9, for a discussion of time in reference to industrial society.

10
On Being Formal

An increasingly significant orientation within sociology is devoted to the development of more precise descriptions and explanations of social phenomena through the application of various kinds of formal language, especially those of mathematics.[1] Sociology as a whole, however, has not taken to this trend with the eagerness of other social sciences, notably economics, where mathematical notations have long played an important part in theoretical formulations and where econometrics is a well-developed field in its own right. In this chapter, I want to look more closely at some other applications, especially those concerned with mathematics as a language for theory. It is beyond the scope of the present volume to give a detailed discussion of particular statistical and mathematical models used in sociology. However, we can pose questions of the kind: Why use formal models? What improvements in knowledge can be claimed for such methods? On what kind of assumptions do they depend? Although the use of formal models is often criticized, it is as well to remember that sociologists use such methods not because, like Everest or the moon, they are there, but because there are felt to be justifiable rationales which underlie their use.

The Nature of Formal Languages

By formal methods is meant mainly the systematic procedures of mathematics and logic. Mathematics, like ordinary languages, consist in the manipulation of symbols according to stated definitions and rules. Unlike natural languages, however, formal ones eliminate, as far as possible, the inherent vagueness which attaches to the languages of the everyday.[2] Compared with the richness and, some would say, the necessary vagueness of natural languages, a formal language is simple but precise in that it allows for the logical development of complex formal structures out of the few simple elements and rules which constitute the nucleus of the language. From the set of initial statements, axioms or postulates, a further set of statements can be deduced and elaborated. This means that once a mathematical language has been learned, uniformity of usage will usually result. A second equally important feature of mathematical languages, and one related to their precision, is their abstractness. In other words, they lack content. Natural languages, on the other hand, have a necessary content which allows them to perform their basic functions of describing, exhorting, explaining, lying, loving and so on, all essential to human interaction. This is one reason why verbal theories are often regarded as inadequate, since they are rich in meaning, innuendo and varied interpretations which create difficulties in seeing *precisely* what they imply. Mathematical languages, on the other hand, are 'poor in adjectives', and having no content, are totally abstract and unrelated to any world. In more technical terms, a mathematical system *per se* is an uninterpreted axiomatic system containing only logical terms, such as 'or', 'not', 'and', and arbitrarily chosen signs, such as '+', '=', '×', which permit deductions and proofs formulated by explicitly logical steps. Such a system has no reference to any empirical world.[3] It simply contains formal meanings and relational definitions specifying how terms in the calculus are related to other terms. Such a formal system, though less rich in implications compared with theories couched in natural languages, has implications more reliably derived and readily available for use.

It is these qualities of logical precision and abstractness which make mathematical languages so powerful for the scientist. The precision forces the scientist to remove ambiguities and vagueness inherent in natural languages, enables him to generate theory and its implications logically, and allows these to be communicated uniformly, while the abstractness helps in generating theories fairly wide in scope. To achieve these aims, some isomorphism must be claimed between certain of the languages of mathematics and aspects of the world (or, more correctly, theories about the world), as, for example, the isomorphism between algebra and mechanics. By doing this, the scientist provides himself with a powerful tool for stating his theories clearly, and also takes a model to act as proxy for relevant aspects of the real world which he can manipulate rigorously. In other words, by interpreting the abstract system— that is, by giving it content in terms of what are held to be properties of the real world—the postulates and axioms within the mathematical language are assumed to have some correspondence with processes in the world, and may even form the structure of scientific laws. As Miller points out, 'Any use of mathematics . . . rests on an analogy: something about the way the symbols are related must resemble something about the relations among the observed phenomena. . . . The task of an applied mathematician is to construct (or borrow) a system of symbols and rules whose structure is isomorphic with the structure that the empirical scientist discovers in his data and his experience.'[4] To achieve this it is obviously necessary to demonstrate the plausibility of the assumed correspondence between the elements of the interpreted mathematical system and those in the world: no easy matter, and one to do with the criteria for testing and validating theories. Moreover, it is a step which can sometimes lead to misconceptions concerning the relations in the formal model. Many of these are formal truths or definitions, not empirical statements in symbolic form or hypotheses to be tested. Their function is defined more by their role within the formal calculus. More of this later.

Measurement Systems and Formal Languages

One of the major attractions of mathematical languages as a language of scientific activity is their use in generating measurement systems. This forms one of the more important credits awarded to the natural sciences: the advances that have been made in the quantitative description of phenomena in their respective universes. It is this quality which perhaps forms the primary justification for the use of mathematics in sociological research. The problems of such applications have already been discussed when we saw how measurement in sociology essentially consists in using, within the data language, a set of rules to enable the researcher to generate numbers which can stand for or describe certain properties or attributes of the phenomena of interest. The procedure embraces the varying levels of measurement from nominal, which allows simple counting, to ratio measurement, which provides for the application of a wide range of sophisticated statistical methods. The rationale of measurement is the claim that it allows the researcher to sort out what is in the data and to provide a more rigorous statement of what has been found. The success of such endeavours depends very largely upon the plausibility of the assumptions contained in the measurement procedure, and their compatibility with those in the theory language. Unfortunately, as far as sociology is concerned, the state of the measurement game is not very satisfactory, and the major criticism levelled against current efforts is that it is measurement by fiat, which 'depends upon *presumed* relationships between observations and the concept of interest'.[5]

Much of the mathematical effort in sociology is statistical at what Coleman calls the 'variable-searching stage'; that is, searching for empirical relationships between variables.[6] To illustrate with an example used by Coleman, Durkheim's pioneering work on suicide was concerned to establish those factors which resulted in a greater propensity of the individual to take his or her own life. Durkheim collected a deluge of data on suicide rates in various countries, among different age groups, religious groups, marital groups and under varying economic conditions, and these were used to generate and test numerous hypotheses about the high suicide rates displayed by certain of these groups, among them Protestants, the elderly, widows, widowers, single men, childless wives, and so on. His analysis revealed factors important as possible causes of suicide, including 'egoism', or a lack of shared purpose. Though a quantitative analysis of the data was an important ingredient in his method, Durkheim's results were non-numerical, and indicated only the way in which the probability of suicide will move, given the presence of one or more of the factors held to be causative. For example, one conclusion could have been stated: 'As lack of shared purpose increased, so did the probability of suicide.' Durkheim's work, therefore, lay primarily in locating the important variables affecting the probability of suicide, and not in further specifying the form of the relation.'[7] Thus, although mathematical-type formulations enter into data analysis, their effect on the form or structure of the theory is often minimal. They are nonetheless important, and there exist quite sophisticated data-dredging procedures.

Formal Methods and the Search for Relationships: Causal Modelling

Causal modelling is one such set of techniques. Suppose a researcher is working in an area where there are a number of major theoretical contributions, involving, at times, different sets of concepts and variables and different orientations and assumptions. Suppose, also, that the field contains empirical findings which have relevance for a series of disconnected theoretical propositions. In short, conditions pertaining in most areas of sociology result in the usual displays of inter-tribal disputes between opposing theories, wide gaps between the abstract concepts used in the theory and the indicators used in empirical research, and a plethora of conceptual schemes. What to do? Give up and try another subject? Or try to use strategies which might sort out the delectable mess? Every so often, someone will attempt to reduce the noise and confusion in various ways: by constructing typologies, by presenting inventories of causes or effects, or both.[8] Unfortunately, such strategies often fail to feed their results back into the process of building systematic theory, and are, moreover, unlikely to offer a set of decision rules which will enable investigators to choose between alternative theoretical formulations abounding in most areas of sociology. Causal modelling, on the other hand, is offered by its proponents as a relatively formal way of eliminating theories or models which do not adequately fit available data.

Illustrative of the logic of the method is the analysis by McCrone and Cnudde of the process of democratic political development.[9] The authors survey many of the ideas and theories in the field of political development which show a reasonably clear delineation of important concepts and variables as well as identifying a number of correlates of democratic political institutions.[10] This prior review of ideas and findings in a field is an essential beginning to the task of building and testing empirical models 'which provide a basis for inferring causal relationships by distinguishing between spurious correlations and indirect and direct effects'.[11] In short, out of these sets of empirical findings the job is to build a model which not only orders the findings into some plausible structure, but also reduces the number of alternative theories to manageable and systematic proportions.

Out of the literature, they select three variables as the most relevant to the process of democratic political development: urbanization, education, and communications; where urbanization refers to the growth of cities, education to the spread of literacy and the increase in levels of education, communications development to the development of mass media, such as newspapers, radio and television; and the dependent variable, democratic political development, the extent to which a political system displays competing sets of political leaders and free elections as the method by which these competing leaders are chosen for office.[12] However, even though only four variables (admittedly complex ones) are involved, there is a whole series of logically alternative models that could be constructed out of them. So, to simplify the process, several assumptions are made. First, political development is assumed to be the dependent variable and urbanization regarded as independent of any other variable in the system. Secondly, relationships between variables are assumed to be linear and additive. Thirdly, other causes of each of the four variables are assumed to be uncorrelated with other variables in the system. That is, it is assumed that if, say, economic development were associated with communications development, it is not also associated with education or the other variables, otherwise it would need to be included within the original model. Of course, if relevant data were available, it could easily be incorporated in the system. Yet, given the impossibility of including every potential variable, an assumption such as this needs to be made at some point. It is a way of getting around the classic social science problem posed by the relatively plausible argument that everything is related to everything. Finally, it is necessary to assume uni-directional causation, though more elaborate models allow for reciprocal causation.[13] Although assumptions such as these might seem to weaken the resulting model by making it too simple or too arbitrary, the act of making them explicit is crucial in that they help to decide the limits of the analysis. Once a model has been developed, it can be elaborated by changing the assumptions in a systematic manner.

Making use of inter-correlations computed from aggregate indicators of the four variables for seventy nations and the assumptions set out above, seven logically possible causal relationships between the variables concerned can be set out and represented as in Figure 21.[14] From here on, matters become a little more complicated. The three components of the first half of the overall model are set out in Figure 22, each representing logically alternative causal sequences and each offering a rather different interpretation of the available data. Model 1 predicts that the correlation between E and C is spurious, owing to the effects of U on both variables. If this model were to fit the data, both educational and communications development would have to be interpreted as the joint consequence of urbanization with no link of a causal nature between them. Model 2 predicts a rather different sequence. The interpretation here is that the sequence from U to C to E covers the relationship between U and E; urbanization produces the spread of communications, which, in turn, produces the growth in literacy and educational levels. The growth of mass media is, in short, a prerequisite of mass

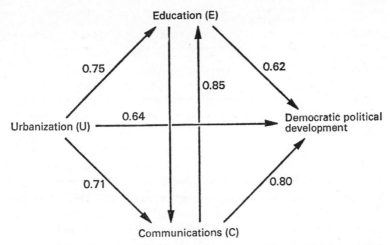

Figure 21. Logically possible causal paths between four variables (including correlation coefficients).

education rather than the reverse. The third model predicts that the causal links proceed from U to E to C, so accounting for the relationship between U and C. Theoretically, this would imply that urbanization is a prerequisite for the growth of literacy and education, and this, in turn, provides the public necessary for the development of the mass media. Note that none of these interpretations is trivial to the understanding of the process of democratic political development. Moreover, if one is able to choose between the alternatives, then this gives some credence to one interpretation over others, so reducing theoretical 'noise'.[15] Table 3 sets out the results of the procedure followed by McCrone and Cnudde in choosing between the alternative models. The prediction equation for Model 1 states that if Model 1 is correct—that is, if the correlation between E and C is spurious owing to the joint effect of U on both E and C—then the correlation coefficient between U and E (·75) and

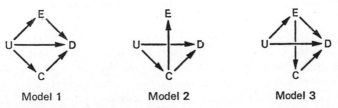

Figure 22. Alternative causal models—first half.

Model	Predictions Predicted	Degree of fit Actual	Difference
1. rUErUC = rEC	(·75) (·71) = ·53	·85	·32
2. rUCrCE = rUE	(·71) (·85) = ·60	·75	·15
3. rUErEC = rUC	(·75) (·85) = ·64	·71	·07

Table 3. Prediction equations and degree of fit for alternative models— first half.

U and C (·71) together should account for that noted between E and C (·85). If the correlation between E and C is spurious, it will be accounted for by the correlations between UE and UC.[16] However, the authors find that the equation rUErUC only accounts for a proportion of the actual correlation found between E and C.

Model 3 shows the firmest fit between the predicted and the actual correlations found in the data, so providing grounds for eliminating Models 1 and 2 and inferring that the developmental sequence is from urbanization to education to communication. It remains to look at the second half of the possibilities inherent in the general model. Figure 23 sets out the possible alternatives.

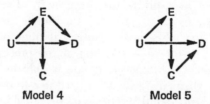

Model 4   Model 5

Figure 23. Alternative causal models—second half.

Since the direction of causation between E and C from Model 3 has already been adduced, only two logical possible models remain. Model 4 says that the relationship between C and D is spurious, owing to the joint effect of E; that is, education not mass media development is the final prerequisite for democracy. The final model predicts instead a sequence from E to C to D interpreting the original correlation between E and D. In this case, communication development is regarded as the final link in the chain of causation. Mass-media communications, encouraged by the growth of an educated public, assist in the integration of a society and lay down the basis for democratic political competition. The equations shown in Table 4 tend to confirm Model 5, namely, that the relationship

| Models | Predictions | Degree of fit | |
	Predicted	Actual	Difference
4. rECrED = rCD	(·85) (·62) = ·53	·80	·27
5. rECrCD = rED	(·85) (·80) = ·68	·62	·06

Table 4. Prediction equations and degree of fit for models of democratic political development—second half.

between education and democratic political development is an indirect one through communications.

A final link remains to be examined: the direct relationship between U and D. A logically possible model would postulate that the entire sequence from U to E to C to D accounts for the entire relationship between U and D; that is, the relationship between U and D is spurious. The prediction equation, $rUErECrCD = UD$ gives (·75) (·85) (·80) = (·51), which is ·13 short of the actual correlation of ·64. This relatively poor fit, the authors conclude, indicates that there is a direct, if rather weak, link between urbanization and democratic political development. The complete model which best fits the available data is U to E to C to D, with a weak link between E and D.

Some Assumptions of Formal Modelling

What does this kind of analysis achieve? Apart from those achievements, or otherwise, concerning the substantive area of political sociology, the procedure is, in effect, using the structure of a certain form of mathematics to 'reveal' a structure in the data. By using the structure of equations licensed by the assumptions, a model is created which orders and patterns the data in ways which make it sensible. In the example used, the various correlations uncovered by previous work have been ordered and the number of logically consistent alternative theories reduced. Not all alternatives have been ruled out, of course: only those not compatible with the assumptions and the data.[17] The point about the formalized elements, the mathematical equations, is that they set out in relatively precise form the criteria to be used to identify substantive rather than spurious relationships, and the manipulation of them enables the researcher to uncover a structure in the data which is both consistent with the theory and valid according to the criteria involved. There are drawbacks, of course, to causal modelling, mainly in that it is a logic appropriate only for certain kinds of data; that is, data which meet the requirements of regression and correlation analysis. If these are met, the logical properties of the models—in this case, prediction equations—impart a quasi-deductive structure to the data.[18]

The development of formal models of this and more sophisticated kinds depends heavily upon techniques and methods that have long been part of the sociological toolkit. Ideas of measurement, of describing relationships quantitatively and of statistical testing, all of which have been around for some time, are some of the basic ingredients out of which formal model building techniques have been created. But the resultant models do not belong to measurement as narrowly conceived, but represent a rather wider aim in developing systematic languages in which to 'talk' data. Sociology abounds with such models, and their formal elaboration has become almost a self-contained and self-sustaining enterprise within the discipline. Such are probability models as developed in statistical theory for sampling and testing purposes as well as for the measurement of phenomena.[19] What, in effect, such models do is to set up formal languages by which data can be created, manipulated and ordered. To this end, their formal deductive properties are important, but their ultimate relevance has to do with the assumptions necessary to the generation of the model, for it is these which determine its appropriateness for any sociological problem to hand. The use of statistical tests is a good example. To cut a long story short, statistical tests are designed to assess the probability that a particular result could have occurred by chance. The methods grew out of attempts to control irregular variations in research situations where all relevant factors were difficult to control. The answer was to randomize the uncontrollable.[20] The logic behind this is fairly familiar from discussion of the experiment: randomly allocated subjects to a control and an experimental group, thereby being able to estimate the probability of a difference in the results between the two groups being the result of chance.

However, for many reasons, such random allocation is not always possible in sociological research. The nearest to it in non-experimental work is random sampling. Thus, if we are looking at the hypothesis that women are more garrulous than men, we randomly sample within the categories 'male' and 'female' and test for differences and their significance. Unfortunately, there is some argument to the effect that such a procedure does not remove all uncorrelated biases: an important condition for applying tests of significance. For one thing, in few surveys is the number of cases large enough to control simultaneously all uncontrolled variables at the analysis stage. For another, all variables known to be relevant may not, for many legitimate reasons, have been included. And, finally, some variables may be so confounded with variables being analysed that control is impossible. For these and other reasons, it is often inappropriate to use statistical tests in non-experimental research, since 'only when all important correlated biases have been controlled is it legitimate to measure the possible influence of random errors by statistical tests of significance'.[21] There is a lot more that could be said on this topic, but the point here is that it illustrates how crucial are the assumptions contained in the model for validating its use: an obvious point, perhaps, but one often forgotten. Moreover, the suitability of the assumptions in the model is not a narrow question of technique alone, but is to be judged in terms of very basic ontological and epistemological postulates concerning the status, nature and subject-matter of the sociological enterprise.

Formal Languages and Sociological Theory

There are, then, relatively formal models which help to create and organize data in systematic ways. Their role often varies, of course, from problem to problem, but their major purpose is to formalize and systematize the data languages. Unfortunately, as said before, such models often fit uncomfortably, or are, at least, only weakly connected with the theory languages involved. Part of the reason for this, some would argue, is that sociological theory languages are inherently vague and are only slightly stricter than natural language. This conclusion has lead some theoreticians to explore the use of mathematics as a language for theory. As Coleman puts it, 'the power of mathematics in empirical science rests on its power as a language for expressing the relations between abstract concepts in a theory'.[22]

What Coleman and similar scholars are concerned about here is not simply measurement or establishing patterns in data, but with exploring the form of theoretical relationships through the logical structure of formal languages. Traditionally, sociological hypotheses are of the form, 'the greater the X, the greater the Y' or 'the variables X and Y are related', which, though useful and indeed powerful in their way, do not really allow the deduction of implications in ways demanded by the kind of theorizing discussed earlier.[23] As a result, complex theories expressed in natural languages are difficult to examine in terms of their deductive structure, internal inconsistencies or unexpected implications.[24] In this sense, mathematically formulated theories are not superior to purely verbal ones; it is simply easier to use the formal languages to derive unexpected hypotheses and to detect contradictions within a set of theoretical propositions.

Willer's Formulation of Durkheim's Theory of Suicide: an Example of Formal Theory

It is difficult to illustrate these points concisely while presuming little mathematical knowledge on the part of the reader, but hopefully, an example from Willer and his mathematical formalization of part of Durkheim's theory of suicide may help.[25] Willer took some conclusions drawn from Durkheim's work where he argued that suicide rates could vary with variations in three social conditions.

1. The rate of egotistic suicide will vary inversely with the degree of social integration in societies or groups in which the norms proscribe suicide.
2. The rate of altruistic suicide will vary directly with the extent of social integration in societies or groups in which the norms prescribe suicide.
3. The anomic suicide rate will directly vary with the rate of economic fluctuations, regardless of the direction of that fluctuation and irrespective of the norms regarding suicide.

These relationships are set out in Table 5.

Social circumstance	Psychological state	Result
Low integration (proscriptive norms)	Egoism	High suicide rate
High integration (prescriptive norms)	Altruism	High suicide rate
Rapid economic fluctuation	Anomie	High suicide rate

Table 5. Willer's formulation of Durkheim's argument.

The forms of the explanation for altruistic and anomic suicide are identical, while that for egoism is that in societies or groups with proscriptive norms, low social integration will result in a certain probability of a psychological disposition, egoism, resulting in a certain probability of suicide and thus a higher suicide rate.

Assuming the relationship between suicide and integration is linear, egoism may be formally expressed as

$$S_1 = \frac{C}{I_1} + K$$

where S_1 is the rate of egoistic suicide and I_1 the extent of integration. C, a constant, must be included, because there is no guarantee that doubling I_1 will reduce S_1 by half. K is necessary, since the zero points of the scales measuring S_1 and I_1 may not coincide. However, if we assume coincidence of the zero points and a one-to-one incremental relationship between the measures of S_1 and I_1, the equation reduces to

$$S_1 = \frac{1}{I_1}$$

The same reasoning gives $S_2 = I_2$ for altruistic suicide. For anomic suicide, if f is economic fluctuation, and S_3 is anomic suicide and K the constant, then the equation is $S_3 = Cf + K$. However, $Cf + K$ may be defined as the social effect of economic fluctuation (F), which reduces the equation to $S_3 = F$. By adding all the separate equations for each type of suicide, we get:

$$S_1 + S_2 + S_3 = \frac{1}{I_1} + I_2 + F$$

So, if the categories of suicide are exhaustive, then S, the gross suicide rate, would yield

$$S = \frac{1}{I_1} + I_2 + F$$

If the original equations are correct, I_1, I_2, F and S are defined in terms of each other allowing the prediction of the gross suicide rate. Moreover, if I_1 and I_2 are known, economic fluctuations can be predicted by manipulating the equations to get

$$F = S - \frac{1}{I_1} - I_2$$

and substituting

$$f = \frac{\dfrac{S - 1 - I_2}{I}}{K} - C$$

If the equation for the gross suicide rate were applied to a homogenous population[26] which had either prescriptive or proscriptive norms, but not both, concerning suicide, it would reduce to

$$S = I_2 + F, \text{ or } S = F + \frac{1}{I_1}$$

The degree of the population's integration would be given by

$$I_2 = S - F, \text{ or } I_1 = \frac{1}{S - F}$$

This simple example shows how a number of concepts can be related by defining each in terms of the others and so enabling the analyst to manipulate them as if they were physical models. The interest in this kind of exercise is often more immediately to do with the form of the relationships than the empirical validation of a theory.

Occasionally numbers are used, but the purpose is mainly heuristic and not directed towards the precise measurement of phenomena. Instead, they are used to illustrate the working of the model and also to see what any data would, in principle, look like in terms of the relationships specified in the model. Compared with those formal models illustrated by causal modelling, formal theory is predominantly concerned with the construction of relational structures and less with the counting, measuring and manipulation of data.[27] To be testable, the formal system needs to be married to appropriate measures or operational definitions. So, if M (X) is an operational definition or measure (M) of a concept (X), then the equation for the gross suicide rate becomes

$$M(S) = \frac{1}{M(I_1)} + M(I_2) + M(F)$$

In this way, the formal structure of the theoretical propositions specifies the relations between the measures and hence becomes testable.[28] Hence this simple illustration exemplifies the ideal involved in some views of the role of theory in the scientific enterprise, the structure of the theory shaping, in a direct way, the structure of the measures and, as such, representing a step beyond techniques exampled by causal modelling. In the latter case, the form of the theoretical model is put together, as it were, after the modelling of the data by the equations. Rarely is any claim made to an isomorphism between the structure of the theory-model and the data-model. Of course, in this example, the expression M(X) conceals any number of essential auxiliary theories of instrumentation as well as assumptions about the level of measurement. One more point: if the theory represented by the equations were confirmed by empirical work, then it could serve as a theory of instrumentation in its own right and be used as a way of generating indicators of concepts from appropriate data.

Some Other Uses of Formal Theory Languages

Though this was perhaps an over-simple example, hopefully it shows how the marriage of a theory with a formal model or system enables the researcher to manipulate the theory according to the rules or rationale contained in the model in interesting and informative ways. One point perhaps less clear is that the model, in its own way, exerts a pressure on the theoretician to specify and define less ambiguously the terms and propositions in the theory language so that they fit the precision of the formal language. Formalization forces the theoretician to check for incompleteness and redundancies in his theory and makes deduction more dependable. This is, of course, a double-edged sword, in that certain of the mathematical languages often require unrealistic or implausible sociological definitions. This is a point which Coleman makes. Unlike mechanics, or even economics, there are no readily available quantitative measurable variables such as mass, distance and time, or quantity and price, which makes it difficult to use the languages of algebra and calculus as languages for much of sociological theory.[29] Nonetheless, there are mathematical languages which allow for the expression of qualitative concepts—agreeing or disagreeing, liking or disliking, marrying or not marrying—more suited to expressions currently prevalent in sociological theory. A number of analysts have used the languages of matrix algebra, graph and set theory to build models ranging from the processes of social mobility, the development of stratification systems, hierarchy in organizations, patterns of social structure, kinship systems and so forth.[30] Also, in the same spirit, game theorists have long been attempting to construct concise models in terms of general theoretical assumptions and have applied them to interpersonal, organizational and international behaviour, the aim being to explain as much as possible in accordance with the canon of theoretical parsimony.[31]

The general character of formal theorizing, as said before, is less directly concerned with the manipulation of data. Although it may at some point be claimed that the formal system connects with the empirical world, the interest and fascination is in examining the model itself. From the initial postulates or assumptions, using the rules of operation or equations, derivations about the characteristics of the model's structure can be made and explored. Application of the formal system to the empirical world involves setting up rules of correspondence or interpretations determining what the calculus in the formal system means empirically. These rules of correspondence often have to do with measurement, but need not be quite so precise or explicit. An uninterpreted formal model can be given any number of meanings or interpretations. The systematization of deductions enables the theoretician to examine the abstract elements within the theory 'as a formal structure relatively independent of its particular embodiment'.[32] The effect of this is to generalize the theory by loosening it from one or more of its empirical interpretations. Thus, Markov chain models have been used to study such different processes as social mobility and voting-decision, and they could, in principle, be applied to any stochastic process in which the transition probabilities of particular states depend, at most, upon the preceeding outcome. Provided this initial assumption can be plausibly made with respect to any social process, then the model could be applied. (In practice, this problem is not as simple. For example, time lag is also important. It may be that a process is not Markovian using short-time periods, but is when longer intervals are considered.)[33] Naturally, the degree of correspondence that any particular analyst wants to claim depends a great deal on his or her purpose. Nonetheless, setting up correspondences or interpreting the formal system involves questions of empirical truth or falsity. Uninterpreted, the formal system is neither true nor false, except in a purely logical sense, about the validity of derivations from the initial postulates. When interpreting a formal system, the terms are given empirical meaning and retain their meaning within the formal calculus. It is important to realize, however, that not all terms within the formal system need have empirical or operational meaning. Some may act solely as connectives within the formal network. Thus, a number of interpreted formal models, or parts of them, often appear to have rather simplistic connection with the real world. In Willer's example above, S_1 is defined as egoistic suicide, which gives the symbol S_1 some interpretation. To root it more directly in the empirical world, the expression $M(S_1)$ is more pertinent, standing as it does for a whole gamut of measurement operations about what kind of phenomena are to count as 'egoistic suicide'. This point is important, since, formally, Willer's equations can be regarded purely as relational expressions defining some terms by others. It is not *necessary* for them to be interpreted as hypotheses or predictions. It may be that a particular analyst will be content to analyse the structure of the formal model as a system of relations using the relational rather than the quantitative power of mathematics.[34] If, however, a formal model is to be given a more direct empirical reference, the formal meanings need to be allied with operational meanings, and once this is achieved, the formal calculus will determine how the terms are to be manipulated, and hence determine how the interpreted model will behave. In sum, then, a formal theory or model contains a calculus and one or more interpretations. The calculus is a structure of relations, and the interpretation some claim is that the structure is isomorphic to aspects of the world.

This barebones discussion probably fails to portray the creative possibilities of formal theorizing. Given some conception of a distinct system, whether a bargaining relations, a conflict situation, a communication network, an industry or organization, processes of social mobility or attitude changes, the provision of collective goods, or whatever, abstracting and deciding upon what sort of relations can characterize this abstract structure may lead to important innovations in thinking.[35] Obviously the choice of characterization influences the kind of theory which can result, and is a further illustration of an earlier point about how basic ontological postulates serve to determine perspectives on the nature of social life. Diesing's illustration is a good one. The idea of perfect competition in economics has long been crucial, and its ancilliary ideas have been part of social science thought for some time. But a radical shift in emphasis occurs if the same phenomenon of personal choice is perceived in a different way; for example, as an $n \times m$ Prisoner's Dilemma game. In this game, a player, by trying to maximize his welfare, serves to destroy both general welfare and his own. The game serves as a method of exploring the parameters governing the interdependence between individual and general welfare by specifying the parameters: (n) the number of individuals, (m) the number of alternatives, and the payoffs to each choice. The perfect competition model fails to note this interdependence in making n and m infinite, with the consequence that the pursuit of individual gain automatically maximizes general welfare, according to the model.[36]

The Choice of Formal Language

Closely related to the characterization of the problem to be modelled is the choice of a formal language to 'talk the model'. The language will frequently influence the characterization as well as vice versa, especially since many subject-matters, as conceived at present, lack an appropriate formal language. A language is appropriate to the extent that its central terms, its semantic structure, match the concepts and logic of the theoretical subject-matter. Thus, in modelling a structure of social relationships, we need a language which can talk about connectedness, such as graph theory. An inappropriate match between the formal language and the theory would lead to distortion and implausible models. In constructing the formal definitions on which to use the language, the theorist may have the choice of taking either abstract or more realistic postulates. Depending on the purposes of the model, as well as on the facilities offered by the formal language, the theorist may make very simple, often unrealistic, definitions, to construct first the basic structure of the model and leave complicating details for later. In other cases, he may have little choice owing to the inability of the formal language to express more empirically adequate complications. Thus, the conception of interpersonal interaction as a two-person, zero-sum game with fixed rules is often a necessary simplification, since a variable-person, variable-strategy game with shifting rules, though empirically more adequate, would be mathematically exceedingly difficult.[37] Nonetheless, simple models can proceed through successive refinements to closer and closer approximations to more complex versions of the world.

As has been pointed out, a large measure of formal theorizing effort is content to build and explore the structure of models which may only have intuitive or heuristic connections with the real world, the aim being to develop theory languages before setting up correspondences in the data languages. The justification is that this is one way in which knowledge about the world can be organized and created in systematic ways. Though necessary simplifications may not matter at the initial stages, sooner or later, such efforts need to be 'fitted' to the world of data. Unfortunately, there are no rigid rules to guide this 'fitting'. A lot depends upon the accessibility of data, not forgetting that simply because one model is consistent with any particular data set, it does not mean that it is thereby validated: any particular data set is likely to be consistent with and deducible from more than one formal theory. Nonetheless, testing formal theories on appropriate data may lead to the gradual modifications of initial assumptions until a sufficiently powerful model has been built. Of course, this, like any other method, is not fool-proof. Although there is no such thing as *the* 'model-building method', model builders generally begin by constructing a first approximation, refining this by heuristic illustration, working out a few derivations and slowly proceeding to fill in details until systematic testing of the model is possible.

Simulation

The advent of high-speed, large-capacity computers has encouraged the development of the computer model which allows the model builder to operate with his model in a simulation. By rewriting the model in terms of a computer language, the analyst can often test out its performance under a variety of conditions. Occasionally models are built which allow for some degree of human intervention by interacting with the model in the machine. Moreover, if the model is designed as a close approximation of the world, various modes can be explored quickly and easily by changing parameters or assumptions. The implications of a model can thus be explored in spite of a world which changes at its own, often slow, pace. It should be added that not all computer models are formally deductive in the sense mentioned, since the behaviour of the parts of the model can be stipulated by rule rather than as a consequence of strict deduction from sets of postulates.[38]

Though the various kinds of formal models have their different uses, their proponents tend to justify them mainly in terms of their deductive powers. Data can be explained by deducing it from a model, thereby verifying an interpretation of the theory represented by the model. Hence, if an interpretation of a formal model has a 'built-in' behavioural theory, it can then enhance understanding of behavioural processes. This deductive quality has a number of advantages. One is that derivations from assumptions or postulates can be rigorously and reliably worked out. Secondly, because the whole system is deductive, only certain accessible elements in it need to be tested or examined since, if these are not empirically valid, then logical rigour requires modification of the primary postulates. Moreover, given plausible data, the terms in the model's calculus can be treated as placeholders for empirical content and data substituted for them. If, then, the calculus describes the relations in the subject-matter from which the data were gathered, further inferences from the data can be made. This practice is often used in forecasting such things as population size in future years.

Conclusions

It has not been easy in the space available to do full justice to the complex subject-matter of formal modelling or theorizing. The reader is advised to read at least some of the relevant literature and even, if really committed, to learn some of the necessary languages. This concluding section discusses points which have to do with the nature of formal modelling in so far as it is part of the sociological enterprise. Compared with some of the so-called 'softer' methods used in sociological research, the use of formal models may appear as far removed from social life as robots are from human beings. However, to the formalists, as Diesing calls them, even human life, at least in its scientifically important aspects, conforms to certain logical principles which they attempt to capture in formal models. Unlike the empiricist, who tries to work with a chaotic and sometimes vague world, '. . . the true [formalist] scientist must penetrate into experience to locate the underlying logical order that produces the surface regularity, and must replace the vague entities of sense with clear and distinct logical ideas'.[39] This implies the claim that apparently dissimilar entities—debates, elections, wars, organizations, patterns of fishing, economic enterprises —are reflections of the same underlying principles which can be talked about in terms of one or more formal languages embodying the principles. 'The empirical finery in which systems appear makes them visible, sensible, real, but also serves to obscure the formal characteristics that makes them knowable.'[40] To those who prefer to take their sociology with a rather stronger empirical flavour, this perspective may seem to rob social life of its *essential* character. Thus, a voting decision is not a game, it is a 'voting decision', and to understand this it is necessary to understand what a voting decision is in terms of the social context in which it has a socially relevant meaning. Social labels and categories are not simple epiphenomena or appearances of some underlying logical principles, but the very stuff of the social life which sociology must attempt to understand.

On the face of it (and perhaps in the guts of it, too), the opposition of these ontologies to each other seems total. Certainly the formal approach to theory construction departs radically from that typical for most of sociology. The greater proportion of empirical and theoretical work in sociology proceeds from data to concepts, an approach termed 'systematic empiricism'.[41] Unfortunately, such an approach does not make it easier to generate truly general theories of social behaviour—theories which have the qualities of those formulated in natural sciences. Whether or not the formal approach will prove more durable in the long run is hard to say. Only time will tell.

Exercises

Since most sociology students are relatively innumerate—and, if it is any comfort, the present author is not much better—it is difficult to devise simple and easy exercises in formal methods. Try your best with these.

This exercise asks you to try your hand at constructing a simple causal model on the lines discussed in the chapter.

Imagine that you have aggregate data correlations among the following variables: 'educational attainment', 'political participation', 'urban residence', 'social mobility'. (Don't worry for present purposes how the variables have been measured or what, in fact, the correlation coefficients might be.) Taking 'political participation' as the dependent variable, construct a causal model diagram to show the logically possible causal relationships. Make clear the assumptions you need to make so as to construct the initial model. Write out the prediction equations necessary to choose between alternative models. Select one of the possible alternative models and write a theory which could account for the relationships. What other variables could possibly affect those included? What assumptions is it necessary to make with reference to these other variables so that they can be regarded as extraneous to the system? Also, you may like to consider more general questions: What kind of things do you think this kind of analysis can achieve? What methodological assumptions underpin it as a method of analysis? What measurement models does it depend upon? The model here assumes simple linear relationships between the variables. What would happen if we assume other kinds of relationships? What would the model begin to look like if we included the idea of 'feedback' between some of the variables?

Notes and References

1. There are a growing number of textbooks in this field, including, J. S. Coleman, *Introduction to Mathematical Sociology*, The Free Press, Glencoe, 1964; P. Doreian, *Mathematics and the Study of Social Relations*, Weidenfeld & Nicolson, London, 1970; R. Mapes, *Mathematics and Sociology*, Batsford, London, 1971; M. A. Beauchamp, *Elements of Mathematical Sociology*, Random House, New York, 1970; and T. Fararo, *Mathematical Sociology*, John Wiley, New York, 1973.

2. This is not to argue, of course, that formal languages cannot be misunderstood and misapplied. Like anything else, people can use them wrongly.

3. H. Hochberg, 'Axiomatic Systems, Formalization, and Scientific Theories', in L. Gross (ed.), *Symposium on Sociological Theory*, Row, Peterson, Evanston, 1969, pp. 407–36.

4. G. A. Miller, *Mathematics and Psychology*, John Wiley, New York, 1964, p. 222. Some have persuasively argued that the development of natural science owes more to the use of mathematical methods than to the experiments; see H. Butterfield, *The Origins of Modern Science*, 2nd edition, Bell, New York, 1957.

5. W. S. Torgerson, *Theory and Methods of Scaling*, John Wiley, New York, 1958, p. 21 (italics in original). See also, A. V. Cicourel, *Method and Measurement in Sociology*, The Free Press, New York, 1964, Chapter 1, for an extended discussion and critique of the modes of measurement currently used in sociology.

6. J. S. Coleman, 'The Mathematical Study of Small Groups', in H. Solomon (ed.), *Mathematical Thinking in the Measurement of Behaviour*, The Free Press, New York, 1960, p. 10.

7. J. S. Coleman, *Introduction to Mathematical Sociology*, The Free Press, Glencoe, 1964, p. 4. Formally Coleman states the nature of Durkheim's problem as follows: what are x_1, x_2, . . . x_n in the relation $p_s = f(x_1, x_2, . . . x_n)$, where p_s is the probability that a person will commit suicide, and where x_1, x_2, . . . x_n are factors affecting p_s? Durkheim's partial solution lay in characterizing x_1 as the lack of shared purpose and in indicating the direction in which p_s varies as x_1 varies. Durkheim could have gone on to take the determining variables, such as religion, marital status, age, etc., as given, and have attempted to characterize p_s as a function of these variables and tried to specify the coefficients of the equation

$p_s = b_1x_1 + b_2x_2 + b_3x_3 + \ldots$, where $x_1, x_2, x_3 \ldots$ are the variables entering into his tables of suicide rates. See W. W. Cooley and P. R. Lohnes, *Multi-Variate Procedures for the Behavioural Sciences*, John Wiley, New York, 1962; and H. M. Blalock, *Theory Construction*, Prentice-Hall, Englewood Cliffs, 1969.

8. See B. Berelson and G. A. Steiner, *Human Behaviour: An Inventory of Findings*, Harcourt, Brace & World, New York, 1967, for the inventory approach; and Blalock, *Theory Construction*, for a discussion of 'noise-reducing' techniques.

9. D. J. McCrone and C. F. Cnudde, 'Toward a Communications Theory of Democratic Political Development', *American Political Science Review*, 61, 1967, pp. 72–9, reprinted in C. F. Cnudde and D. E. Neubauer (eds.), *Empirical Democratic Theory*, Markham, Chicago, 1969.

10. Most of this literature is reprinted in ibid.

11. McCrone and Cnudde, 'Toward a Communications Theory', loc. cit.

12. Alternative definitions of democracy are more than possible.

13. See Blalock, *Theory Construction*, for details. See also selections in H. M. Blalock (ed.), *Causal Models in the Social Sciences*, Macmillan, New York, 1971.

14. The original data was taken from P. Cutright, 'National Political Development: Measurement and Analysis', *American Sociological Review*, 28, 1963, pp. 253–64. Reprinted in Cnudde and Neubauer, (eds.), *Empirical Democratic Theory*, pp. 193–209.

15. Alternatives could, in some cases, be decided upon *a priori* grounds in terms of the internal consistency of the theories. The obvious difficulty is that internally consistent theories may not fit the data.

16. Note that even if E and C are only related because of the common effect of U on them both, they will still be correlated. The test is to see if U accounts for *all* the variance noted between E and C. See H. Simon, 'Spurious Correlations: A Causal Interpretation', *Journal of the American Statistical Association*, 49, 1954, pp. 467–79.

17. There are other sets of theories based upon different ontologies and epistemologies which are not ruled out either.

18. Abell calls such models 'quasi-deductive' because 'the data will, in general, be equally compatible with other models. Furthermore, since we are dealing with a probabilistic phenomenon, a failure to establish the predicted values does not refute the model outright but gives it a low probability of being correct'—P. Abell, *Model Building in Sociology*, Weidenfeld & Nicolson, London, 1971, p. 243.

19. The literature on this is impossibly large. D. E. Bailey, *Probability and Statistics*, John Wiley, New York, 1971, gives an interesting and comprehensive account of the applications of mathematical probability theories to behavioural problems.

20. The statistical thinking behind this argument is largely the work of R. A. Fisher; see his *Design of Experiments*, Oliver & Boyd, London, 1951

21. H. Selvin, 'A Critique of Tests of Significance in Survey Research', in D. E. Morrison and R. E. Henkel (eds.), *The Significance Test Controversy*, Butterworth, London, 1970, pp. 98–9. This reader contains an excellent selection of readings on aspects of statistical testing.

22. Coleman, *Introduction to Mathematical Sociology*, p. 34.

23. Blalock, *Theory Construction*, pp. 15–16; H. Costner and R. K. Leik, 'Deductions from Axiomatic Theory', *American Sociological Review*, 29, 1964, pp. 819–35.

24. Attempts have been made to recast sociological theories into deductive form relying on natural languages to do so; the most notable being Zetterburg's formalization of Durkheim's division of labour; see *On Theory and Verification in Sociology*, The Bedminister Press, New Jersey, 1965. Costner and Leik, ibid., criticize such efforts on two main grounds: (a) propositions of the form, 'The greater the X, the greater the Y' are ambiguous in that it is not clear whether causal asymmetry is implied; (b) if, in an empirical test, unexplained variation is found, the strict deductive argument implied in axiomatic theory will not apply unless one adds auxiliary assumptions about the behaviour of uncontrolled variables. Diesing refers to such attempts as 'implicit formal theories' because their structure is incompletely developed owing to the inadequate language used. P. Diesing, *Patterns of Discovery in the Social Sciences*, Routledge & Kegan Paul, London, 1972, p. 30.

25. D. Willer, *Scientific Sociology*, Prentice-Hall, Englewood Cliffs, 1967, pp. 10–13. Willier's example is intended, as he himself points out, as illustration and not a critique of Durkheim's work.

26. This qualification is important, otherwise the equations would apply only to homogeneous sub-groups appropriately defined.

27. Diesing, *Patterns of Discovery*, p. 35, points out the importance of this distinction when tempted to apply the justly unflattering label of 'quantophrenia'. The use of mathematics to study relational structures is qualitative not quantitative.

28. Willer, *Scientific Sociology*, is an extended discussion of these ideas.

29. Coleman, *Introduction to Mathematical Sociology*, p. 102. The argument is not that the calculus cannot be applied to sociological

problems, simply that the level of measurement available prohibits its use extensively. But see Simon's treatment of Homan's work in *Models of Man*, John Wiley, New York, 1957.

30. See Diesing, *Patterns of Discovery*, p. 33, for discussion of these ideas. He points out that the 'various branches of mathematics and logic deal with different kinds of relations, and whenever a new kind of relation is clearly and distinctly conceived, a new branch of mathematics or logic can be invented to deal with it'. Some examples of mathematical applications to sociological problems are to be found in O. J. Bartos, *Simple Models of Group Behaviour*, Columbia University Press, New York, 1967; F. Harary *et al.*, *Structural Models*, John Wiley, New York, 1965; J. Berger *et al.* (eds)., *Sociological Theories in Progress*, Vols. 1 and 2, Houghton Mifflin, Boston, 1966, 1972; P. F. Lazarsfeld and N. Henry (eds.), *Readings in Mathematical Social Sciences*, MIT Press, Cambridge, Mass., 1966; and R. McGinnis, *Mathematical Foundations for Social Analysis*, Bobbs Merrill, New York, 1965.

31. See M. Shubik (ed.), *Game Theory and Related Approaches to Social Behaviour*, John Wiley, New York, 1964; and W. Riker, *The Theory of Political Coalitions*, Yale University Press, New Haven, 1962.

32. Diesing, *Patterns of Discovery*, p. 116.

33. Bartos, *Simple Models of Group Behaviour*, p. 316.

34. Diesing, *Patterns of Discovery*, pp. 40–41.

35. ibid. This section of the chapter owes a great deal to the discussion in Diesing. His Chapter 3 contains an excellent account of the process of formal theory development.

36. Accounts of this and other games appear in H. Alker, *Mathematics and Politics*, Macmillan, New York, 1965; A. Rapaport, *Fights, Games and Debates*, University of Michigan Press, Ann Arbor, 1960; Shubik (ed.), *Game Theory*; Bartos, *Simple Models of Group Behaviour*; and, of special interest to the problem of relating individual to collective welfare, M. Olsen, *The Logic of Collective Action*, Schoken, New York, 1968; and K. Arrow, *Social Choice and Individual Values*, John Wiley, New York, 1951.

37. Diesing, *Patterns of Discovery*, p. 51.

38. See D. Meadows *et al.*, *The Limits to Growth*, Earth Island, London, 1972, for a computer simulation of the end of the world. Other readings include Diesing, *Patterns of Discovery*; and H. Guetzkow *Simulation and International Relations*, Prentice-Hall, Englewood Cliffs, 1962; and for discussions of simulation methods in general, M. Inbar and C. S. Stoll (eds.), *Simulation and Gaming in Social Science*, The Free Press, New York, 1972.

272 SOCIOLOGICAL ANALYSIS

39. Diesing, *Patterns of Discovery*, p. 126.

40. ibid., p. 132.

41. D. and J. Willer, *Systematic Empiricism: A Critique of Pseudo-Science*, Prentice-Hall, Englewood Cliffs, 1974.

11
Conclusions: Research Methodology, and Sociological Perspective

Throughout this book I have tried to give an honest account of some of the methodological issues arising from the various research techniques and approaches used by sociologists. Although I have tried to be as comprehensive as possible within the limitations of space, a good deal has obviously had to be omitted or discussed only briefly. There has not been much discussion of the practicalities of research or the kind of expertise that can only be found through experience in trying to make sense of some relevant data.[1] Nor have I dealt with statistical methods in any great depth, apart from making some general points about their role in some areas of sociological research. This omission is not due to a feeling that statistics is unimportant, but simply to considerations of space.

Instead, what I have attempted to do is to introduce research methods as an integral and essential part of the sociological enterprise and not simply as 'neutral "atheoretical" tools'.[2] While there is an important sense in which research methods can be regarded as neutral instruments designed to do a particular job (in this way, they are practical procedures for doing research), equally important from the perspective of this text is the fact that any method also involves a theory or theories of instrumentation. A questionnaire, an attitude scale, participant involvement within a social group or a sample survey rest on theoretical justifications which licence them as valid tools of research. A further major point made throughout was the importance of the researcher looking for alternative theories which could explain the findings he or she has observed and recorded. In other words, the major substantive theoretical problems which constitute the focus of the research, the reason why the data was collected in the first place, may not be the only plausible theories consistent with the data.

One inescapable fact, often ignored by sociologists, is that the research act is also a *social* act, and, many of the theories of instrumentation which underpin the various research methods are accordingly also substantive sociological theories in their own right. So, among the alternative explanations which may be consistent with a set of data, will be theories which have to do with the way the data is generated as part of the research process itself. In this way, every act of research can be regarded as a test situation for those theories of instrumentation. To take a familiar example, the interview is a test situation for those theories of instrumentation which state that valid responses will be produced by certain socially recognized behaviours on the part of the interviewer. That is, it is a statement of the necessary conditions to produce verbal behaviours —replies, opinions, attitudes—which are an accurate reflection of a respondent's thoughts, ideas and intentions. In a similar way, the participant observer will have to act upon certain theories about taking-a-role, and about the presentation of a *persona*. If he is adopting the role of a complete participant, the problem of managing two identities has to be faced: one as a member of the group under study, the other as a member of the sociological community. In any event, the 'solutions' he adopts are the acting out of implicit, often taken-for-granted, sociological theories about the nature of social interaction. One final example, the coder, when transferring questionnaire responses for machine processing and tabular analysis, often makes sense out of 'ambiguous' responses by using implicit, commonsense knowledge or theories about the social worlds in which the respondent lives.[3]

These social elements which arise because the research act is also a behaviour setting are traditionally treated as intrusions to the process of obtaining valid results. In the experiment, for example, realization of its social characteristics, in terms of such things as subject anticipation, cultural definitions of the context of the experimental setting, and the like, lead to refinements in study design. Similarly, a considerable amount of effort is devoted to removing the 'biases' that arise from the social interactions between interviewer and respondent. Moreover, the question of instrumentation is relevant to a fairly common problem in sociological research, namely, the comparability of results derived from different methods. To what extent, for example, are findings, and the theories based upon them, derived by a survey compatible with those provided by, say, participant observation or experiment? To what degree do the different methods complement each other? Is it possible that different methods focusing upon different units and used by different researchers can produce an accumulative and consensual body of sociological knowledge?

The Issue of Inter-Method Comparability

These questions are most difficult to answer, especially since the answers are dependent upon what happens to the sociological 'trade' in the future: a most unpredictable matter. However, conventional wisdom tends, I suspect, to regard the present-day debate over methods and approaches to be an interim phase characteristic of a youthful science. It is the belief that, ultimately, sociology will mature into a discipline which displays a greater degree of unity of approach resulting in a body of knowledge which is cumulative and consensual. But this is for the future. Most admit, at least, to the fact that sociology, for all practical purposes, will still be characterized by different methods of approach and varying inter- pretations. Such differences have their source in the varieties of methods used, the sociologists' differing interpretations, varying unit definitions, and the changing state of the reality being ob- served.[4] However, many practitioners believe this state of affairs to be not only inevitable but also a cause for hope rather than des- pair. After all, no method or approach is entirely encapsulated im- moveably within its system of meaning. If this were so, there could hardly be any theoretical development, no means of evaluating the knowledge gained from the methods used, and no way of redefining the meaning of the data we have. In short, no way of looking at the social world with new eyes and, perhaps, a fresher vision. In- deed, an argument put throughout this text has been that, by regarding methods as theories of instrumentation, sociologists would be forced to re-examine not only the utility of the method or tech- nique, but also, by treating it as an empirical theory, help the development of substantive sociological theory.

Methodological Triangulation

One interesting perspective on this issue of inter-method compara- bility is Denzin's notion of triangulation: triangulation of data, method and theory. The argument is that, given 'sociology's em- pirical reality is a reality of competing definitions, attitudes and personal values', research must acknowledge this, and to 'raise sociologists above the personalistic biases that stem from single methodologies', multiple methods and theoretical approaches must be used.[5] Denzin's four basic types of triangulation are data with respect to time, place, person and level; investigator in terms of multiple *versus* single observers of the same phenomenon; theory, by using multiple *versus* single perspectives in relation to the same set of objects; and, finally, methodological involving both within-method and between-method triangulation.

In more detail, this research strategy would involve, as far as data triangulation is concerned, for example, using as many data sources as possible to illuminate the same subject-matter. So, if studying the social meanings of death, to use Denzin's own example, the same method could be used to examine this phenomenon in as many different settings as possible: hospitals, families, primitive societies, highways and so on. 'By selecting dissimilar settings in a systematic fashion, investigators can discover what their concepts (as designators of units in reality) have in common across settings. Similarly, the unique features of these concepts will be discovered in their situated context.'[6] Using this principle with respect to different points in time, different kinds of unit, whether person or collective, and so on, a fuller and more rounded interpretation of a phenomenon could be obtained. Theoretical triangulation, more difficult to achieve, involves listing all the propositions in a field and subjecting them to empirical test until a reassessed and reformulated theoretical system grounded in empirical testing is attained.[7] Within-method triangulation is employed when the observational units are regarded as multi-dimensional. In this case, the researcher takes one method, such as the questionnaire survey, and develops multiple strategies within that method to examine the data; for example, by using different scales to measure the same unit. On the other hand, between-method triangulation means using dissimilar methods to measure the same unit. Since it is possible to regard the flaws of one method as often constituting the strengths of another, a combination of methods would seem to use the best of each while overcoming their separate deficiencies.[8] For example, it can be argued that surveys are best suited to studying relatively stable patterns of interaction over a large scale, while participant observational methods are more appropriate for revealing the subtleties and complexities of smaller-scale interaction. Moreover, according to Denzin, the theoretical value of a study can be enhanced by combining methods that might initially seem inappropriate, since even weak methods may reveal aspects of a problem that a theoretically stronger method might overlook. It is possible, then, that different methods can reinforce and complement each other. For example, comparing the results produced by participant observer methods and those by a survey of prestige ranking in a small town, two researchers reported that 'the techniques of participant observation and the sample survey are not competitive. . . . The survey provides representative information which is given meaning by the anthropological observer . . . surveys may be used to test hypotheses developed out of the less formal experience of the observer, particularly in those areas where information is admissable at a public level and where replication is both possible and meaningful.'[9]

The advantages claimed for the triangulation strategy are that it encourages a more systematic continuity of both theory and research. 'By combining multiple observers, theories, methods, and data sources, sociologists can hope to overcome the intrinsic bias that comes from single-method, single-observer, single-theory studies.'[10] Apart from the obvious practical difficulties which would arise in attempting to mount research incorporating the principle of triangulation, there is a good deal to commend it as a research strategy. It is, in an important way, a stronger statement of the culture of scientific inquiry itself: a culture which stresses objectivity, interchange and theoretical development through competition in the testing-ground of empirical verification. Moreover, crucial to the perspective are the theories of instrumentation, since any argument for comparability must demonstrate that factors intrinsic to the research act are neglible in the production of results, and unless such theories are known, no account can be taken of them. The theories of instrumentation are, if you like, the lynch-pin between data and theory and affect the theoretical relevance of a method.

Critique of Strategy of Triangulation

Unfortunately, this is not all that can be said on the matter. It was pointed out in Chapter 2 that sociological research tools, and the theories of instrumentation upon which they depend, are embedded in a meaning system which gives them sense. In this text, the predominant systems of meaning with relevance to sociological inquiry were identified as 'positivistic' and 'humanistic'. The former stresses the unity of approach between the natural and the social sciences, and while allowing for different methods of inquiry, argues that the social sciences, like the natural, are concerned to search for the causal laws which govern human behaviour. On the other hand, the latter perspective draws a sharp distinction between the 'social' and the 'natural' and seeks for explanations in terms of 'meanings', 'understandings', 'reasons' and 'purposes', so, it is claimed, preserving the distinctively human element in social inquiry. Furthermore, these perspectives cannot be regarded solely as disagreements about the right way to do research: they are statements about what forms the very 'stuff' of sociology and set up criteria of sociological understanding, defining when and how inquiry should be judged. As systems of thought they can be thought of as a structure consisting of the following kind of levels:

1. Epistemology: theory of knowledge and how it is to be acquired—views on what sort of knowledge of the social world we can hope to achieve.
2. Philosophy: substantive and generalized world views, which incorporates certain values and puts limitations on the substantive theoretical postulates which also form part of the system.
3. Theory: substantive hypotheses to account for and explain observed facts, phenomena and events.
4. Methodology: lower level prescriptions as to the methods to be used in research, e.g. hypothetico-deductive method, subjectivism.
5. Description, or field of study, actual method of describing observations.[11]

Although the connections between the levels may not be strictly determined in any strong logical fashion, it does illustrate the point that each method is, to a degree, embedded in such a system or structure of thought. Moreover, at the most abstract levels of epistemology and philosophy, disagreements cannot be solved by evidence and empirical demonstration since they define what is to count as evidence and what are to count as phenomena. If this is correct, it suggests that the principle of triangulation presumes too much about the way in which disagreements about theory and method can be resolved. It assumes, in other words, that there are criteria upon which all agree and which can be used to decide between alternative theories, methods and inconsistent findings. If a survey should provide one pattern of results, participant observation another, and an experiment still another, how are we to decide which result to accept?[12] Resolution can only be achieved if the parties to the disagreement agree on the same domain assumptions and beliefs regarding the nature of the discipline. In practice, of course, particular theories and ideas may be consistent with more than one set of epistemologies and philosophies, but ultimately, there is a point beyond which disagreement must prevail. Accordingly, on this view, sociology can never be a coherent body of knowledge, but only an arena of competing and irreconcilable paradigms.

Abandoning Method

What are the implications of this view for research methods and research strategy? For one thing, it would seem to deny that there are any *absolute* criteria by which sociologists can assess the validity of their theories. This is not to say that there are *no* criteria, simply that there are no absolute rules by which to evaluate the worth of sociological efforts. What, then, is the source of the rules by which we do judge, for judge we do? One answer is the community of scholars, the practitioners of the discipline. As Phillips puts it, 'every discipline's practitioners must agree on the criteria which, for that group and that time, determine what is to be regarded as factual and as constituting knowledge. In science, then, truth cannot be regarded as conformity with the "real" but rather as conformity with standards held in a scientific community.'[13] If this view of the status of 'truth', 'objectivity' and so on is accepted, it effectively places the sociologist along with the persons being studied in that, like them, the sociologist is involved in a process of making sense out of a social reality. Like social actors, the sociologist constructs versions of the social world, marshals evidence to support these versions and tests them out in an on-going process of social interaction. In short, the social character of the research act is not something of passing interest, something to be corrected so that 'bias' can be removed, but is of fundamental importance and an inescapable source of the very criteria by which research is judged. 'Sociological research is behaviour: it is action which is covered and guided by rules.'[14]

Teaching people to become sociologists means that they are exposed to rules of procedure which, if followed successfully, will lead to the kind of outcomes which the community of sociologists would define as normatively adequate. In other words, the sociologist is distinguished from the layman in that he or she belongs to a specific community along with other men and women who call themselves sociologists, and although he or she may possess more 'facts' or know more about what other sociologists have written or said, there is no specific method, no ultimately warrantable method, which puts the sociologist's skill and expertise superior to or beyond that of the layman. Sociology, in Phillips's borrowing of Wittgenstein's phrase, is simply a 'form of life'.[15] The criteria for knowledge, truth, objectivity and so on, are not given in nature, but derive from language and are only intelligible in the contexts of modes of life. The social reality which concerns sociologists does not exist independently of the methods for studying and hence producing it. Objectivity, bias, truth are part of the conventional wisdom of the sociological way of life, and, as such, are entirely the products of social actors: they are wholly social constructs.[16]

If these arguments are plausible, their implications for methods and research strategy could be serious indeed. Such conceptions put the sociologist in a paradoxical situation in that, while he is studying social patterns and relationships, he must use procedures which are themselves rooted in social patterns and social processes. No appeal can be made to ultimate and given standards by which to judge the extent to which his theoretical constructions fit some 'external reality'. Indeed, that 'external reality' is itself the production of the very methods designed to understand it. Are then the methods discussed in this book simply toys with which a group of people can play games to keep themselves off the street? If so, this would seem to argue for an 'anarchist methodology' in which anything goes.[17] Rules should be broken, theories which are inconsistent with well-established facts should be actively introduced and elaborated, and accepted points of view constantly questioned. Sociology is a playful activity, not guided by formal rules or methods, but engaged in as an end in itself, a context ruled by fancy, imagination and creativity rather than method.

It would be understating the obvious to point out that this conception of scientific activity differs in its epistemological assumptions from that which has traditionally informed scientific life. Moreover, it is a view which, I suspect, few will accept easily, since it effectively not only robs the scientist of his privileged and unique status as a producer of knowledge but also reacts strongly against all that has been inculcated through his membership of a particular society and a profession. Nevertheless, whatever the merits of this perspective (and it does point to the importance of communication, language and meaning as elements in the social construction of reality), just because there is no ultimate justification for the sociological enterprise beyond the enterprise itself, this does not mean that anything can pass for sociology. Whether we regard sociology as play or as some more serious-minded pursuit (although play can be serious), these alternative paradigms suggest a need for sociological inquiry, especially with regard to that aspect with which we have been most concerned in this text, namely research methods, to be aware that it does not use unalterable procedures—fixed, God-given rules for obtaining knowledge. Research methods are theories for looking at the social world, and if used creatively and imaginatively, they can improve our understanding of the worlds which people create and in which they live.

Notes and References

1. See P. E. Hammond (ed.), *Sociologists at Work*, Basic Books, New York, 1964, for an interesting selection of essays by some eminent sociologists on the 'hidden', normally unreported, aspects of their research.

2. N. K. Denzin, *The Research Act*, Aldine, Chicago, 1970, p. 298.

3. See A. V. Cicourel, *Theory and Methods in a Study of Argentine Fertility*, John Wiley, New York, 1974, for an analysis of the commonsense, taken-for-granted knowledge used by interviewers and coders.

4. Denzin, *The Research Act*, pp. 298–9.

5. ibid., p. 300.

6. ibid., p. 301.

7. See B. G. Glaser and A. Strauss, *The Discovery of Grounded Theory*, Aldine, Chicago, 1967, for a discussion of this process. Also, F. R. Westie, 'Toward Closer Relations Between Theory and Research: A Procedure and Example', *American Sociological Review*, 22, 1957, pp. 149–54.

8. E. J. Webb *et al.*, *Unobtrusive Measures*, Rand McNally, Chicago, 1966, pp. 173–4.

9. A. J. Vidich and G. Shapiro, 'A Comparison of Participant Observation and Survey Data', *American Sociological Review*, 20, 1955, p. 33; reprinted in N. K. Denzin (ed.), *Sociological Methods: A Sourcebook*, Butterworth, London, 1970, pp. 512–22.

10. Denzin, *The Research Act*, p. 313.

11. Taken from M. Glucksmann, *Structuralist Analysis in Contemporary Social Thought*, Routledge & Kegan Paul, London, 1974, p. 10.

12. D. L. Phillips, *Abandoning Method*, Jossey-Bass, San Francisco, 1973, p. 91.

13. ibid., p. 117. See also an interesting point on this, W. W. Sharrock, 'On Owning Knowledge', and D. H. Zimmerman, 'Fact as a Practical Accomplishment', both in R. Turner (ed.), *Ethnomethodology*, Penguin Books, Harmondsworth, 1974, pp. 45–53 and 128–43 respectively.

14. Phillips, *Abandoning Method*, p. 100.

15. ibid., p. 125, and L. Wittgenstein, *Philosophical Investigations*, Blackwell, Oxford, 1958.

16. A. F. Blum, 'Theorizing', in J. D. Douglas (ed.), *Understanding Everyday Life*, Aldine, Chicago, 1970, p. 333.

17. P. K. Feyerabend, 'Against Method: Outline of an Anarchistic Theory of Knowledge', *Minnesota Studies in the Philosophy of Science*, 4, 1970, pp. 17–130.

Postscript, and a Concluding Exercise

It would be good if, at this point, one could say, 'Right, go out and do your own research project.' Unfortunately, time, money, inclination and experience as well as knowledge must make for pause. But perhaps, after all, this is over-caution. In my view, essential to learning sociology is experience in creating and using data, whatever that data might be. Too much sociology teaching consists of reiterating what other sociologists have said, and while this is clearly important and necessary, it should be balanced by allowing the student to generate theories and to use them on data. After all, most of the great masters of sociology, including the trinity of Marx, Weber and Durkheim, were trying to make sense out of an empirical reality by constantly moving, in their differing ways, between theory and data. By some standards, at any rate, their methodology may leave a lot to be desired. Nonetheless their magnificent mistakes have formed the basis for subsequent advances in both theory and method. According to their example, sociology has to be a unity between theory, method and data.

However, it should be no surprise by now to point out that the relationship between theory, method and data is not unproblematic. Indeed, one of the points made once again in this chapter was that the act of sociological research is itself an area worthy of investigation precisely because of its social character and the questions it raises about the putative connections between theory, method and data. And, although this self-inquiry might well raise awkward epistemological and philosophical issues, greater awareness of the social character of the research act may at least result in more 'newsworthy' research.

Possibly, by now, you have already developed an inclination to one or the other (or maybe to quite a different one) of the perspectives outlined on the nature of the sociological enterprise. If you have, well and good, but speaking as one who was once a convinced and rather aggressive positivist, but who is now inclined towards an alternative perspective, intellectual fashions have a habit of changing, and not necessarily in a whimsical way. The point is to try to understand each perspective as honestly as possible. After all, few of the adherents to any position are dupes or fools.

Look back over the exercises you have done and try to evaluate them anew. Try once again to formulate alternative theories, especially those which have to do with the social nature of the research. Think about the implicit assumptions you have made about such things as the nature of human interaction, including that interaction in which you were involved as a researcher, the implicit knowledge and the taken-for-granted reality that are necessary to make a method workable. Then try to relate these to the more abstract conceptions of the character of social life and the knowledge necessary to understand it. Be as creative as you like. What implications can you draw about sociological theory, areas of interest, and questions that need to be looked into?

Alternatively, pick an area of sociological concern—education and social class, small-group dynamics, organizations, political socialization or whatever—and try to design a project, assuming reasonably unlimited resources, incorporating the principle of triangulation. Since this will require a considerable amount of reading to gather material already available, it would be an advantage to regard this as a class project. You will have to draw up a list of available theoretical perspectives and propositions, as well as a summary of findings to date. Formulate researchable questions: what areas are to be looked at, what data is to be gathered and by what methods, and so on? Try to point up areas of epistemological and philosophical concern to see whether or not they fundamentally prevent the development of a consensus of knowledge. Think about where such disagreements might lead in terms of the conceptions of sociological inquiry. Do they point to new ways of looking at the social world, new questions that need to be asked, new areas of inquiry and, more difficult, new conceptions of knowledge?

May the enterprise be enjoyable.

Index